Restigouche

Also by Philip Lee

Home Pool: The Fight to Save the Atlantic Salmon

Frank: The Life and Politics of Frank McKenna

Bittersweet: Confessions of a Twice-Married Man

The Next Big Thing: The Dalton Camp Lectures in Journalism (ed.)

Restigouche

THE LONG RUN OF THE WILD RIVER

PHILIP LEE

Edited by Susan Renouf.
Cover and page design by Julie Scriver.
Cover image and interior section pages: *Restigouche River*, copyright © 2013
by Jean-Michel Cormier, www.instagram.com/jmcormierphotography.
Interior maps: Copyright © 2020 by Lena Beckley, www.instagram.com/lenabeckley_art.
Printed in Canada.
10 9 8 7 6 5 4 3 2 1

Library and Archives Canada Cataloguing in Publication

Title: Restigouche : the long run of the wild river / Philip Lee
with an introduction by Roy MacGregor.
Names: Lee, Philip, 1963- author.
Description: Includes bibliographical references.
Identifiers: Canadiana (print) 20190181885 | Canadiana (ebook) 20190181958 |
ISBN 9781773100883 (softcover) | ISBN 9781773100890 (EPUB) | ISBN 9781773100906 (Kindle)
Subjects: LCSH: Restigouche River (N.B. and Québec) | LCSH: Restigouche River (N.B. and
Québec)— History. | LCSH: Restigouche River (N.B. and Québec)—Description and travel. |
LCSH: Lee, Philip, 1963-—Travel—Restigouche River (N.B. and Québec) |
LCSH: Stream conservation—Restigouche River (N.B. and Québec)
Classification: LCC FC2495.R48 L44 2020 | DDC 971.5/11—dc23

Goose Lane Editions acknowledges the generous support of the Government of Canada, the Canada Council for the Arts, and the Government of New Brunswick.

Goose Lane Editions
500 Beaverbrook Court, Suite 330
Fredericton, New Brunswick
CANADA E3B 5X4
www.gooselane.com

For Butch and Marty
and the Expeditionary Force

Contents

Foreword **9**
by Roy MacGregor

TIME **15**

WATER **103**

FLOW **183**

Acknowledgements **261**

Notes **263**

Foreword

Here's hoping Philip Lee will forgive me for calling him The Mole. It is intended as a compliment.

Mole, of course, was a main character in Kenneth Grahame's 1908 children's novel, *The Wind in the Willows*. Mole, Grahame wrote, "was bewitched, entranced, fascinated" by the river that ran through the forest and meadows where Toad and Ratty and Badger and Grahame's other imaginary creatures lived. For Mole, "happiness was complete" only when he sat on the banks "while the river still chatted on to him, a babbling procession of the best stories in the world, sent from the heart of the earth to be told at last to the insatiable sea."

Mole, meet Philip Lee. Kenneth Grahame's river, meet the river that runs through this magnificent book.

What Philip Lee has done in *Restigouche* is compose a compelling, poetic love letter to the forever river of his life. Like Mole, he sees the Restigouche as a living creature, perhaps not quite the "sleek, sinuous, full-bodied animal" that Mole liked to watch, but the beloved main character in a grand and sweeping tale that is also the story of New Brunswick, of the Maritimes, of Canada. There are history lessons inside these covers and also geological lessons, hydrology studies, philosophy teachings and even a touch of theology, as might be expected from the son of a Presbyterian pastor who brought his young family to New Brunswick in the late 1960s. In the more than half century that he has lived in the province, this river has become his spiritual core.

9

For years, I knew of Philip Lee as a byline on many of the most readable newspaper stories coming out of New Brunswick. Later, when he became a professor of journalism at St. Thomas University in Fredericton, we connected at a one-day forum on the national game. I knew he believed in good journalism and that he liked hockey, but I knew little of his other passions until the summer of 2016, when I was working on a series on the great rivers of Canada for the *Globe and Mail*, an examination of sixteen rivers that would later be expanded into a book, *Original Highways*.

Knowing that one of the rivers would be the Saint John, "the Rhine of North America," I contacted Philip after finding out that he had published a book on salmon fishing called *Home Pool: The Fight to Save the Atlantic Salmon*. He not only agreed to meet with me and connect me with others along the river, but he also said he would personally get me out on the water. So on a lovely and calm late June day, Philip Lee, looking like a "gillie" about to set out for a secret pool on a Scottish salmon river, poled his square-stern canoe up to our hotel dock. That's right, dock—the Delta Hotel in Fredericton has a dock as well as a parking lot. "Climb in," he said. "We're heading upstream to Burpee Bar."

Ellen and I climbed in and spent the rest of the day spellbound by the slow grace of the river and its banks, the silent whisper of a canoe being poled rather than paddled and the intelligence and information that poured out of the man standing at the stern while working a four-metre pole along the river bottom. We saw no salmon at Burpee Bar, but on the way back downstream, we did see two bald eagles. And we learned about another river a few hours away, which our guide said was once the most famous salmon river in the world, a place where a US president was once part of an exclusive club, where the Duchess of Windsor once outfished the duke, where the man who gave the world standard time once built a bridge. It was a gentle river where, paradoxically, some of the great battles of Canada—French against English, settlers against First Nations, industry against conservation, ownership against public access, common sense against greed—had been fought and were still being fought from the river's source in the high hills to where it empties into salt water at Chaleur Bay. For centuries, the Restigouche has been a cat's cradle of competing interests. And in too many ways, it still is.

Philip Lee said he was writing a book on that river — and here it is.

Restigouche is canoe tripping with the best company imaginable. Not only is Philip a great storyteller, but he is a fabulous researcher. You will, of course, meet the rich and famous — the Irvings of New Brunswick, Teddy Roosevelt, the Vanderbilts, the Marquis of Lorne and his wife, Princess Louise, daughter of Queen Victoria — but you will also meet, and often fall in love with, the ordinary people who live along the Restigouche: loggers, fishers, French, English, Mi'gmaq. It is a river that has experienced its own rough waters, from the horrendous expulsion of the Acadians nearly three centuries ago to as recently as 1981, when police and game wardens from Quebec descended on the Listuguj First Nation and beat and arrested members of the Indigenous community for netting salmon.

Salmon, of course, are at the heart of this superb book, just as they are the prime attraction in the crystal clear waters of the Restigouche. Philip is clearly on the side of the salmon, detailing what overfishing, logging, pollution and climate change have done to the fishery. This book is his plea for conservation, protection and restoration.

But it is also, happily, a book filled with love of the river and hope for its future.

— ROY MacGREGOR

He did not need to get his map out. He knew where he was from the position of the river.

— "Big Two-Hearted River"

Time

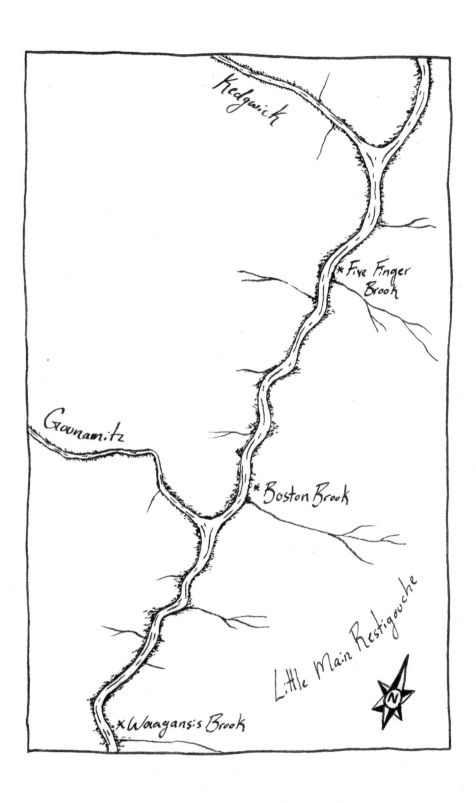

Kedgwick

*Five Finger Brook

Goonamitz

*Boston Brook

Little Main Restigouche

×Waagansis Brook

N

For here too there are gods.

—Heraclitus

1 The wild river flows down from the northern reaches of the Appalachian Highlands where for almost half the year it is encased in ice and buried in deep layers of snow. In early spring, as the days grow longer and the heat of the sun grows stronger, the ice begins to crack and shift until it shatters into a rugged slurry that rumbles downriver, scraping shorelines, plowing down trees, rearranging boulders, scouring gravel beds, dividing islands and forming new ones. Every year the ice run leaves behind scars on rocks and trees, witness marks in a story of change that passes through a vast measure of time.

The freshet follows the ice run, the snowmelt from the hills running into a torrent that breaches the banks and spills into the floodplains, back channels, gullies and swamps. As the flow subsides, the water clears, and the river recedes into its banks. Summer blooms in a rush of greens, sweeping across the floodplains and hills, as if in a hurry to make the most of the season. When cool nights sprinkle frost in the valley, mists swirl over the water, and hardwoods on the hillsides turn orange and crimson until winter winds strip the trees bare and the ice and snow return again.

The wild river is creation in motion, yet each season when we return to the valley, we recognize landmarks from stories centuries old, the names passed on from one generation of travellers to the next: Campbell's, Jimmy's Hole, Cheyne, Trotting Grounds, Stillwater, Devil's Half Acre, Three Sisters, Shingle, White Brook Island, Pine Island, Cross Point, Two Brooks, Chamberlain Shoals, Chain of Rocks, Rafting Grounds.

We know these places as we know the timbre of the river's voice, the texture of its waters, the shape of its meanders, the colour and polish of its stones. No two rivers are the same; in all the world, there is only one Restigouche. That's why long ago the river gods were many and the sea god was one.

The Restigouche River runs northeast for 200 kilometres, marking the border between the Canadian provinces of New Brunswick and Quebec, before spilling into Chaleur Bay. The narrow bay, 130 kilometres long, bends northeast toward the Gulf of St. Lawrence and the Atlantic Ocean. The headwaters of the Restigouche rise in streams that spill into the Little Main Restigouche from the southwest and the Kedgwick River from the northwest. The main river begins where the currents of the Kedgwick and Little Main collide in a deep, swirling pool we call the Junction. Below the Junction, the river continues to collect water from countless small streams and three major tributaries: the Patapédia from the north, the Upsalquitch from the southwest and the Matapédia from the northeast.

The Matapédia, which runs through the province of Quebec, is the only tributary that passes through towns and villages. The others flow through wild spaces broken by a scattering of logging roads and isolated fishing lodges, some of them more than a century old, built by a handful of the wealthiest people of their time who came to the river when Canada's Intercolonial Railway connected this valley to the outside world in the summer of 1876.

There are small cities in New Brunswick on the south side of the Restigouche estuary, Campbellton and Dalhousie with its deep-water harbour, and the remote hills of Quebec's Gaspé Peninsula across the river to the north. Listuguj is on the northern shore opposite Campbellton, Ugpi'Ganjig on the southern shore just beyond Dalhousie, both communities of Mi'gmaq, the First People of this river. Their territory is called Mi'gma'gi, and it includes the Gaspé Peninsula, the islands in Chaleur Bay, the Atlantic provinces of Canada and part of the state of Maine. The Restigouche flows through Gespe'gewa'gi, the last land, the seventh and largest district of Mi'gma'gi, extending from the Miramichi

River in the south to the farthest reaches of the Gaspé Peninsula in the north.

Each of the Restigouche tributaries has its own personality, yet they all share the primary characteristic of the main river, which is the startling clarity of the water. Over the years, I have floated hundreds of kilometres by canoe on these waters. On clear days I can see every stone on the river bottom from bank to bank. And when I look down into the deep ledge-framed pools and hollowed-out pockets below cold-water brooks, I see silver Atlantic salmon that have returned to spawn on the same gravel beds where they spent the first seasons of their lives before migrating thousands of kilometres to distant oceans and back again. For generations, the Restigouche salmon has defined, united and divided this valley and the people of the river.

A well-travelled American journalist who came here in the 1860s wrote of a great river flowing through one of the most "superb and fascinating" landscapes on the continent, where mists swirl along cliffs and chasms and across "far-reaching sweeps of outline and continually rising domes," the water "gleaming like polished steel." He published a long feature in *Harper's New Monthly* magazine in March 1868 that opens by stating matter of factly that the Restigouche valley affords "unquestionably the best field for the sportsman to be found in America, east of the Rocky Mountains." The writer suggested that if artists followed him and captured what they saw on canvas, they would paint another *Heart of the Andes* or *Valley of the Yosemite* and call it *Restigouche*.

2 The course of my life turned toward the river when my family moved north from Montgomery County, Maryland, to the seaport city of Saint John, New Brunswick, where my father had taken a job as the pastor at a downtown Presbyterian church. It was the spring of 1969, three months after my sixth birthday. In Maryland we lived in a two-storey brick manse across the road from a country church with a white clapboard steeple, surrounded by farms, flat dirt roads and wire fences. In Saint John we moved into a duplex in a working-class Irish Roman Catholic neighbourhood on the west side of a deep-water harbour where weathered saltbox row houses lined the streets that ran up the hills that frame the mouth of the Saint John River. There the water rushes into the Bay of Fundy through a deep gut carved by the current known as the Reversing Falls, named for the dangerous rapids that turn and run upstream on the incoming tide.

We came to this rough-hewn town at a time when mothers and fathers pushed their sons and daughters outside in all seasons and told them to return only for meals or treatment of serious injury. When I stepped out my front door, I fell into the embrace of gangs of boys and girls who mapped their playgrounds through a maze of grassy clifftop paths, rugged beaches and railway yards, through the remains of crumbling cattle sheds, longshoremen's shelters and the long cargo sheds along waterfront docks. In the days of my youth, we were all explorers, and the freedom I discovered in my new Canadian home suited me just fine. This was the time of my second birth, when I awoke to feel the salted winds on my face and the rocky earth beneath my feet.

My father grew up in Tampa, Florida, exploring the sandy Gulf coastline and Everglade swamps with fishing rods and rifles. Later, when we lived in Maryland, he fished and hunted along the wild streams of the West Virginia hills. We arrived in Saint John at a time when the calamity of the Vietnam War and the assassinations of a president, a civil rights leader, and the president's brother had caused my father to lose his passion for shooting. He stored his hunting rifles and shotgun when he came to Canada, but it was not long before he started looking for places to fish. When I was old enough to hike through the forest and wade in flowing water, my father started taking me with him as he explored the rivers and streams near our home.

My father is slight but sturdy, straight-backed and deceptively strong. In the southern tradition, I was named after him, as he was named after his father. Like many men of his generation, he has perfect manners and tidy presentation. He fearlessly took up winter sports when we moved north, teaching himself to ski and skate, although he never learned to do either particularly well. One Sunday morning he processed into the sanctuary sporting a weeping black eye that he earned by falling on his face playing hockey on a frozen pond the day before. He always preached the revolutionary message of the New Testament, that we must love our enemies and the meek shall inherit the Earth. I learned to write by listening to the cadence of the sermons that he scribbled on unlined paper and read aloud before leaving for church.

One summer we launched a canoe into a stream called New River to search for a stretch of water called the Diamond Pools. A man at a rural general store had told my father that the pools were filled with brook trout. We didn't know precisely where they were, only that they lay somewhere above the highway bridge. So that's where we set out, in a canoe filled with camping gear and fishing rods, pushing against the current in a stream so shallow and rocky that we were soon wading and dragging instead of paddling.

Our trips were often this kind of Presbyterian enterprise, based on the assumption that good fishing waters would be reached after a long slog that only those of sturdy faith would have the fortitude to endure. For two days we dragged the canoe upstream, portaging around a small waterfall, camping at night on grassy bluffs above the stone beaches beside the river. We never found the Diamond Pools on the New River, but I've always carried with me memories of that trip, the anticipation of turning another bend with nothing but unexplored territory ahead. Most importantly, I was learning to seek grace through perseverance, that the inevitable difficulties and hardships we encounter on trips such as these, and in the passages of our lives, are necessary obstacles to overcome. Sometimes we have no choice but to pull our canoe over a shallow gravel bar or shoulder it across a portage. In my life, I've done my share of both.

As the years passed, my father and I ranged farther north to the remote border region of New Brunswick and Quebec, into the valley of the Restigouche, and after our first season on the river, we returned to it at every opportunity. For more than two decades, first with my father and later with my friends and other members of my family, I've been following the clear currents of the Restigouche along high-cut banks, dropping over the tumble of rapids into deep pools. At the end of long summer days, we've swung our canoes out of the flow, pulled them into the high grasses on the shore and camped in splendid isolation on wild islands. We've watched eagles and osprey dive for fish in the shallows and moose ford the river with spring calves. We've climbed mountain trails that follow the river's feeder brooks cascading down from cold springs over moss-covered rocks, cooked over open fires on polished gravel beaches, slept in rustic cabins, and cast flies for salmon on cool mornings and at dusk in driving rainstorms. We've made our beds beside the water, watched the last light reflect off the tops of towering balsam firs heavy with moss, and then stood in a warm circle of first light by the river to drink a cup of coffee brewed over a morning fire.

3 For me, the Restigouche has always been an expression of nature's fragile grace flowing through a world that affords little value to wild rivers and the lands that sustain them. In each new season I watched assaults on natural systems spread through the valley. Some I have seen with my own eyes: the logging trucks rumbling down from the hills twenty-four hours a day; the cuts growing larger and creeping ever closer to the river; feeder brooks that once flowed through the summer now dry and choked with sediment washed down from nearby logging and more distant industrial enterprises. The hills have been sprayed from the air with pesticides and herbicides, and the old mixed forests transformed into new monoculture tree plantations. Through it all, the salmon still return to spawn in the river, although they are now engaged in a grim survival game, both in their home waters and in warming and rising seas.

We recognize that the river and all the life systems that it supports are not what they once were, even in my lifetime. But how did this happen? This is a complex and challenging question, but one surely worth exploring, for it goes to the heart of understanding how we might preserve the natural systems that support life on Earth. We know the river is thousands of years old. We know that on this river, the greatest changes in natural systems came during the past 150 years, accelerating during the last fifty. We know that the changes to the Earth's climate that began a century before that now threaten the river's systems in ways we never imagined possible. There are many things we don't know about the history of the river and the great mysteries of nature, but there are many things we do know to be true. The enduring mysteries don't cancel out the facts, although we often interchange the words believe and know, as if they carry the same meaning and weight in the life of a wild river.

Since the dawn of the Industrial Revolution humans have accepted that disruptions in natural systems are the price of progress, preordained and unstoppable. The one thing each new generation could count on was that their world would not be the place of their mothers and fathers. The all-consuming idea that we could impose our will and reason on nature, that everything new was superior to a distant past, has been so compelling that we are still seized by it today. Only now we are beginning to recognize with some alarm that perhaps all the world was not ours for the taking, and many things have been done that should not have been done.

Our knowledge of natural systems is deeper and richer than at any time in human history, yet it is still so awash with mysteries that our actions run ahead of our understanding of their consequences. Our imperfect knowledge is used to dismiss both those who call for caution when we seek to disturb the natural order and Indigenous communities who suggest their ancient and traditional knowledge of the ways of lands and waters and the lives they sustain might well provide a foundation for modern systems of understanding. Instead the debate has been and continues to be confined in a strongbox of utility, calculating the greatest good for the greatest number, measuring what we save and what we can afford to lose. The case for disruption of natural systems is supported by measures of economic necessity and acceptable risk, and the inevitable imperfections and lack of definitive evidence in the Indigenous and conservationist appeals are used to dismiss their warnings and concerns as sentimental and idealistic. What's good for the wild river is rarely factored into the equation, as if its waters are disconnected from us, as if we ourselves are not children of nature.

The arguments for resource extraction and destruction of natural systems are supported by reports that predict the numbers of direct and indirect jobs that will be created and tax revenues that may be collected. To counter this argument, conservationists commission reports about the economic value of the sport fishing and tourism industries in a river valley. Or they argue that preserving wild spaces will help us to better understand the effects of changes in climate in our communities, or that wild spaces contribute to human health and general pleasure. Or more abstractly, they assign spiritual value to wild spaces, making vague references to their sacred contributions to the human psychological condition.

How different the conversation would be if we were to begin by stating that we hold this truth to be self-evident: that a wild river supports a grand tapestry of life, and since the moment of its creation, and in every movement since, it is in itself beautiful and complete.

When I worked in the newspaper business, a great editor and friend taught me how a true story well told becomes a parable. He was a libertarian editor in the old school who saw his newspapers as daily journals of moral conduct. When something is broken, it is the work of the moralist, the storyteller, to place a finger on it and then ask who's responsible for fixing it. I've carried his lessons with me throughout my life, for once a person adopts the habits of the moralist, it's hard to let them go. This compulsion, I admit, tends to drive those I love most to distraction. We now have a house rule that I'm not to engage in this kind of talk at least until the morning coffee has been poured, and talking back to radio newscasts in the kitchen is strictly forbidden. I've learned to honour the contract, but the questions still run hard through each passing season.

How did it come to be that all the great political movements of the industrial age have proven themselves incapable of pursuing their ends without destroying the life sustaining systems of the Earth itself? What marked the turning point when we set out to become alienated from that upon which we depend for life itself? Was it when Henry the Navigator sent his sailing ships out from the beaches of southern Portugal to explore what lay beyond the seas, or when Copernicus and Galileo championed the heliocentrism that helped to launch a scientific revolution, or when the steam engine and railway lines released us from the constraints of time and place?

What has allowed us to treat our wild rivers and the lands that sustain them so carelessly? In T.S. Eliot's poem, we lost sight of the river gods, seeing them first as a frontier, "useful, untrustworthy, as a conveyor of commerce," then as problem for builders of bridges. But when that problem was solved, the rivers were all but forgotten. By the time the first railway lines and bridges were being built in the wilderness of the Restigouche valley, the Industrial Revolution had been fouling European rivers for a century. In the opening passages of *Bleak House*, Charles Dickens wrote of the Thames that flowed through London, where the fog rolled "defiled among the tiers of shipping and the waterside pollutions of a great (and dirty) city." New York City was using the Hudson River as an open sewer and garbage dump, and the Chicago River was so polluted that engineers had reversed its flow into the Mississippi River and away from the city's source of drinking water in Lake Michigan. Rivers such as the Thames and Hudson have gone through extensive rehabilitation since then, but they are nothing like what they were in their pre-industrial state. Rivers are remarkably resilient, but they do not wash away our sins.

The more I thought about the wild river the more I began to consider a new kind of inquiry. I began to wonder if, in all our evaluations of what's worth saving and what we can afford to lose, we were even measuring the right things. Could a truer measure of what's worth saving be found in the story of the life of one wild river?

I set out to test this proposition by travelling into the headwaters of the Restigouche River and over the course of one season following its lines and stories to the head of tide. When I set out, I had no idea what I might find. When I returned, I lay awake long into the winter nights, trying to unweave and unwind all that I had seen and learned. At the end of my exploring I didn't have all the answers and still wondered what the future might hold. What I did know was, like the man who washed his eyes in the Pool of Siloam, I had come back seeing.

4 The thaw came late that spring. By the third week of April the ice was still holding in the Restigouche as I drove four-and-a-half hours north from my home in Fredericton, New Brunswick's capital city, into a village called Tide Head to discuss my plans with a man who knows the Restigouche as intimately as anyone on Earth. Alan Madden is the former New Brunswick government biologist in the region, a scientist by training, a naturalist and natural theologian by vocation.

Alan and his wife, Annette, live in a bungalow beside the river, just below the head of tide, surrounded by untamed gardens, a fish pond, bird feeders and projects in various stages of completion, the habitat of a man with an active mind and restless disposition. When they settled here in 1973, he began to plant grapes, flowers and shrubs and an orchard, grafting dozens of varieties of trees onto rootstocks, and now he has forty apple, thirty plum and two pear trees bearing fruit in the fall.

For thirty years his responsibility was to study and help manage the Restigouche River. He left the office two decades ago but his life's work has continued without pause. He's tall and lean, still fit enough to hunt and fish and run the river as he always has. He keeps an old canoe on the shore and when the river ices over and the snowfalls come, he and his wife travel to wild spaces where he takes photographs and later compiles journal notes that document where he has been and all the birds, animals and fish he has encountered. His journals show that in just the first five years of his retirement he fished 156 named bodies of water.

That afternoon the spring sun melted the snowbanks outside his kitchen window and the ice creaked in the river while we sat in his living room drinking his home-pressed apple cider and discussing various scenarios for my river trip. He suggested I begin at an old portage route in the headwaters of the Little Main Restigouche. This long-forgotten route was once the most important link between the Restigouche and the Saint John River, the longest and largest of the great rivers of New Brunswick. The Saint John rises in northern Maine, flowing the length of the province from north to south, through the Grand Falls gorge, the highest waterfall east of Niagara Falls, and empties into the Bay of Fundy at the Reversing Falls in the city of my youth. The First People of the valley call the river Wolastoq, the beautiful river, and they are Wolastoqiyik, the people of the beautiful river. A tributary of the Saint John River, called La Grande Rivière, near Grand Falls is the first stage in the old portage trail to the Restigouche that continues twelve kilometres overland through the forest to a narrow, swampy waterway called Waagansis Brook. The Waagansis winds through marshland and alder thickets and empties into the upper reaches of the Little Main Restigouche. Once the railway came to the mouth of the river in 1876, the trail was followed less frequently and today it is followed not at all. I decided that afternoon that I would attempt to make Waagansis Brook my starting point.

Through the rest of the afternoon Alan and I talked about fly fishing, canoeing and various books he thought I should read. As the sun dropped in the sky, our conversation turned to the difficulty we all have in perceiving change in the natural world. The work of the naturalist demands both attentive observation and the collection of data to track patterns of change over time. For decades, in addition to the records of his own observations on the Restigouche, Alan collected historical accounts of the commercial fishery and records from fishing lodges and filed them in his office. When he canoed over pools and gravel bars to supervise the counts of salmon and their nests (called redds) in the fall, he compared these numbers with the historical data.

Alan has studied the reports of Moses Perley, a Fredericton lawyer who in the 1840s was commissioned by the colonial government to describe and quantify the various commercial fisheries along the coastlines of New Brunswick. Perley's comprehensive report included the salmon catches of a Scottish trader named Robert Ferguson who in the early 1800s introduced commercial net fishing to the Restigouche. He exported an average of 1,400 barrels of salmon a year. Each barrel held between eleven and fifteen fish, which means that Ferguson caught between 15,400 and 21,000 large salmon every season for many years. During the same period, a fisherman named Robert Christie was exporting two thousand tierces of salmon a year. A tierce, which is an old English unit of measurement, holds between twenty and twenty-five salmon, so his catch amounted to between forty thousand and fifty thousand large fish. Madden thinks Christie fished at a place known today as Christie's Run, one of the four channels among the lowermost islands in the river about two kilometres upstream from the head of tide. Therefore, Ferguson and Christie captured and exported fifty-five thousand to sixty thousand large salmon every year. That was the harvest of two netsmen. There were many other unrecorded harvests at the same time, and still enough salmon left to spawn and maintain the population at these levels. One fisherman reported that he fished six nets tied in tandem upriver from Ferguson and Christie and captured three thousand salmon in a two-night operation and others had taken a great many more than that. The entire commercial salmon catch in upper Chaleur Bay during the season of 1971, the last year of the commercial salmon fishery there, was three thousand fish.

What this tells us is that the size of the Restigouche River salmon runs in a not-so-distant past was prodigious. Yet instead of measuring what we've lost, we sweep away these historical records as if they were stories from a long lost mythical age that has little connection to the river we know today. How did it happen that the runs of salmon have been reduced to what they are today and what is the larger ecological significance of this change? Instead of addressing that question, we lower the bar and declare the salmon runs to be healthy when the river meets the government's new conservation targets of fifteen thousand spawning fish.

Late in the afternoon I left Alan Madden's home and drove back through the valley across the Upsalquitch River where the road rises and crosses a high plateau with clearcuts of the logging companies stretching in all directions as far as the eye can see. At the foot of the plateau, I passed the sawmill at the entrance to the town of Kedgwick and stopped at a store on the corner to buy a bottle of wine. I turned off the main road and wound down deep into the valley to the village of Kedgwick River, crossed the Little Main Restigouche just above the Junction Pool at the Montgomery Bridge and turned down the dirt road toward Chalets Restigouche, a collection of cabins and a campground owned and operated by sisters Manon and Pascale Arpin.

I arrived just before dark and parked on a layer of slushy snow that covered the driveway beside a cabin that I had called to reserve earlier in the day. The Arpin sisters had gone home but they left the cabin door unlocked and the key on the kitchen table. In the fridge, I found they had left me a mason jar of chicken stew and half a loaf of home-baked bread. I warmed the stew on the stove, opened the wine and sat with a glass at the kitchen table. I was the only person staying in the cabins that evening. There's no cell phone service in the valley, so for the first time in a long time I was alone and disconnected. The forest all around me was dark and the silence was deep. The river ice moaned and cracked in the distance.

In the morning I drove back across the Montgomery Bridge to visit my friend Marie-Christine Arpin, who is Manon and Pascale's cousin. As I crossed the bridge I could see patches of open water and bubbling bands of current and I figured the ice would be moving before long. Marie-Christine lives at the top of the hill but I was meeting her at her father's house down in the valley beside the river next to her business,

Arpin Canoe Restigouche. For years she and her father, André, have been shuttling me and my friends and family and our canoes to various points throughout the valley. I parked by the office, which was still closed for the winter. The canoes were racked on the edge of the trees above the melting snow banks.

Marie-Christine walked across the yard to greet me. She is small but powerful, with a wild tangle of long dark hair. Her staff call her *boss des bécosses*, an untranslatable expression that means something like the Big Boss, which is an inside joke. She drives trucks and buses, loads canoes and grows vegetables in her gardens that she cooks and serves on guided river trips. She also raises chickens, works in the maple syrup industry in the winter and plays guitar in an all-female gypsy jazz band. She built her house with the help of her father and friends out of lumber sawn from trees harvested from her property using a portable mill. It's the way everything happens in this valley: if you want something done, you do it yourself; if you need help, you know who to call.

Marie-Christine's business now sends about six thousand people in canoes on the river each season. Her partner, Rémi Bergeron, nicknamed *le barbu*, the bearded one, is an Arpin guide and an infinitely resourceful man on a river trip. He has a side enterprise crafting wooden canoe paddles, a business he has named Waagansis.

André Arpin is a gentle man with a long grey beard and a fierce energy that supports the many enterprises he has taken on during his life beside the river. He worked as a carpenter and raised sheep until one fall he counted his assets at the end of the season and concluded that all he had to show for his work was a large manure pile behind the barn. He sold his sheep and in 1993 bought six canoes that he stacked on a trailer at the end of his driveway under a For Rent sign. Seven years later, he had a hundred canoes for rent and the first adventure tourism business in the valley, its headquarters strategically located a short walk above the confluence of the Little Main and the Kedgwick. This allowed him to shuttle canoeists upstream to various points of departure so they could paddle down to their vehicles parked in his yard, or they could set out from his beach into the main river and he would collect them at pre-arranged times at landings downstream. When André decided to retire, Marie-Christine, his eldest daughter, took over the business.

That morning we drank coffee in the kitchen of André's log home and discussed the logistics of a trip from the old portage route as well as various other arrangements that would need to be made for shuttles and pickups downstream. Marie-Christine said she would be happy to drive me into Waagansis Brook but we would have to pass through a two-hundred-thousand-hectare tract of industrial forest owned by the multi-billionaire Irving family, more precisely by the forestry company J.D. Irving Ltd. All roads into the land around the Waagansis portage are now gated. The company has transformed this land it calls Black Brook into one of the most intensively managed tracts of private industrial forestland in Canada with more than 40 per cent of the landbase converted into spruce plantations. Marie-Christine promised to send me a phone number to call to try to secure permission to pass through what the company calls the Veneer Gate.

I wasn't surprised at this news. J.D. Irving Ltd. is named for James Dergavel Irving, the father of industrialist Kenneth Colin Irving who, in the years following the Second World War, swept into the forests of New Brunswick and New England to assemble a network of timberlands and mills. He also built the largest oil refinery in Canada in Saint John. He was known in New Brunswick and beyond as K.C., and his influence and the work of his sons and grandchildren and great grandchildren, now dominate the economic landscape of the province. When we travel the roads and rivers of New Brunswick, we are surrounded by the Irving presence. Almost every community has an Irving gas station and store. The family owns five sawmills in the north, three sawmills in the centre of the province and pulp and paper, tissue and cardboard mills in the south, the largest in Saint John beside the Reversing Falls. It owns trucking companies, a railway line, a building supplies chain, a modular home manufacturer, the refinery in Saint John, a nearby liquified natural gas terminal and a chain of newspapers where I once worked as a reporter and editor. None of the businesses dominate the landscape more than J.D. Irving Ltd., which controls 2.4 million hectares of forestland, about half of it freehold and half public land where it holds timber rights. Within its holdings, many rivers and streams flow, including, I now learned, the upper reaches of the Restigouche River.

I left Marie-Christine and André and drove back toward the Saint John River valley across the highway that runs through the Black Brook property where every side road is barricaded and posted with no trespassing signs. I thought that while this was an obstacle, it surely defined one of the central issues of the inquiry from the outset. What responsibilities do those who hold legal title or timber rights on a property have to the natural systems on the land? What responsibility do we have to the land around our property, to the water that flows through lands we occupy, to the atmosphere above us? What responsibilities do we have to each other? What responsibilities do we have to the other forms of life that share these spaces with us? What does it mean to have legal title to a property in New Brunswick? What does it mean to have title to property in Mi'gma'gi, on lands that were never ceded to the Crown? These questions came at the beginning of the journey, and I would continue to grapple with them long after I returned.

5 Two weeks after my trip to Tide Head, the Saint John River overflowed its banks and spilled into my city. We live in a century-old house in an elm-shaded neighbourhood a block from the river in downtown Fredericton. Every spring we watch the river levels with apprehension as the crest of water from the snowmelt in the north migrates through Grand Falls toward us. Below Fredericton is a vast chain of lakes and wetlands called the Grand Lake Meadows. Most years, the meadows act as a giant natural sponge as the river fills up during the freshet and gradually drains. But there is a delay in the drain at the mouth of the river caused by the powerful Bay of Fundy tides that turn the river currents back upstream at the Reversing Falls twice a day. The heavy tide runs all the way back up to Fredericton, 125 kilometres above the mouth of the river. In the spring of 2018 the Grand Lake Meadows were swollen with water after a sudden thaw accompanied by heavy rain. But we didn't worry too much because government forecasters who have tracking systems up and down the river were predicting that levels in Fredericton would stay below eight metres above sea level, the danger point for my neighbourhood and most of the city. Since our house had been built, the water had exceeded eight metres only three times: in 1926, in 1973 and in 2008, the one flood we had experienced when the river water pushed up through the city storm sewers and filled our stone basement.

I woke at dawn on the morning of May 2, 2018, walked out onto the street in front of my house and found the river bubbling up through the storm sewers. I went back inside and turned on the radio news. The river had risen faster than anyone had predicted to 8.36 metres. I went down into the basement, checked on my electric sump pump and started moving the few odds and ends we keep down there to higher ground. For the next eleven days my singular focus was the rising river and protecting the house. It took a couple of days for the neighbourhood to fill and then the water began seeping in through the stone walls of the basement. During the flood a decade earlier, my electric pumps had controlled the flow as the water came and went within a couple of days. This time the water came and stayed, rising up against the outside walls of the basement. I placed sandbags along the foundation and bought a gas-powered pump when the electric pumps were overwhelmed.

I was setting my alarm through the night to start and stop the gas pump to keep the water levels below the electrical systems in the house without draining the basement completely because the water pressure outside without equal pressure inside could crack the foundation. It was a strange time in the neighbourhood. I'd wake up at four in the morning and go outside to manage the pump and see my neighbours splashing around their yards in waders, the sound of their pumps rumbling up and down the street. Meanwhile, south of the city the situation was far worse. The crest roared downriver, swamping homes in the farming communities below us. The Grand Lake system rose to the highest levels on record, and then during a day of high winds the waves kicked up and smashed against the sides of waterfront homes and cottages, tearing some of them off their foundations and leaving them as piles of rubble in distant fields. In Saint John, families with waterfront homes raced to build sandbag barriers as the river there rose to record heights before finally releasing into the sea.

This wasn't the first time the Saint John River had spilled into Fredericton. But there was a feeling that this flood was different. The river wasn't behaving in a predictable way and the reasons why remained unclear. Why did the snowmelt come so quickly from the northern hills? Could it be related to years of intensive logging that has removed forest cover that regulated the melt? Why didn't the Grand Lake Meadows do its job as a sponge when the water came? Could it be that a new four-lane highway that filled in and divided the meadows forever changed this sensitive landscape? Were weather patterns changing in a warming climate? There were no immediate answers. But one thing was clear. We all had a front-row seat to witness the untameable power of a river, which should be a reminder of our hubris in imagining that such a grand and complex natural system might operate within our control. It also should have woken us up to the fact that the changes we had made and continue to make in the river valley and beyond have not been benign, but rather are a high-risk experiment that might result in all of what we have built being washed away, but I'm not sure that it did.

6 When the flood waters receded, I packed away the pump and hoses and turned back to my Restigouche inquiry with a greater sense of urgency. I spread topographical maps of northern New Brunswick on the floor of my office, tracing the meandering lines of Waagansis Brook

to the Little Main Restigouche. For thousands of years rivers were the
only highways through this wilderness. Indigenous travellers established
trails that linked these rivers in the area around a small mountain range
in the centre of the province where the three highest points in the
Canadian Maritime provinces — Mount Carleton, Mount Sagamook
and Mount Bailey — rise more than eight hundred metres above sea level
on a delineative plateau. From there water flows north into Chaleur Bay,
south into the Bay of Fundy and east into the Northumberland Strait and
the Atlantic Ocean. The chain of cold-water lakes at the base of Mount
Carleton are the source of both the Tobique River, the major tributary of
the Saint John to the south and the Nepisiquit River to the north. The
Nepsiquit, which empties into Chaleur Bay east of the Restigouche, is
connected by an overland trail to both the Upsalquitch River and the
splendid sprawl of the Miramichi River system that empties into the
eastern ocean.

I sketched a plan for a river trip in three stages that would begin
at Waagansis Brook during the last week in June. I would follow the
Waagansis to the Little Main Restigouche, then descend to the Junction
Pool at the mouth of the Kedgwick. This would be the most remote part
of the trip over a band of water I had never travelled. The following week,
I'd resupply, then push off from the Junction Pool and follow the main
river to the landing at Two Brooks, about halfway to the tidewater. That
part of the river I had run before for it passes through the heart of the
famous Restigouche salmon angling waters, past many of the grand old
fishing lodges built by Americans of the Gilded Age who came to the
Restigouche at the end of the nineteenth century. Later in the season I'd
return to Two Brooks landing and complete the trip to the sea, taking a
side trip up the Matapédia, before exploring the archipelago on the lower
river above the head of tide.

To prepare there were many inquiries to make and much I needed
to learn. I began by searching for accounts of past trips through the
Waagansis Brook passage to the Restigouche. One of the earliest written
mentions of the Waagansis is in the strange tale of the mapping of

the border between Canada and the United States. At the end of the American Revolution, the new government of the United States sent representatives to Great Britain to negotiate a treaty and determine the boundary between the new country and the British colonies to the north. In 1783, the treaty defined the northeastern border of the United States as "a line drawn due north from the source of the St. Croix River to the highlands, along the said highlands which divide those rivers that empty themselves into the St. Lawrence, and those which fall into the Atlantic Ocean." This was all fine and clean on paper, except no one knew where the line along the highlands was. In the summer of 1817, a team of surveyors led by Joseph Bouchette of Montréal and John Johnson of Vermont set out to define the line, beginning in the headwaters of the St. Croix River, which now marks the southern border of Canada in New Brunswick. Bouchette pushed up through the old portage route from the Saint John River in September, and when he came to Waagansis Brook and found water flowing to the northeast, he assumed he had found the line of water flowing into the St. Lawrence River and declared the job done. His assumption was wrong, for had he continued on he would have found himself floating down the Restigouche into Chaleur Bay far south of the St. Lawrence. Bouchette was dismissed the following year. His mistake left the border in dispute until the present-day boundary was established farther north along the Saint John River in the summer of 1842.

The fall of that same year a geologist named Abraham Gesner, his son Henry and two Wolastoqey guides organized an expedition through the Waagansis portage. Abraham Gesner, who was working for the colonial government in New Brunswick, told the story of the challenging trip in a report to the lieutenant-governor the following year. A fire that had swept through the area three years earlier had reached the overland route, blocking the trail with fallen trees. Ice had formed in the Waagansis by the time they arrived in mid-September, forcing them to drag their canoes fifteen kilometres through frozen swamps to the river. Once they reached the main river, the water was flowing free to the tidewater.

In the same report, Abraham Gesner told the story of his trip earlier that year to the lower Restigouche to search for deposits of coal. In the course of his travels he turned his bark canoe north across the estuary of the river to explore a crumbling crimson shale and sandstone shoreline at a place now called Miguasha, an adaptation of the Mi'gmaw word for red rocks. "Crossing the harbour at Dalhousie, and on the Gaspé side of the Restigouche below Escuminac Bay, I found the shore lined with coarse conglomerate," he wrote. "Farther eastward the rocks are light blue sandstones and shales, containing the remains of vegetables.... The shale is very soft and yielding, and the cliffs are yearly retreating before the tides and currents of the river." Among the rubble of sandstone and shale at the base of the cliffs, Gesner reported that he found fossils of fish, one with a heavy armour of scales and leg-like appendages that he misidentified as a small tortoise. Gesner's account led me into the world of geology, allowing me to see the story of the river in the context of the long history of an evolving world.

The broad-shouldered Abraham Gesner was the first geologist appointed in the British colonies. His father had fought for the British in the Revolutionary War, alongside his twin brother, before settling in the Annapolis Valley of Nova Scotia as a United Empire Loyalist refugee. Abraham was the sixth of twelve children. As a young man he had been shipwrecked twice during a failed attempt to establish a horse-trading business between Nova Scotia and the Caribbean. Deep in debt, as he would be for much of his life, Gesner travelled to London, England, to study medicine. In London, Gesner discovered his true passion: the study of geology and chemistry. This would lead him later to a measure of international fame as the inventor of the process to distill kerosene.

During breaks in his medical studies, he attended lectures by Charles Lyell, one of the pioneers of modern geology. Lyell's grandly ambitious *Principles of Geology* advanced the theory of uniformitarianism, that the Earth was formed not in a moment of divine creation, but gradually, through processes we could see in the world around us. Lyell was not the first to adopt this theory but he expressed it with such force and style that it couldn't be ignored. Charles Darwin took the first volume of Lyell's work with him when he began his voyage of discovery on the HMS *Beagle* in 1831. When Darwin returned from his voyage, the geologist and the botanist became life-long friends. Lyell wrote that rocks told the story of a world that was much older than previously thought, and that changes came slowly over a grand expanse of time. Fossils suggested a history that could be divided into epochs, during which species of plants and animals had come into being and passed away. The way rivers carved deep valleys was the clearest evidence of a creation process that extended far into a distant past and would continue long into the future.

Lyell would later come to Nova Scotia to go fossil hunting with Abraham Gesner. He would also visit Fredericton to reunite with an old friend from his school days, Sir Edmund Head, the lieutenant-governor of New Brunswick. I found a record of Head's journey through the Waagansis portage in the archives of the Beaverbrook Art Gallery in downtown Fredericton. Edmund Head and his wife, Anna Maria Yorke, arrived in Fredericton in April 1848 and that summer struck out together for the Restigouche. Head was an angler and was no doubt one of the first to hook a salmon on the river with a fly rod. Anna Maria was an artist who created pencil drawings in her notebook on the way downstream, and those I found in the gallery archives. One is of a campsite on the upper reaches of what appears to be the Little Main Restigouche downriver from the mouth of Waagansis Brook, their tall canvas tents pitched beneath towering fir trees. Another is a portrait of her guide standing in the bow of her bark canoe holding a pole and wearing tall boots, a floppy broad-brimmed hat and a sash tied round his waist. The archivist at the gallery also located a watercolour of a wider expanse of water framed by gentle hills on the lower Restigouche painted by her husband on the same trip.

I found an account of another vice-regal trip through the Waagansis portage in 1862. Arthur Hamilton Gordon, who had been appointed lieutenant-governor of New Brunswick the previous year, travelled through the portage route and descended the Restigouche with a well-known Wolastoqey guide named Gabriel Acquin, and he later wrote of his journey in a long essay, "Wilderness Journeys in New Brunswick," that he published in London. Gordon, a lean man with a drooping moustache and heavy beard, was a thirty-two-year-old bachelor when he came to New Brunswick the year after his father, George Hamilton Gordon, the former British prime minister, had died. Arthur Hamilton Gordon had served as his father's private secretary and had been seeking a governorship in the colonies.

When he arrived in the colony he found that he had entered a political maelstrom. The debate about the formation of a new country called Canada was raging through the colonies and New Brunswick, though small, was seen as a key jurisdiction for the pro-confederation forces. Gordon played a critical role in keeping a pro-confederation government in power in New Brunswick that helped lead to the formation of the Dominion of Canada in 1867.

Gordon's escape from politics was the New Brunswick wilderness, and whenever possible he arranged for expeditions with Gabriel Acquin. I found a photograph of Gordon and Acquin with a group of men and a map spread out on the wide stone steps of the Government House mansion beside the Saint John River, and another of them preparing to depart on a hunting adventure with bark canoes and rifles on the shore of an unnamed river.

Gordon was drawn to the freedom of forest life although he admitted that the hardships in camp, such as biting insects, rain and cold, might appear insane to his readers in the cities of England. He admired the play of sunlight on leaves, rocks and water, the sight of kingfishers startled from their nests, foaming rapids, wildflowers and ferns. He took to bathing in the river and fishing for salmon and trout that were cooked over an open fire and eaten off plates made of birchbark. His account of the journey through the Waagansis portage route gave me some idea of what I could expect. The stream turned every moment through a succession of muddy shallows and deep holes. The tangled growth on the banks hung over the brook, and they had to break down two beaver dams to pull their canoe through to the river. Every mile of progress took an hour and they were relieved to float out into the open air and clear waters of the Restigouche and leave behind what Gordon called the "detestable" Waagansis. I wasn't particularly concerned by this account. I figured he was a sensitive British aristocrat; what he described sounded like a regular day on the river with my father. What I didn't know then was that he wasn't the only one to use the word detestable to describe the Waagansis. It may have been a way to the Restigouche but it was no easy passage.

7 While the stories of previous expeditions were useful in mapping my own, it was the geologists who expanded my understanding of the frame of time and transformed vague images of a distant past from the abstract to the specific. Geologists sometimes place the timeline of the history of the Earth on a twenty-four-hour clock to help us understand the context of time, evolution and change. These clocks are often modified to reflect new fossil discoveries that adjust the timelines by hundreds of thousands of years. A geological time scale presented as a clock might look something like this: if we mark the formation of the Earth at midnight, single-cell organisms appear at four a.m., photosynthetic organisms at five-thirty. (Here we must pause to consider this critical moment in the history of the Earth. Photosynthesis allows an organism to draw energy from the sun into a molecular power plant that converts carbon dioxide and water into glucose, releasing oxygen as a biproduct.) Photosynthesis resulted in the atmosphere becoming infused with oxygen by noon on the geological clock, opening the world to a further explosion of life. Fish arrive at eight p.m., land plants take root at nine-thirty, land animals arrive in numbers at ten. Dinosaurs roam the land at ten-forty and disappear by eleven-forty. The ancestors of human beings join at one minute to midnight. We were late arrivals to the party.

Within these broad parameters, we can trace the origins of the river itself, beginning with the fossil that Abraham Gesner misidentified as a tortoise. In the years following the publication of Darwin's *On the Origin of Species*, Gesner's tortoise was correctly identified as a fish called *Bothriolepis*, a placoderm that was abundant in these waters 380 million years ago, in a period we now call Devonian. It was the age of fishes, when the evolutionary stream of life was dividing and turning toward the land. In the Devonian age, Miguasha was part of a sprawling deltaic plain at the mouth of a great river. The mountains around the river were still being formed, pushed up from the bottom of the sea as continental masses collided and began to draw the first rough draft of North America. Cascades of fresh water washed down from the new mountains, depositing silt on the delta and spilling into the salt sea, creating a brackish aquatic ecosystem teaming with fish.

During the epochs that followed, the land cooled and warmed, glaciers advanced and retreated, the sea rose and fell. Fossilized spores suggest that 120,000 years ago the mountains and valleys in this corner of eastern Canada were covered by towering hardwood forests. When the Earth cooled, softwoods and tundra grasses grew in place of the hardwoods, until the snow stopped melting in the summer and the land was covered by ice and snow for 100,000 years, give or take.

We call our current geological epoch Holocene, which begins at the end of the last ice age. The river we know as Restigouche began to run to the sea fifteen thousand years ago when glaciers from the last ice age began to melt and migrate down from the Appalachian hills, by then weathered remnants of the young mountains that in the Devonian age had been one of the greatest mountain ranges in the world. As the glaciers retreated, they carved new valleys, grinding the rocks beneath them into gravel, sand and silt, marking the path of the river to the sea. For four thousand years the ice melted and the glacial till washed down with the water during seasons of freezing and thawing, settling in the valleys.

As the land warmed, winds and water distributed seeds and spores of pioneer plants that took root in the till. They fertilized and stabilized the soil, creating the conditions for the growth of trees, such as willows and alder. Then forests of spruce, aspen, birch and pine grew in the Restigouche valley, followed by maple, beech, cedar and hemlock, creating what today we call the Acadian mixed forest that in the fall paints the hillsides in brilliant reds, oranges, yellows and greens.

Archaeological evidence suggests that Indigenous people were living on this land at least ten thousand years ago, perhaps having migrated from the west after the last Ice Age. They were joined by an eastern Algonquin people who came to the territory from the southwest. These two groups merged into one to become the ancestors of the Mi'gmaq of the Restigouche, who have lived for five thousand years in Gespe'gewa'gi, the seventh district of the distinct and defined political community Mi'gma'gi. They are an ancient people with a history as old as the cities of Mesopotamia, older than the wars at Troy and the world described in the epic poems of Homer. In the early 1500s the Mi'gmaq encountered the Basques and Portuguese fishermen who crossed the Atlantic in small sailing ships. They were among the first Indigenous people in North America to encounter Europeans and some of these first contacts were in the estuary of the Restigouche River.

In the world of the geologists, I came to understand how difficult it is for us to conceive of the scale of time in the life of the river in the context of the short passage of our own lives. As I explored the history of the Restigouche, I tried to expand the context of the story by creating new timelines based on a simple mathematical experiment. I began to imagine that the Restigouche was one hundred years old. And in that context, I began to place events on an imaginary timeline.

If the river were a hundred years old, it ran free from human interference for its first ninety-nine years. All the major disruptions in the watershed would have come at various times during the last year and the great acceleration of change during the past six months. On my new timeline there was nothing gradual at all about the changes that were sweeping through the natural systems in the river valley.

8 During the first week of June, I made one more trip north into the river valley to prepare for the first stage of my canoe run. I crossed the main river just below the mouth of the Matapédia and drove up the Quebec shore. The ice had released from the river a month earlier, the spring freshet had come and gone, and the water was flowing in its banks already at summer levels, the gravel bars on the shorelines drying in the sun. I said a silent prayer for rain as I drove into the riverside town of Matapédia past the post office and parked beside the railway tracks. I climbed the stairs to a second-storey office to meet David LeBlanc, the executive director of the Restigouche River Watershed Management Council.

The Restigouche watershed, 1.3-million hectares of land that drains into the river and its tributaries, is divided between the provinces of Quebec and New Brunswick. This region has been a jurisdictional challenge, to put it nicely, with administrators from the Canadian government, two provincial governments, Mi'gmaq Nations, private fishing clubs and municipalities all exercising their authority through the watershed. In much of the Restigouche valley, the river has been managed by a different set of rules depending on whether you happened to have anchored your canoe on the New Brunswick or Quebec side of the river. The various governments had their own mandates and agendas; they spoke different languages, literally, politically, socially and philosophically.

In 2002, representatives from Listuguj and Ugpi'Ganjig, recreational salmon groups and fishing clubs incorporated the Restigouche River Watershed Management Council as a non-profit organization. The intention of the founding members was to create a local management group that could begin to address the jurisdictional challenges as well as the conflicts among river users and concerns about the increasing encroachment of industries such as forestry, agriculture and mining throughout the watershed.

The council's members now include representatives from the Mi'gmaq Nations, the fishing lodges, forestry companies, local towns and villages and ecotourism outfitters. The federal and provincial governments are partners, as well as various conservation organizations. The membership list itself is a significant accomplishment. The council is designed to share information and help people who weren't talking to each other begin to have a dialogue and, when possible, fix things that need to be fixed. This allows a diverse group of people in the valley who had often been in competition or conflict to focus their energies on their common desire to protect and enhance the Restigouche watershed. The council's success is in no small part due to the energy and character of its level-headed young leader.

Matapédia is David LeBlanc's hometown. After studying biology and wildlife management he returned to the valley, started an adventure canoe business and worked for a forestry co-operative before taking the job to run the council. He has been running the council's affairs for the past eleven years, supervising staff who are working on the river, organizing volunteers, running research and river enhancement projects, raising money, applying for grants, making presentations to governments, organizing and chairing meetings, and in general bringing steady leadership and calm competence to the council's work in the valley.

He's a problem solver and a fixer. For example, in the summer of 2017 when he received reports that potato fields were spilling silt into Five Finger Brook and then into the Little Main Restigouche after heavy rains (I was on the river fishing with friends when one of these floods of brown muck came down), he identified the source of the problem, organized meetings with the farmers, raised money from various sources and designed a solution. Then he put on his work boots and spent several days in the field helping the farmers install berms and silt traps to correct the problem. He applies a simple formula to his work. What's broken? What's the solution? Let's work together to fix one problem at a time. In each season he organizes and supervises fish counts, measures and monitors water temperatures and conducts surveys of logging in the headwaters to identify areas being overcut. When we met that day in June, he was making plans to remove log jams in the headwaters of the Little Main Restigouche that would block the migration of salmon in the fall. He was also making plans to begin a systematic program of breaching beaver dams in feeder streams to open up new areas of spawning habitat where juvenile salmon can live until they migrate to the sea. It would be a gentle intervention; once the spawners migrated above the obstructions and deposited their eggs, the beavers would return and make repairs to their dams.

We left the office and drove in his truck across the river bridge that crosses the Matapédia in the centre of town and followed the river upstream. David lives in a log house he built himself on the site of an old homestead farm on a high hill that overlooks the river. He dug an old-style root cellar into the hill to store the vegetables he grows in his gardens, and that afternoon he warmed up a pot of soup he had made from last season's crop of root vegetables.

We sat in his kitchen and talked about his work, and about the things that worry him these days, most of all the effects of clearcutting in the headwaters in a time of climate change. It is a lethal combination of land transformation and new weather patterns that bring powerful storms to the valley, causing the river to rise suddenly and fall quickly, and the water to warm in extended periods of summer drought. What a wild river in this part of the world needs is to be surrounded by forested hills that shade and protect feeder brooks and weather patterns that deliver days of steady, soft, dripping rain, followed by a gentle rise and a gradual drop.

We also talked about the things that give him hope, such as the Harmony Project, in which the council is a partner, that brings together children from schools in Listuguj and neighbouring communities to plant trees along the river valley, an exercise that promotes both stewardship and reconciliation. After lunch we drove back into the town and I left him at his office, promising to stay in touch through the season.

I drove downriver on the Quebec side, past the chain of islands where the river widens before it meets the tidewater, and turned into the community of Listuguj, passing rows of bungalows along the river. The spring crews hired by the local government were out mowing lawns and painting fences. In the centre of town are government offices and the headquarters of the police and fire departments and the Listuguj Rangers, who patrol and manage the salmon fishery. Across the street the afternoon sun reflected off the grey rounded steeple of the old stone Sainte-Anne Church. Capuchin friars built Sainte-Anne beside the river in 1903, near the site of the first chapel on the river built by Recollect missionaries in 1745 on what was then called Mission Point.

I parked by the river and walked down to the landing beside the highway bridge that crosses back into New Brunswick. There, Mi'gmaw fishermen were launching small motorboats to begin setting their nets on opening day of the salmon season. Uniformed Listuguj Rangers were on the wharf and in their own boats on the river, checking safety gear and beginning the monitoring program that will continue through the season. It was a peaceful, orderly scene. But it had been a long and hard road for this resilient community before they could return to a day like this.

9 It was during this trip north that I began to realize this journey was far more challenging than I imagined. The pieces of the story were scattered, and each one that seemed to fit would lead me to another that didn't. It was an unsettling experience, to be lost for a time in pursuit of a story that on the face of it should not have been so elusive. I had been travelling on rivers and writing about salmon angling and conservation at home and abroad for years. I had flown into river valleys in small planes and landed on airstrips maintained by millionaire anglers and fished out of lodges that served lobster and steak at midnight and champagne and orange juice for breakfast. I'd lived through a float plane crash landing on a remote river in Labrador. I'd mingled with sporting artists, nature writers and professional anglers, edited a magazine for a salmon conservation organization, volunteered for community watershed management groups, worked with academics on research projects and given public talks about river management.

I was expecting to find new and surprising facts through my research, but not to be overwhelmed by this sense of things jumbled and hidden. This was the river I knew more intimately than all the others, and I was starting to feel as if someone had poured the pieces of a large puzzle on the table and thrown away the box. This is what happens when dependable narrative lines collapse. As difficult as it was to face, I found a measure of consolation by reminding myself that surely this was a necessary stage in an inquiry such as this.

As I gathered the pieces of the story of the Mi'gmaq and Europeans that came to the Restigouche valley, I began to consider how the variations in their relationships to the natural world had contributed to a divide that Canadian society five centuries later is still struggling to cross. This caused me to reconsider my own relationship with the natural order that first came from my father and a Sunday School education that taught me the Genesis creation account, a story at once simple and deeply mysterious, where in the beginning the spirit of God moves over the waters and darkness lies on the face of the deep. Creation begins when God brings light into the world, then creates the heavens and the Earth, the oceans and rivers, all living creatures and finally humans from the dust of the ground. My father always reminded me that at the end of all this creating, God "saw all that he had made, and it was very good." At the same time, my father taught me how to read the Genesis account as myth, how it did not stand in opposition to our understanding of theories of evolution and the long history of the Earth. During a trip to New York City in the fall of 1979, my father introduced me to his teacher and mentor, the theologian Paul Lehmann, who presented me with a gift of an illustrated copy of Charles Darwin's *The Voyage of the H.M.S. Beagle.*

Then when my father began reading *The Odyssey* aloud to me in the evenings before I went to bed, he inadvertently converted me to paganism. In Homer's verses I fell for Ancient Greek theology, and I imagined living in a world in which gods were close at hand, among them the gods of rivers. When Odysseus was near drowning in an ocean storm on his long journey home to Ithaca, he came to the mouth of a river and prayed to the god before swimming up into the calm of the estuary and collapsing on the bank in safety, covered in brine. The sea was vast, dark and dangerous, ruled by the vengeful Poseidon. River gods responded to our prayers.

When I left home to study at university, I was introduced to the works of Aristotle, who had come to Athens to study at Plato's academy when he was seventeen and stayed for two decades. After Plato died, Aristotle left Athens, married and settled for a time on the island of Lesbos where he turned his extraordinary mind beyond his teacher's search for universal first principles and immersed himself in the particulars of the world around him, the study of nature itself. He made friends with fishermen, took to the water and dirtied his hands, collecting and dissecting specimens, systematically documenting and categorizing what lay before his eyes and so began to compose his remarkable works on biology, botany, cosmology and physics. He approached his inquiry from his experience in nature where he saw something simple and complex and wondrous in the same moment: the natural world he studied on the Island of Lesbos was endlessly at work striving to be what it was meant to be.

Aristotle looked up into the night sky and in the precise patterns of the movements of the stars and planets saw an intimation of the divine that he called the eternal world as opposed to the material world in which we lived. Both worlds had their special charms, he wrote, for "every realm of nature is marvellous," and even the most modest forms of life reveal "something natural and something beautiful." Aristotle's god is the primary source of all motion; every movement in the natural world is of divine origin. He wrote that when our ancestors told stories through myth about how the divine is present in the whole of nature, these were inspired words and should be preserved like a relic of an ancient treasure.

I found myself circling back to the Christian teachings of my father when I found Aristotle's vision of the essential goodness of creation preserved and expanded in the theology of Thomas Aquinas, the brilliant Dominican who was nicknamed the Dumb Ox because of the size of his girth and his halting manner of speaking. In 1265 he began writing the volumes of his *Summa Theologica* until he famously put down his pen in early December 1273 and declared all that he had written to be nothing more than straw. In the *Summa*, Aquinas referred to Aristotle simply as the philosopher. Aquinas and the philosopher shared the view that the intention of creation is revealed to us in the beauty and diversity of the world, in the participation of the many in a perfect order: "For goodness, which in God is simple and uniform, in creatures is manifold and divided and hence the whole universe together participates in the divine goodness more perfectly, and represents it better than any single creature whatever."

Pope Francis, in his 2015 encyclical *Laudato Si: Care for Our Common Home*, turned to Thomas Aquinas to support his assertion that everything in the created world is related, "and we human beings are united as brothers and sisters on a wonderful pilgrimage, woven together by the love God has for each of his creatures and which also unites us in fond affection with brother sun, sister moon, brother river and mother earth."

The vision of Earth as mother also appears in Mi'gmaw creation stories that come from a long oral tradition. In all the Mi'gmaw accounts, humans are the youngest form of life in a world that existed long before our arrival and will continue long after we depart. Creation begins with a life-giving energy called *Gisu'lgw*, "we have been created," from which came the sky and the sun. Dry earth was transformed into a green land that gave life to plants and animals. In time the energy gave life to a creative force called *Glusgap* that later took on human form. In his wanderings, *Glusgap* meets Grandmother, who was created from stone, an elder whose wisdom was expressed in language; Nephew, who rose from the energy of the foam of the ocean, sweet grass and the midday sun; and

Mother, who was born from the leaf of a tree and the morning dew and carried with her the teachings of the cycles of life.

"Our notion of Creation is not as a singular 'big bang' when everything began to be created nor is our story grounded in a Garden of Eden and the expulsion of Adam and Eve," writes Stephen Augustine, a hereditary chief and dean of Unama'ki College at the University of Cape Breton. "Mi'kmaq generally understand that our world is a cyclical motion of events, we have been created, we are being created; in the future, if we wake up in the morning and see our world before us, then we are continuing to be created."

For the Mi'gmaq, all things in the world have a spirit; therefore a river might require a gift from a traveller. Animals that die in a hunt offer the gift of their lives for the well-being of the hunter's family. All life decays, but life forces persist as a new tree rises from the earth where an old tree has fallen. The world is full of life and the potential for life to be renewed.

The language of the Mi'gmaq is an expression of an active relationship with the natural world. It has eleven consonant sounds and six vowel sounds and in the terminology of linguists is polysynthetic, which means that complex words are formed through fragments of words that when combined are rich in meaning. Mi'gmaq is verb-based and highly efficient; much is said in few words. For example, *a'sugwesugwijig* means to meet on the water in a canoe; *paqasa'latl*, to place something in the river; *alkumi*, to push oneself around in a canoe with a fishing spear; and the almost untranslatable *pemie'plewinatawijika'sit*, she walks along so close to the edge of the shore that she almost falls in but because of her skill does not. In the Mi'gmaw tradition, the sounds of their language came from the energy that moves among land, waters and sky, and anyone who has heard Mi'gmaq spoken knows that it is a gentle language that sounds like wind in the trees or water washing against a riverbank.

Fred Metallic, a salmon fisherman, scientist, historian and the director of natural resources in Listuguj, says the Mi'gmaq learned to live in accordance with the flux of creation. The Mi'gmaq knew when the salmon arrived in the river by observing the cycles of the moon and tides, the arrival of birds, the hatching of insects and the shifting patterns of the wind. Metallic explains that when the salmon return to the Restigouche, when they have returned to their home waters in their cycle of life, the people of Listuguj are in the same place in the cycle of their own lives. The Mi'gmaw language expresses relationships rather than subjects and objects, focusing on the processes that create life.

In speaking, the Mi'gmaq express their way of being in the world. That way of being is based on an understanding that they are all part of a divine process in an ever-changing world that is greater than themselves. Therefore the order of the world is divine and sovereign, but unlike the cosmological empires of the ancient world in Egypt, Mesopotamia, China and Japan, there were no rulers who carried with them the mandate of the divine. In the Mi'gmaw world view there is no division between human and the natural world, for they live with the particular ecology of their place where everything is alive and *msit no'kmaq*, "all my relations."

That way of being is not so far removed from the vision expressed by Pope Francis when he wrote that everything in nature has its own particular goodness and perfection, and that we have a moral responsibility for the care of the order of the Earth, "to avoid any disordered use of things." Pope Francis composed his letter to compel Christians to seek a correction of what he argues has been humanity's grave mistake — to think we "can substitute an irreplaceable and irretrievable beauty with something which we have created ourselves." We can trace this break away from the natural order to a particular time and place.

The first contacts between the Mi'gmaq and settlers came during an age of discovery that began to transform the way the people of Europe regarded their relationship with nature. A century after Jacques Cartier sailed into the Restigouche estuary, the French mathematician and philosopher René Descartes declared that a revolution in science had appointed humans "the lords and possessors of nature."

The transformation accelerated in Europe as an agrarian society was overturned by a new age of industry fueled by the burning of coal and the harnessing of steam. This was a time when the world was transformed by science and the Enlightenment, by a society not strictly bound and compelled by Christian teaching but freed from its constraints, as if human life on Earth had been reborn in the tumult of revolution. This relatively short period in human history radically changed both the way we think about the world and the way we live in it. As the printing press was spreading literacy throughout Europe, Copernicus positioned a motionless sun at the centre of revolving planets, Galileo perfected the telescope that confirmed a new cosmology and Newton extended our horizons to infinity. In England, Francis Bacon systematically unravelled the science of Aristotle by exposing its errors in fact and finding it barren on the subject of the production of works from nature that would benefit humans. Steam engines would come to move ships and locomotives, and hot air balloons were taking to the skies. Factories processed steel from pig iron and manufactured the Portland cement that laid the infrastructure for new landscapes. Power looms wove sheets of textiles and gas spread light into the dark corners of the world. In the rush of progress, the lessons of the past were abandoned like forgotten luggage on the platforms of railway stations throughout Europe and across the continent.

"If we are to understand the feeling of life which surged through the whole of Europe, we must not underestimate the significance of the hopeful excitement which was also stirred by these discoveries," wrote the Swiss theologian Karl Barth in his study of the transformation of society in the eighteenth century. "Here is manifested the existence of the absolute man, the man almost capable of anything."

On my drive downriver from Matapédia to Listuguj that June afternoon, I passed the railway bridge across the Restigouche that had opened the river valley to the world in the summer of 1876. The railway line and bridge were designed by the Scottish-born Canadian railway engineer Sandford Fleming, who supervised the construction of the Intercolonial Railway to the east and helped build the Canadian Pacific Railway to the west. Fleming was tall and strong with a large personality and intellect. He travelled for weeks through the wilderness to survey the route of the railway line, designing the railbed to withstand the northern climate and defying the lumber merchants by insisting that all new railway bridges be constructed from steel that would rest on piers built to last.

The Intercolonial's route followed the Matapédia River valley, turning almost at a right angle to cross the Restigouche. There, a steep embankment blocked the route, an obstacle that was removed by damming streams and directing water through wooden troughs in jets that pushed the entire hillside down into the river. Fleming was pleased that such an immense amount of material could be removed with little manual labour, calculating the reductions in cost, the disturbance of dumping a small mountain of gravel into the river not part of his equation.

Four piers were required to build the bridge across the Restigouche, and they had to be designed to withstand the force of the annual ice run and freshet. All would rest upon bedrock, no matter how far down they had to go. At the first pier, they found rock 16 metres below the summer level of the river, at the second pier 23 metres, at the third pier 19 metres and at the fourth pier 16.5 metres. The work began in 1869, using pumps powered by steam that could discharge 22,000 litres of water per minute. They drove 18,000 lineal metres of timber into the bed of the river continuously from August 1872 until April 1874. The piers were constructed of huge granite stones weighing as much as nine tons each, and 4,500 cubic metres of Portland cement all bound together with massive iron clamps so that not a single stone could be carried away without moving the whole mass. Fleming had seen bridges dispatched by northern rivers and he wasn't having that happen here. "Every precaution has been taken to render the piers of the bridge capable of resisting the formidable forces, to which they will periodically be exposed," Fleming wrote. "It is believed that they will remain uninjured." One hundred forty-two ice runs and freshets and counting, his prediction has held true.

Fleming was a devout Presbyterian who produced a prolific collection of writing in elegant prose. He wrote about how the railway was the link that allowed for the creation of a country, connecting the Maritime provinces with central Canada, binding us in common purpose, offering a passage over the struggles of the past. He saw with great clarity how technological advances were dramatically changing the human condition on Earth. Nature could now be exploited economically on a large scale and tamed for the pleasure and advancement of the human race. In the Restigouche valley and throughout America, the wilderness was being transformed with astonishing speed. It was as if humans weren't doing it at all. These were the new laws of nature that were transported to a new world by successive generations of immigrants. "The traveller, who is borne onwards, moving in an hour a distance which would have taken weeks to traverse through the tangled forests, scarcely casts a thought on the thousands of the sons of labour who toiled so many days and years in making smooth his path," Fleming wrote.

He saw how the application of steam power to travel on land and water and the telegraph that revolutionized communications had "rudely shaken customs and habits" that were centuries old. "We have undoubtedly entered upon a remarkable period in the history of the human race," he wrote. "Discoveries and inventions crowd upon each other in an astonishing manner. Lines of telegraph and steam communications are girding the earth, and all countries are being drawn into one neighbourhood."

Fleming saw in technological advancements the promise of progress, but he identified what he considered to be a fundamental flaw in the way we measured time. All of Europe had started to run on railway time. Large clocks were displayed in public places and pocket watches that kept accurate time became a matter of life and death for those who supervised the new flow of traffic on the tracks. But when he travelled through Europe and across the continent by rail, he would find "the hands of various clocks pointing in all conceivable directions." He began advocating for a worldwide standard time and a division of the Earth into time zones. In 1884, Fleming helped to organize the International Prime Meridian Conference in Washington that led to the universal adoption of standard time, a global reform of profound consequence for the conduct of human affairs that began with the worries of a railway engineer who wanted to make sure the trains ran on time.

We all now live according to the practical and predictable rhythms of the same clock that is regulated by the artificial lines we have drawn across our maps. But the river still keeps its own time. We who run rivers in canoes know this. For when we're on the river, the position of the sun in the sky becomes the measure of a day in which all motion is determined by the ebb and flow of the water, the direction of the winds, the stroke of the paddle and the push of the pole. We arrive at our destinations when the river allows us to be there, and in every moment of the day we remain fully conscious of all that is above and below the surface of the water. On days when we allow ourselves to fall into river time, we are released from the prime meridian and slip back into the embrace of the created order, reaching out toward the still point of the turning world.

10 Late in the afternoon I left the landing in Listuguj, crossed the bridge back into New Brunswick and drove upstream and down into the valley of the Kedgwick River. Just above the Montgomery Bridge, rows of Restigouche-style canoes, each with small outboard motors attached to the flat stern-end, were anchored along the gravel beaches. Most of the Restigouche canoes are 26 feet long and the best ones are made by a family named Sharpe in a workshop in Mann Mountain Settlement, a community on the lower end of the river. The Sharpe canoes are the workhorses on the river, heavy and stable with a wide, flat bottom, constructed of cedar strips covered by fibreglass, painted forest green, designed to carry large loads while running over shallow water. They all have a block anchor attached to the bow with a pulley system that extends the length of the canoe to the stern. The operator stands and runs the outboard with an extended tiller handle. The rows of canoes above the bridge belong to local anglers who fish the waters of the Little Main Restigouche.

I checked into a room at Chalets Restigouche and that evening, about an hour before dark, I pulled on my chest waders, strung up my fly rod and walked down to the river. I followed a trace of a path upriver through the woods until I reached the bottom end of an island behind which a stretch of swampy ground impedes the back channel of the river to create a shallow pond. I waded through the stream flowing out of the swamp and then crossed the island to the other side where the main channel runs fast and deep along a high bank, and then I walked up the gravel beach as far as I could go without getting myself into any wading heroics on slippery rocks. I knew it was too early for salmon to be ascending because the first fish in the spring generally run up the Kedgwick River below me. Each of the tributaries has its own distinct genetic strain of fish and the most experienced guides on the river can often identify a Kedgwick salmon or an Upsalquitch salmon by their shape and the timing of their run into the river. The early-run Kedgwick salmon tend to be large multi-year spawners, some weighing more than thirty pounds. The remarkable thing about Atlantic salmon is that they return to the river where they were hatched. How they navigate their grand journeys from their home waters to the coastal waters of Greenland and back again to spawn, sometimes repeating the trip two or three times, remains a mystery that has led to lots of scientific speculation about how they follow the Earth's magnetic fields and ocean currents and can recognize the chemical composition of water. I've read enough speculation on this topic to conclude that this is one mystery that will endure. The one thing we can say for certain is that we know this happens and we hope the day will never come when it doesn't.

That evening I was casting for trout, and at the lower end of the run I hooked one, reeled it into the shallows, slipped the hook from its jaw and released it back into the river, a brief moment of connection before sunset. It was a lovely little fish, about a foot long, copper coloured with red and green spots, one of the native fish species on the Little Main. I reeled up my line and bushwhacked my way back downriver and reached my room with the last light of the day fading from the sky.

11 I spent the next day beside Chaleur Bay, gathering material from the Restigouche Regional Museum in Dalhousie, a town that was once the heartbeat of New Brunswick's industrial revolution. Today Dalhousie is struggling to find a future a decade after a giant paper mill, chemical plant and power generating station all closed. Three generations of Dalhousie families earned a good living in the world of heavy industry, so it's difficult for the people here to recall that before the arrival of the mill this town was an international travel destination known for its natural beauty, clear air and clean water filled with fish where the great river meets the salt sea at the head of the bay.

The British travel writer John Rowan visited Dalhousie before and after the opening of the Intercolonial Railway when it was a sleepy town built where the bay narrows, beside a deep harbour. When the railway opened, Dalhousie was twelve hours by rail from Quebec City and five days by ship from the west of Ireland. On all the coastline between New York and Quebec, Rowan found no place with clearer water, purer air and finer scenery than the estuary at Dalhousie. "The whole of this vicinity seems to have been upturned by some convulsion of nature, and the hills are piled upon hill and rock upon rock in the most fantastic forms imaginable," he wrote.

Rowan, who had lived in Canada for some time before the construction of the railway, had written essays about the region under the pen name Cariboo for the widely read British sporting publication *Field*. These essays and other observations were incorporated in his expansively titled book *The Emigrant and Sportsman in Canada: Some Experiences of an Old Country Settler with Sketches of Canadian Life, Sporting Adventures, with Observations on the Forests and Fauna* published in London in 1876, with a large folding annotated map of Ontario, Quebec, Nova Scotia, New Brunswick and Prince Edward Island, showing every place he mentions and the route of his travels.

Rowan noted that the almost eight hundred kilometres of Intercolonial Railway, the most well-built railroad on the continent in its day, was a public works enterprise that would likely never pay for itself as it ran through "as wild and barren a country as there is in the world." He did suggest that the railway would create tremendous opportunities for summer tourists. "The dried-up New Yorker can in less than forty-eight hours breathe about the most bracing air on the world; and the English tourist, fresh from the trim fields or smoky cities of the old country, can in ten days without hardship or fatigue make the acquaintance of the illimitable wilderness." He wrote of a bay lined with sand beaches and warm salt water in summer for bathing, teeming with salmon and trout, shoals of herring and mackerel, and runs of smelt so prolific that farmers paddled down the Restigouche and scooped them out in handheld nets to use as fertilizer for their potato fields. He saw schools of white porpoises chasing herring through the waves at the mouth of the river.

He expected the railroad to open the market for fresh salmon in the big cities of the United States. He described how before the coming of the railway, salmon were shipped in sealed tins, as much as two hundred thousand pounds in a single season. In the mornings he watched canoe after canoe delivering loads of salmon from the nets. In the spring whole loads would contain fish that averaged twenty-five pounds each, and he saw some weighing up to fifty-six pounds. They were laid on benches and the scales were scraped off. Then they were gutted and washed in a cistern, cut into chunks and packed in large tins and sealed. A hole was punched in each cover and they were carried to a boiling house, after which the hole in the tin was soldered the moment the steam stopped rising. Then the cases of tins were doused in cold water, painted and labelled for export.

Inch Arran House, the first of Canada's grand railway hotels, was built in 1884 with expansive dining rooms and wide sweeping verandas on the promontory at the mouth of the river, four years before the construction of the Banff Springs Hotel and almost a decade before the opening of Chateau Lake Louise and Chateau Frontenac in Quebec City. But when Inch Arran House burned in 1921, it was never rebuilt. By then the provincial government was consumed by the fallout from the collapse of the sawmill industry that it hoped to replace with new mills that would manufacture paper from the forests of Restigouche County.

The logging industry in New Brunswick had first been a supplier of masts for sailing ships. Crews would search for towering pines, thirty metres high, straight and free of rot, preferably near a river so they could be felled in winter and floated to the sea in spring. At its peak, the industry exported about three thousand masts a year. As the demand for masts declined and the supply of two-hundred-year-old white pine disappeared, the industry began shipping raw timber to markets in Europe.

The timber merchants hired gangs of lumbermen who took to the woods in winter and lived in camps they built themselves from rough-hewn logs, sleeping on mattresses made of fir and spruce boughs. The lumbermen harvested trees with crosscut saws and axes, piling them on sleds. Horses run by skilled teamsters hauled the heavy sleds over ice-covered trails to rivers and streams where the logs were stacked and stamped by their owners on the banks.

In the spring the logs were pushed into the freshet and floated in huge drives downriver to the mills. The log drives were the first major stress on the river's systems. Lumber companies used whatever methods they could devise to move the logs to the mills. They dammed small brooks to create backwater ponds that were released to create greater flows in the spring. They clearcut steep shorelines so they could roll logs down into the river. The logs changed the course of the river and filled in pools with debris. When piles of logs jammed and dammed the river and couldn't be released by the men with their pike poles called picaroons, they were moved with dynamite.

In the mid-1800s through the turn of the century, lumber companies began to build sawmills in New Brunswick. "Sawmilling was a much more appropriate industry for facilitating the transition of New Brunswick from a resource frontier to a settled colony," writes University of New Brunswick historian Bill Parenteau. "Surveyor General Thomas Baillie, for example, remarked in an 1832 immigration pamphlet that 'a large and well conducted sawmill is a little town in embryo, and from experience I am fully convinced that no schemes for the formation and erection of inland towns will ever prove effective, unless combined with manufacturing.'"

By the turn of the century, the government had granted two thousand ten-year licenses to cut timber in Crown-owned forests to 280 companies. While the residents of rural communities worked the woods and mills, the lumber barons who controlled the timber leases turned their attention to the economic and political life in the province. "In the rough and tumble world of New Brunswick politics, the lumber barons dominated the legislature," Parenteau writes. "Generally, an average of about 50 per cent of members of the legislature were directly involved in the lumber industry well into the twentieth century. They were also patrons of their communities, intimately involved in the churches, education system, health care and other aspects of social development."

In the 1920s and 1930s, about the time that the forest industry throughout North America was moving from the production of lumber to pulp and paper, the post-war recession was driving the New Brunswick lumber barons into bankruptcy. This created a crisis for the government that lost almost half its revenue and had to face the political and social problem of thousands of laid-off forestry workers. The government responded by cutting deals with companies that would establish new paper mills in exchange for generous long-term leases of Crown lands or the wholesale transfer of large tracts of private land. Bill Parenteau tells how the premier of New Brunswick, John Baxter, had a vision for a new industrial revolution in the press room of a newspaper in Montreal. "Partly closing my eyes, I could vision the forest. Looking again, I saw the newspapers rushing from the press by hundreds, until the two visions seemed to blend, and I could almost see a tree transform itself into the printed sheet."

The new paper mills had three requirements: a wood supply for fibre, a source of hydroelectricity and a body of water that could be used both for the production process and as a dump site for its liquid effluent. All of these requirements were a direct assault on river systems. Baxter's vision was realized by three large companies: the Fraser Company that would operate mills in Edmundston on the Saint John River and in Atholville just outside of Campbellton on the Restigouche River; the Bathurst Company that ran a mill on the Nepisiquit River; and the International Paper Company, the largest paper maker in the world, that would transform Dalhousie into a paper town. Bill Parenteau has documented how all three companies began buying forestland and securing Crown leases from the failing sawmill operations, eventually sharing among them 70 per cent of all Crown forest holdings in the province and wielding the kind of bargaining power that turned the province into a client state.

When International Paper negotiated the rights to hydroelectric development on the Saint John River at Grand Falls, the new industrial revolution began in earnest. "After more than twenty years of holding substantial wood and power resources in reserve, International Paper began industrial developments of an unprecedented scale in New Brunswick," Parenteau writes. The company blasted what became the largest hydro pressure tunnel in Canada through the rock beneath Grand Falls, more than eight hundred metres long and seven metres in diameter. It ran a transmission line from the powerhouse directly to Dalhousie where it began to build a $15-million newsprint mill, the largest and most technologically advanced mill of its kind in the world on the shore of Chaleur Bay. The company created space for the mill by building a seawall around a cove, pumping out the water, digging down to the bedrock, filling in the hole with cement and levelling it with more than five million bricks. It dammed the nearby Charlo River to create additional power for the mill. The Dalhousie mill was opened in March 1930. Premier Baxter started the paper machines while a children's choir sang "O Canada" accompanied by the Canadian National Radio

Orchestra. A plane was dispatched from the capital city with copies of the Fredericton newspaper and landed on the Restigouche River ice to deliver the printed news of the opening.

In 1948, the Toronto newspaper the *Globe and Mail* marked the fiftieth anniversary of International Paper and the economic miracle it had brought to Canada, making special mention of the mill in Dalhousie. It included a passage from the company's anniversary book that suggested the paper-making industry would continue its work in perpetuity, supported by the new technology of scientific tree farming that was described as an act of conservation: "Every large-scale pulp and paper manufacturer must aim to have and maintain a perpetual source of wood and to encourage the growth of trees as a crop. The goal of the International companies today is about 5,000,000 cords a year. The modern papermaker is a conservationist by instinct and by necessity." This was a conservation ethic driven by the need to protect assets and manage forests to maximize profits, and it transformed an ecosystem into cubic metres of fibre and the Acadian forest into a new crop scheduled for future years of production.

In the early 1960s, the provincial government began looking for ways to expand the industrial footprint in Dalhousie. In particular, it was hoping to convince Canadian Industries Limited, a company that manufactured explosives, pesticides and fertilizers, to build a plant there. To make the site more attractive, the government decided it needed a new supply of fresh water, and in 1963 it built a dam across the Eel River that flows through the Mi'gmaq community of Ugpi'Ganjig, formerly known as the Eel River Bar Indian Reserve. The Mi'gmaq had been living there since 1807 when the government encouraged them to create a year-round community beside the bay and end their traditional migrations from the shore to inland winter hunting grounds. The Mi'gmaq had adapted to their new circumstance, which in the beginning was little more than a swampy stretch of coastline, by harvesting clams from the sand flats at the mouth of the river and fishing eels and salmon. The dam stopped the tidal flow that replenished the clam beds and blocked the migration of eels and salmon into the river and those that remained were contaminated by effluent discharged into the river and were no longer safe to eat. The result was an ecological and economic catastrophe for the Mi'gmaq community.

A community member would later tell a commission studying the effects of the dam: "When everything was all said and done, I moved my people, my family out of the community to get away from this creature that was plaguing my people. Whether it was a demon, or whatever you wanted to call it, it was a curse to our people."

The New Brunswick Power Corporation built the Dalhousie Generating Station in 1969 to produce electricity for the mill by burning coal and heavy fuel oil. A reporter from the *Globe and Mail* visited Dalhousie in February 1974 and came upon a scene that was about as far as we can imagine from the place John Rowan encountered a century earlier: "On a bright wintry day as you travel down Highway 11 toward the water, it seems a near perfect setting for a town — until you turn the corner on to William Street and are confronted with the massiveness of the New Brunswick International Paper Co. mill. The mill sits across from the town's main business section and its smoke hangs over the town like a straight arm."

The young mayor of Dalhousie, Allan Maher, told the reporter: "It is in a bad place as far as scenery goes. But it's the mainstay of the community, and if you took that out our heart would be gone. They're pumping out black smoke today and that's unusual. They converted to oil three or four years ago. They must be burning bark or something." The reporter noted that the mill employed 1,200 people in the town of 6,400.

The power station was expanded in 1975 to burn high-sulphur coal mined near the small town of Minto about an hour outside Fredericton and then in 1988 an even dirtier fuel called Orimulsion that was imported by tanker from Venezuela. I won't even try to explain the tortured economic and environmental justification for the supply chain that was powering the paper town by the time the Venezuelan link was added. When the Orimulsion supply was lost, that was the beginning of the end for the Dalhousie power station.

The pulp and paper miracle lasted about another two decades, with the New Brunswick government propping up and expanding the industry with infusions of public cash. During this time, Parenteau notes, the industry developed an "extraordinary sense of entitlement to the public forest and financial resources of the province." It was all held together with this masking tape of public financing until newsprint and paper use began to drop in the electronic information age. Then the North American housing market crashed early in the twenty-first century at the same time as paper production entered a global marketplace, moving to warmer regions of the world where trees grow faster and labour costs are lower.

I visited the Restigouche museum on the recommendation of Tony Tremblay, one of my colleagues at St. Thomas University in Fredericton. Tony grew up in Dalhousie in a family of mill workers and did his own shifts in the mill before he left to study at St. Francis Xavier University in Nova Scotia. Now he's a professor of New Brunswick Studies, and after the Dalhousie mill closed he turned his attention to his home-town. He produced a documentary film called *The Last Shift* about the closure of the mill in 2010 and the life of the company town back when Dalhousie was one of the most stable and affluent communities in the province.

Tremblay recalls that the people of Dalhousie in his youth had what he calls a "nobility of spirit" about who they were and the work they did. They were not environmentally reckless. They were trying to make ends meet. The paper makers took pride in their work and maintained a deep connection to the lakes and rivers and forests that sustained their community. Most sacrificed themselves for the dream of seeing to their children's futures. Tremblay's father and many of his friends died shortly after retirement. "The place was hardest on its people, and they had no choice or say in the matter," he says.

His film is a record that might otherwise have been lost of the vibrant life of this community during the paper-making years. It is also a reminder of how transitory our works in this world can be. Those who are living in a mill town can't help but imagine that the enterprise will go on for all time—until the day it ends, and they recognize that conservation meant something different to them than it did for the company. "The real secret is the damn mill was never ours anyway," writes David Adams Richards, who grew up in a boom-and-bust paper and lumber mill town beside the Miramichi River. "That is Canada's true tragedy, which goes beyond my region."

When the mill closed, the chemical plant that produced chlorine, caustic soda and sodium hypochlorite also closed, along with the power station. The Eel River dam was removed in 2011, and the river and clam beds are slowly healing, but there remains a long hard road to repair the damage to the people of Ugpi'Ganjig. Today the mill and the power station have been demolished. The future of Dalhousie is uncertain, and like many rural places in the province, the population is declining with a median age closing in on sixty. The vast vacant lots are reminders of all that has come and gone.

We now know after samples were taken from sediment, water, and mussels that the industrial enterprises contaminated the Restigouche estuary with mercury. The mussels sampled in the Dalhousie area were small, contained heavy metals and had enzyme changes in their digestive glands. The memory of the grand wilderness that John Rowan described was swept away in the vapour trail of an industrial journey whose final toll is yet to be determined and paid. The idea that the industrial revolution once started would never end was myth and political illusion for, unlike the life of the wild river, we can measure the beginning and end of this episode with precision. The papermaking era in Dalhousie lasted about eighty years. Or if we place it on the timeline of our imagined one-hundred-year-old river, the mill made paper for about twenty-eight weeks, and the Eel River dam held back water for about fourteen weeks. And the river still flows on into the bay.

12 The morning after my visit to Dalhousie I was back in Kedgwick River to reconnect with my old friend Danny Bird, the manager of the Kedgwick Lodge, one of the oldest fishing lodges on the river. His first party of anglers would be arriving that afternoon for the opening day of his season. I met Danny three decades ago when I came to work for the Atlantic Salmon Federation, a conservation organization based in Saint Andrews. I was hired to edit the federation's magazine and Danny was the regional manager for New Brunswick. I was struggling that year with the moral shift from journalism to advocacy, and as a young idealist, I thought the ultimate objective of a conservation organization should be to put itself out of business. This was an unhelpful proposition for my employer, but I found a friend in Danny, who had worked as a river guide in his youth and is an iconoclast by nature. Most of all, I admit, we shared an aversion to anyone telling us what to do. After Danny left the federation, he was asked to be the manager of this lodge.

I found him in his office that morning, answering the phone and worrying over the few final details of the day. The guides were moving into their quarters and preparing three Sharpe canoes for the evening fishing. Windows in the lodge still needed to be caulked. Someone needed to go to town and buy new sponges that are used to mop up water from the bottom of the canoes during the season.

The lodge was completed in 1897, during a time when wealthy New York sportsmen had discovered the Restigouche River and its fabulous opportunities for salmon angling. William Kissam Vanderbilt, the grandson of Cornelius "The Commodore" Vanderbilt, heir to a shipping and railway fortune, and a member of one of the wealthiest families in America in their day, hired local craftsmen to build the lodge out of squared logs with dovetailed joints. One of Vanderbilt's fishing companions, Stanford White, among the most renowned New York City architects of the Gilded Age, designed the lodge. White was a partner of the firm McKim, Mead, and White, which designed New York's Penn Station, Madison Square Garden, the Savoy-Plaza Hotel, the Boston

Public Library, Washington Square's triumphal arch and mansions on Fifth Avenue.

By Vanderbilt standards, the lodge was a modest structure, but White's design was elegant in its simplicity and perfectly functional. The walls were made from timbers cut in the valley of the Upsalquitch River in the winter, transported by sled to the site, split and squared with adzes. The main lodge is one octagonal room finished in lightly stained spruce and birch, with three banks of windows facing the river and a massive stone fireplace against the rear wall. The ceiling is twenty-five feet high, with a chandelier made from antlers hanging over a long table where all meals are served. The kitchen is attached to the main building. There is a large porch on three sides of the building covered by a shingled hipped roof. The posts are made of cedar trees with the bark and stubs of branches still attached. Four bedrooms, each with its own fireplace, are in a separate building, connected by a breezeway. The lodge still stands much as it did in 1897, including a mounted elk head in the main room that, so the story goes, was shot by Teddy Roosevelt.

It's a plausible story. When Vanderbilt had the lodge built, he was leasing the land from a man named Archibald Rogers, a member of New York's high society and a railway engineer of inherited wealth who married into more wealth. Six years later, Vanderbilt turned the lodge back over to Rogers, whose mansion on the Hudson River was built in the French Renaissance Chateauesque style, an homage to sixteenth-century country homes in the Loire Valley. Rogers's mansion was designed by the same architect who had designed the Vanderbilt family's summer estate in Newport, Rhode Island. These mansions were the architectural statements for a new American aristocracy. Rogers and his wife Anne Coleman Rogers hosted parties at their estate and ran a school on the property for their own children, as well as some others, among them Franklin D. Roosevelt.

Archie Rogers lived a double life. He raced yachts and lived in the public eye in New York, and then every spring he would disappear into the wilderness for months to hunt and fish on the Restigouche. He discovered salmon fishing during a trip to the Miramichi River, and from there he made his way to the Restigouche. He bought land just below the mouth of the Kedgwick that bordered on a pool with the modest name Jimmy's Hole. An argument can be made that Jimmy's was then and remains the finest Atlantic salmon angling pool in the world. Archie Rogers was fit, wiry, and argumentative, an accomplished sportsman and writer with a large moustache. On the river, he often wore a tall, floppy, broad-brimmed hat. Once he established himself at the Kedgwick Lodge, he returned almost every season until he died in 1928.

That June morning I pulled old leather-bound logbooks off a shelf next to the fireplace and read daily fishing diaries meticulously recorded in Rogers's neat handwriting that noted every fish taken, the weight, location, weather conditions and type of fly he used. He would arrive in mid-June, usually from Matapédia on a wooden scow drawn by a team of horses. The river scows were made of spruce, sixty-five feet long and nine feet wide, with rugged gunwales and a wooden tiller extending from the stern. Two to three horses with a rider on the "high horse" on the left hauled a fully loaded scow that weighed more than fifteen hundred pounds, the team hitched to a hundred-fifty-foot tow rope. Once he was settled in at the lodge, Rogers would stay until early August and go fishing every day. Most seasons he brought a friend, although he came some years on his own and at various times he hosted other guests for shorter periods. In 1894 he brought along his eleven-year-old son to introduce him to the Restigouche and salmon angling.

Rogers hired Mi'gmaw guides and they poled his bark canoes, one standing in the back and another in the bow. Today the Kedgwick Lodge is the only lodge on the river that still employs exclusively Mi'gmaw guides, a chief guide and a bowman in each canoe. In the new guides' quarters situated across the lawn from the old lodge, Mi'gmaq is the first language spoken and it remains the first language for all boat commands and exchanges between head guide and bowman on the river.

The lodge is situated at the base of what's known as Broderick's Hill, named after Michael and Bella Broderick, who arrived on the beach in front of the lodge on June 10, 1906, with their three small girls, one still a babe in arms. They had come up the river from Matapédia by scow with all their belongings. Michael, who had come to New Brunswick as a teenaged stowaway on an Irish freighter, had been hired by Rogers to be the lodge manager. The Brodericks moved into the caretaker's home, an unfinished farmhouse with just one walled bedroom upstairs. They drew water from a spring near the river. A week after he arrived Michael planted his first potato crop. They inherited a modest collection of farm equipment and livestock, including four cows, six sheep, a mowing machine, two plows and a variety of hand tools. Rogers owned twelve hundred acres of land on which the Brodericks were given permission to cut wood, farm and sell their produce.

Bella cooked at the lodge, a life defined by long days in the kitchen preparing an early breakfast, an afternoon lunch and then a late-night meal when the guests returned from fishing at sunset. In the summer this would be as late as ten p.m. When the anglers departed late in the summer, the lumbermen arrived and they would often stop for meals or spend the night with the Brodericks. Michael and Bella Broderick occupied the caretaker's home for decades, eventually passing on the management job to their son John. On early maps, the community of Kedgwick River is simply called Broderick. The only access was by river and rough forest trails until a truck road was cut through the forest and down over Broderick's Hill in 1944. It remained an isolated outpost in the northern wilderness, occupied by hard-working settlers and loggers, Mi'gmaw guides and sportsmen of astonishing wealth and privilege, a social order that continues today.

When the party arrived for opening day, I met them on the porch. Among them was Danny Bird's eldest son, Andrew, a military veteran who had put the group together as part of a program called Connecting Veterans with Atlantic Salmon. The program has two objectives: to connect military veterans who may be suffering physical or emotional trauma from their service with others who have had similar experiences, and to offer them healing time on the river. Andrew spent twenty-five years as a combat engineer with tours in Bosnia, Eritrea and Afghanistan. When his mind is racing "a million miles an hour," he says, the river slows everything down, and he can just breathe again. The river pulls him back into the world. On the water he sees something new every day, in every run of current. "The river is a story of life," he says.

Later that afternoon I stopped in to see Herbie Martin, the senior guide at the Kedgwick Lodge, in his summer quarters, an immaculate travel trailer in a small campground beside the Little Main Restigouche. He was about to begin his fiftieth season at the lodge. Herbie is a tall man with silver hair who speaks softly and moves with graceful power. His father Alexi had been a guide before him and used to travel from Listuguj by horse and buggy for two days to get to the lodge, stopping to camp the first night near the Upsalquitch River. In the years before the construction of the lodge, the guides and fishing parties lived in tents, supplied by boats that came by twice a week to deliver mail. Herbie's parents spoke Mi'gmaq at home when he was a child, but when he went to school, the priests tried to make him stop speaking his language. He first came to the lodge as a teenager to work as a bowman for his father when John Broderick was the camp manager. He's worked for the lodge every season since.

That afternoon we looked through a collection of old photographs. In one, he and his father are standing together in long ponchos, leaning against a car as a light rain falls on the river. He has a file of photographs of his guests, including several of Robert Goodyear, a businessman from a prominent Buffalo railway family who took over the lodge after Archie Rogers died. Bobby the Bull, as he was known, was a powerful man and a fine athlete. He had attended Yale where he was a baseball teammate of George H.W. Bush, who remained a lifelong friend.

Herbie told me why the pools have the names they do: Cow because there used to be a cow pasture there; Soldiers because that's where the army patrols would stop and camp. He told me the difference between Jimmy's Hole and Jimmy's Hat and Looking Glass that receives cool water from the brook that flows into the river below the lodge. He told me about the night he and Bobby Goodyear got caught in a storm at Jimmy's and a tree on the bank that had been struck by lightning burst into flames. He spoke of his concerns about clearcutting, how the river isn't holding water like it used to and how much the landscape is changing. He remembers how in the 1950s when the forestry companies and the government started spraying the pesticide DDT to combat spruce budworm, the eagles disappeared for a time and then when the insecticide was banned they returned, a story that he witnessed long before it became known to the world in Rachel Carson's *Silent Spring*.

Later that evening Andrew and his friend Dave Walcott, the operations officer from his last tour in Afghanistan in 2010, went fishing in Herbie Martin's canoe with bowman Rene Martin, who is also from Listuguj. That evening they were fishing the Junction Pool using a system that those who fish the Restigouche by canoe call drops. The bowman drops the anchor and one of the two anglers in the canoe "covers the water" with a series of casts. When Herbie decides it's time to move, he asks Rene to pull the anchor and allows the current to pull the canoe downstream into a new stretch of water. When he's where he wants to be, he asks Rene to drop anchor. The word drop is used in a sentence as a noun, as in "let's take a short drop," or, "I'm going to give us one more drop here."

Herbie explained to Dave how salmon angling is a sport of "when you least expect it." Darkness was falling, but Herbie decided to take a final drop. Andrew had made a couple of casts when a large salmon broke the water and took a fly called a Green Highlander that Danny had created on the tying bench in his office. The fish was so strong it pulled the canoe downriver out of the Junction Pool and through another pool called Campbell's before Herbie brought the boat to shore. There Rene Martin netted a thirty-pound silver Atlantic salmon fresh from the ocean that they released back into the river. "It's those times when the weight of the world is lifted and the demons are put to rest," Andrew later told me. "You feel nothing but the power of the salmon, and the peace of the river."

All these stories swirled through my mind as I returned home to make final preparations for my own trip down the river.

13 In the early records of first contacts between Europeans and Mi'gmaq in the Restigouche valley, I found a narrow window into the world of Herbie Martin's ancestors. The first written account is in the journals of Breton explorer Jacques Cartier, who called the bay Chaleur, or Bay of Heat, when he sailed into the Restigouche estuary in search of a northwest passage on his first voyage across the Atlantic Ocean in the summer of 1534. For three days in July Cartier explored the bay where he encountered hundreds of Mi'gmaw men, women and children with whom he traded knives and iron wares for furs. Cartier later wrote in his journal that the river valley was as temperate as Spain, the hills blanketed by towering forests, the lowlands bursting with wild wheat, white and red currants, strawberries, raspberries and wild roses. The pools in the river were filled with silver Atlantic salmon.

This kind of welcoming encounter wasn't a singular event. In the records of early contact of Mi'gmaw people with French settlers, all their interactions were peaceful. In Mi'gma'gi, where the hard winters would kill those without the skill to survive, the relationship between these newcomers from France and the Mi'gmaq was a matter of life or death. They would continue to live together as neighbours until they became caught up in the European wars that spilled across the Atlantic.

The oldest detailed account of the lives of the Mi'gmaq of the Restigouche valley was written by the French missionary Chrestien Le Clercq, who lived in the Gaspé region between 1675 and 1687. Le Clercq was a member of the Recollect order, reform Franciscans who became the first missionaries in New France. Le Clercq wrote a book about his experience, *Nouvelle Relation de la Gaspésie*, published in 1691 in Paris that New Brunswick historian William F. Ganong translated in 1910. Ganong wrote a cautionary note in his introduction about the distortions in the text and the author's tendency to embellish matters. Nonetheless, Ganong recognized the value of Le Clercq's account, as do Indigenous researchers who are now working to develop a more comprehensive understanding of the history of Gespe'gewa'gi. A careful reading of the text allowed me to see how Le Clercq came to appreciate both the beauty and the unforgiving harshness of the land and to admire the character of the people who welcomed him into their world.

Le Clercq was thirty-four years old when he arrived at a fishermen's outpost on the Gaspé Peninsula in late October 1675, his ship having been almost lost in a storm in the Gulf of St. Lawrence. He called the Mi'gmaw people *Gaspésiens*. He had an uncommon capacity for language and spent the first fall and winter both learning Mi'gmaq and devising a system of characters to help him teach the Christian faith during his mission. Le Clercq's writing system, modified by missionaries who followed him, was used for hundreds of years. In the summer of 1676, he began living with the Mi'gmaq of the Restigouche.

Throughout his book Le Clercq calls the Mi'gmaq *sauvages*, which Ganong translates as Indians. However, Le Clercq maintains that they were not "wild men" as many Europeans had been persuaded to believe. One of the purposes of his writing, he said, was to "disabuse the public" of this misconception. He praised their eloquence and use of language, which he described as "very beautiful and very rich in its expressions," lending itself to public speeches. "It is necessary to admit that some persons in our Europe are persuaded too easily that the peoples of North America, because they have not been bred in the maxims of civil polity, preserve of the nature of man nothing but the name of wild men, and that they have none of the finer qualities of body and spirit which distinguish the human species from the beasts of the field," he wrote. "It is well, however, to correct an idea so stupid, so unjust and so unreasonable."

Le Clercq described the celebrations beside the Restigouche River upon the birth of a child. The newborns were washed in the river then placed on a board covered with the skin of a beaver decorated with paints, beads and porcupine quills and the community celebrated with a feast and speeches. He wrote that the Mi'gmaq had a deep understanding how the cycles of the moon, constellations and stars related to the movements of animals and the return of the salmon to the river. They drew maps on bark that showed all the rivers and streams in the lands through which they planned to travel. "They know five kinds of winds," he wrote. "They have so exact an idea that, provided they have the sun in view, they never wander from their route; and they know all the rivers so exactly that, however slightly a certain wigwam may be indicated to them, though it be distant eighty to a hundred leagues, they find it at the place named, even though it is necessary to traverse very dense forests. They say that the spring has come when the leaves begin to sprout, when the wild geese appear, when the fawns of moose attain to a certain size in the bellies of their mothers, and when the seals bear their young. They recognise that it is summer when the salmon run up the river, and when the wild geese shed their plumage. They recognise that it is the season of autumn when the waterfowl return from the north to the south."

They moved with the seasons where the land and water afforded them the greatest opportunities for hunting, fishing and gathering. They prepared "the greatest feasts in the world." They considered themselves equal in life and death, and loved their children, giving them "a thousand kindnesses and the best of everything that they have." The *Gaspésian* chief dressed modestly and resolved disputes "through friends and arbiters." After the arrival of the French, many of the *Gaspésian* clothes were made from blankets, cloaks and cloths that came from France, but previously their clothes were made from "skins of moose, beaver, marten and seal." They adorned themselves with "collars, belts and bracelets," but they were "foes of luxury and vanity." They valued the moose above all other game. They dried and smoked the meat and from the marrow of the bones and the grease made a kind of paste. They crushed the bones into a powder that they boiled and used as stock for soup. They boiled water in wooden pots by filling them with hot stones and in the same way melted snow for drinking in winter.

Le Clercq learned of the true danger of the winter in 1687, when he decided to make a journey from the Nepsiquit River that flows into the south side of Chaleur Bay to the Miramichi River to visit the Mi'gmaq there and the Seigniory of Miramichi. The seigniory was run by Richard Denys, the son of the French trader Nicolas Denys, governor of the lands along the coast of the Gulf of St. Lawrence from Gaspé to what is now Cape Breton. In 1653 the land granted to Nicolas Denys included the Seigniory of Restigouche that he largely ignored until he established a temporary trading post near the ancient village called Tjigog in 1669. He soon abandoned the post, passing it on to his seventeen-year-old son Richard three years later. Richard rebuilt the trading post and constructed a house and warehouse where he dried fish for export and traded furs, attracting a handful of French settlers.

It was Richard that Le Clercq set out to see, with a Mi'gmaw man, his wife, and a child in arms as well as a man named Phillippe Enault, who was the most prominent French resident of the area after Nicolas and Richard Denys. They packed twenty-four small loaves of bread, a portion of flour, three pounds of butter, a small keg of brandy and a box of hyacinth confection that had been a gift from the nuns in Quebec. Le Clercq baptized the infant boy before they left. They walked on snowshoes and dug hollows in the snow and slept on fir branches at night. Instead of following the river upstream along the portage route to the northwest branch of the Miramichi, they decided to traverse a section of forest that had been burned and in so doing they lost their way. Then they were slowed by a snowstorm that created such deep drifts they sank to their knees every step. They began to run out of food and were reduced to drinking water boiled with flour and planned to begin eating moccasins to stay strong enough to continue. When crossing a small river, Le Clercq fell through the ice, requiring the party to stop and build a fire to dry his clothes. That night, they ate the last of their flour. The next day they proceeded slowly, all extremely weak, until they came across the tracks of a Mi'gmaw hunter. Later that day they heard the sound of his snowshoes cracking in the distance and waited for him to arrive. He made a camp for them and cut wood for a fire. He had one partridge and killed two more that they boiled for dinner. The man guided them to his camp, and from there the party proceeded on to the Miramichi.

One of the most remarkable passages in the book is Le Clercq's account of a speech given by one of the Mi'gmaw leaders to a group of missionaries. The man was responding to suggestions that his people should adopt the French fashion of living. He asked Le Clercq to act as an interpreter when he gave his response: "My brother, hast thou as much ingenuity and cleverness as the Indians, who carry their houses and their wigwams with them so that they may lodge wheresoever they please, independently of any seignior whatsoever? We can always say, more truly than thou, that we are at home everywhere, because we set up our wigwams with ease where ever we go, and without asking permission of anybody. Learn now, my brother, once and for all, because I must open to thee my heart: there is no Indian who does not consider himself infinitely more happy and powerful than the French." He said he could call himself the sovereign of his own country with the right to travel and hunt and fish where he wanted, more content in the woods and in his wigwam than if he were in palaces and at the tables of the greatest princes of the Earth. Here, a Mi'gmaw chief was lecturing a group from France about the possibility of a radical human freedom and religious tolerance within a political community a century before the French Revolution. Le Clercq wrote that even though the *Gaspésiens* were pagans, he recognized that what he had been told was true. *Je les estimerois incomparablement plus heureux que nous*: I should consider these people incomparably more fortunate than ourselves.

Le Clercq's book was not particularly well received and was largely ignored. Instead, the word *sauvages* and the political, social and racial baggage it carried with it persisted and would define Mi'gmaw relations with Europeans for centuries. The word savage carried with it two false narratives. The first suggests a people consumed with the hard necessities of staying alive, without political or social order or the self-awareness of the people of Europe. The second was of a romanticized noble savage, and this had no more connection to reality than the brutish savage. The Indigenous as noble savage found its culmination in nineteenth-century literature, such as Henry Wadsworth Longfellow's *Song of Hiawatha*, published to great acclaim in 1855, which I remember reading in school as a child. The novelist Thomas King notes that as Hiawatha prepares to die, he urges his people to give all of their lands to the Europeans: "Longfellow's poem was romantic wishful thinking, but, more than that, it confirmed that Indians, understanding their noble but inferior nature, had willingly gifted all of North America to the superior race."

By the time Chrestien Le Clercq was making plans to return to France, Europeans wars had come to Mi'gma'gi. The Treaty of Utrecht in 1713 ceded the lands of Acadia to the British, but the European powers couldn't agree on the borders of this territory, which the French maintained included only lands in what is now Nova Scotia. The French set out to defend the territory in what is now New Brunswick by building forts along the rivers, including Camp des Reserves on the north shore of the Restigouche at the head of Chaleur Bay. Behind a palisade, the French built a small arsenal, blacksmith shop, stores and a hospital, and anchored a fleet of sloops and schooners in the river.

The French joined forces with the Wabanaki Confederacy, an alliance that included the Mi'gmaq, the Wolastoqiyik of the Wolastoq valley, and the Passamaquoddy, Penobscot and Abenaki people from lands that are now part of southern New Brunswick, Southern Quebec, Maine, New Hampshire and Massachusetts. In June 1755 France's strategic Fort Beauséjour on the Isthmus of Chignecto, the narrow strip of land that connects Nova Scotia and New Brunswick, fell to the British.

The Acadians had hoped to remain neutral in the conflict but refused to swear allegiance to the British Crown. The presence of Acadian militias inside Fort Beauséjour when it fell undermined their case for neutrality. That year the British began expelling French-speaking settlers from their lands. The British burned farms and villages and forced ten thousand Acadians to board ships during the great tragedy of *Le Grand*

Dérangement, scattering them as refugees in Europe and as far south as Spanish Louisiana. Hundreds died of disease and drowning during these voyages. Some escaped into the northern wilderness with the assistance of the Mi'gmaq and built a community on the northern shore of the Restigouche River. By the winter of 1760 fifteen hundred Acadians were living in a community they called Nouvelle Rochelle, behind a rough palisade in about two hundred log homes, barely surviving by hunting and fishing. As if starvation were not enough, by chance, war found them again.

Quebec City had fallen to the British army of General James Wolfe on the Plains of Abraham in September 1759. In April the following year, six French supply ships loaded with flour, salt meat, wine, spirits, weapons and clothing, led by the frigate *Machault*, set sail from Bordeaux on a desperate mission to sail up the St. Lawrence River to resupply the garrison at Quebec City. Almost immediately, the convoy was pursued by British warships. In mid-May the French captured a British ship in the Gulf of St. Lawrence and learned that a British fleet was already in the St. Lawrence River. The French fleet retreated into the Restigouche estuary. The British dispatched a fleet of warships to find them.

On June 22, 1760, British warships blockaded Chaleur Bay. The French, with the assistance of the Mi'gmaw and Acadian militias, operated the batteries on the shore. The Acadians sank boats in the river to create an underwater barricade, and for days the two sides skirmished as the British commander searched for a channel to move his warships within range of the French fort. On July 3 the British ships found their way through a narrow channel on the south side of the river, and with their cannons now in range began to bombard the Acadian community. A British landing party torched the log homes. On July 8 the outgunned French scuttled the last of their ships, including the *Machault*, ending the final battle of the Seven Years War in North America.

John Rowan wrote about finding cellars and stone chimneys at the site of Nouvelle Rochelle. Cannons, muskets and shot had been dug up and kept as trophies by later settlers, and the remains of one of the

French ships could be seen, its oak timbers protruding from the sand. The wreckage of the *Machault* lay on the bottom of the river for two centuries. In 1969 Parks Canada archaeologists began excavating its remains, and a collection of artifacts from the bottom of the river are now displayed in a museum at a National Historic Site on the northern shore of the Restigouche estuary, a short drive upriver from the community of Listuguj.

In the years that followed the end of the war, British and Scottish settlers arrived in the Restigouche valley, now a British colony, followed by United Empire Loyalists at the end of the Revolutionary War, then immigrants from Ireland and Acadians who returned home from exile. The Mi'gmaq had signed a series of Peace and Friendship treaties with the British, but they remained apart from the growing settler society. "Their society remained alive, with its own focus, its own structure, its own religion, its own folklore, its own reason for existing," the historian L.S.F. Upton writes. "In a sense, though they made peace, they refused to admit defeat." In the course of two centuries of history, the divide had grown, and for the Mi'gmaq, the worst consequences of that were yet to come.

14 By the third week in June I was facing a problem that might derail my plans for the river trip before I even started. A week before I was scheduled to leave for the Little Main Restigouche, I was still trying to secure permission to pass through the Irving Veneer Gate. As well, Marie-Christine and Rémi were worried that there would be beaver dams on the Waagansis that I would need to either pass over or portage around and that the cedar strip canoe I had planned to bring would be too heavy. Then I received a message from David LeBlanc: he had been surveying the headwaters to prepare for an obstruction removal project, and he had seen log jams on the Little Main that would force us to portage.

I consulted my friend and long-time river companion Marty Stewart, who is a professional hunting and fishing guide. He suggested I borrow his twenty-foot Tripper built by the Old Town Canoe Company in Maine. The Tripper is made of a light and indestructible plastic compound called Royalex that revolutionized canoe manufacturing in the 1970s by producing a boat that could run hard against a rock and live to float another day. Marty uses the Tripper for his fall expeditions on shallow tributaries of the Miramichi. He had modified the canoe for this purpose, taking out the front bench seat and replacing it with a folding wooden chair for his clients, allowing him to stand in the stern and run the canoe with a pole. In recent years I had also taken up poling, which is the way canoes were run on the Restigouche in the days before outboard motors. Poling allows me to move a canoe with the current and against it, and to control the boat more easily in the swift shallows when I'm searching for a channel. From a standing position in the stern, I have an expansive view of the landscape and the river. Marty had carved me a ten-foot pole from a young spruce tree, light but strong. I sanded it smooth and fastened an iron point on one end to give it weight when I drop it into the water and to protect it when I push against rocks.

When I finally made phone contact with a Black Brook supervisor, he responded to my request with a flat no: the company didn't allow canoe parties on its property and didn't want people travelling its roads or camping on the riverbanks. I've never been one to take the first no for the final answer, but this was discouraging. I decided to send a message to Mary Keith, the vice-president of communications for J.D. Irving Ltd., asking her to call. My phone rang late in the afternoon as I was pulling into my driveway with Marty's canoe tied to the top of the car. I explained to Mary the purpose of my trip and she promised to see what she could do. She made some things happen quickly, and I received a call back from the same Black Brook supervisor later that evening telling me I could pass through the Veneer Gate. He gave me a number to call when I reached the area; a security guard would meet us there. I called Marie-Christine and told her I would be coming the next day. Then I called my travelling companion, Tommy Colwell, and confirmed that we would leave in the morning. Tommy said he would be there, that he was packed and ready to go.

Tommy is as complete an outdoorsman as I have ever met, a fisherman, hunter and former trapper. He and his wife Denise live in a house Tommy built on the shore of Maquapit Lake on the outskirts of Fredericton. When he and Denise were young and beginning a life together, he hunted moose and deer, learned to butcher his own meat and ran traplines to supplement their income. Tommy says a day on the river is always a good day because he learns something new every time he steps out into the wild. "With fishing and hunting, I like to put in the time," he says.

I went over my packing list that evening: a tent, tarps, propane stove, utility box of tools, flashlights and fire starters, a cooking kit and waterproof kitchen box, maps, notebooks and camera, rain gear, hats, bug spray, sunscreen, a first aid kit, two canoe poles and a paddle, life jackets, anchor and rope, fishing rods, fly boxes and waders, sleeping bag, mat and pillow, and a cooler filled with ice and drinks. Tommy had packed another cooler with food, with each meal planned so we would not carry more than we needed. All of this was stowed in plastic waterproof barrels or dry bags. One thing I have learned the hard way is that even if it doesn't rain, everything in a canoe gets wet on a river trip.

Tommy arrived shortly before eight a.m. Light rain was falling as we drove north up the Saint John River valley. A couple of hours later we passed La Grande Rivière where in earlier times we would have launched our canoe with arrangements to continue by horse and wagon to the Waagansis. At the town of St. Leonard, where J.D. Irving Ltd. has a large automated softwood lumber mill, we turned east on the desolate Highway 17 that passes through the Black Brook industrial forest where the spruce are planted in rows, the various years' plantings stretching in neat blocks to the horizon. At the end of the Black Brook forest, we drove through the town of Saint-Quentin, a bustling francophone community of two thousand people supported by a growing maple syrup industry and Group Savoie, a homegrown company that cuts maple, birch, aspen and ash from its private lands and from blocks leased from the Crown. The company manufactures hardwood pallets, produces hardwood lumber, and from the remains creates pellets for fuel and pulp for fibre.

The main street runs past a collection of small businesses and the stone Roman Catholic church. That morning the town had strung flags across the street, and the businesses were decorated with life-sized cut-out silhouettes of people wearing western boots and cowboy hats in preparation for the annual rodeo, known as the Festival Western. Since 1984 Saint-Quentin has been an official stop on the North American rodeo circuit. I've always thought that this was a curious celebration in this remote eastern town. What connection do the people here have to the traditions of the Wild West? None really, except that New Brunswickers of Acadian descent know well the story of their ancestors' expulsion and their hard journeys home, and so tend to carry themselves with the spirit of a gunslinger who swaggers through the swinging doors of a saloon after returning from a long ride across a desolate plain. The Festival Western culminates in a community parade of flatbed floats and a showcase of the latest wood harvesters and skidders that crawls slowly through town, the drivers tossing candy out the windows while children scramble to gather them from the roadside.

We stopped for gas and ice, then drove past potato fields and down into the Five Finger Brook gorge that drains into the Little Main Restigouche. When we reached the village of Kedgwick, we turned off the main road and began to drop into the valley. We pulled into the Canoe Restigouche yard, the parking lot now filled with cars, the outfitting season in full swing. André Arpin was up on scaffolding, putting a new green tin roof on his log home. The rain had stopped, but dark clouds were swirling overhead as we transferred our gear into Marie-Christine's truck and tied the Tripper onto the rack on the back. I parked my car in her yard and left the keys in the office. Because we were heading into unknown territory, she suggested that I take her satellite phone in a waterproof box, and she showed me how to make an emergency call if we ran into trouble. I told her that we planned to be back in three days, and she made a note in her book. If we didn't appear and I hadn't called in, she promised to come looking.

We climbed into the truck and drove back through Saint-Quentin where I placed the call to the J.D. Irving office and said we were on the way. A security guard met us at the Veneer Gate, and Marie-Christine followed his pickup down groomed dirt roads through a landscape that looks more like farmland than forest, each block squared off and numbered, some of it planted with seedlings, some with trees in various stages of growth and some clearcut and plowed for planting. The roads all ran straight in geometric patterns.

We rolled along these long straightaways for about half an hour before turning down a one-lane side road that cut through a plantation until we came to a steel-reinforced wooden bridge that crossed an unmarked stream with thick tangles of alders on both sides. We had arrived at Waagansis Brook. I walked out onto the bridge and looked down into the muddy flow and then got to work. I climbed down over a rock pile and stood just below the bridge while Marie-Christine passed down the canoe. I settled it in the brook, and she and Tommy began passing down the gear. I set up Tommy's chair in the front and distributed the cooler, barrels and dry bags for balance. I secured the canoe to the bank and hoisted myself back up onto the road so we could take photographs on the bridge. Then we climbed back down and Tommy took his seat. I picked up my pole and pushed off into the lazy flow of the brook, leaving Marie-Christine on the bridge behind us. By the time we turned the first corner we felt the silence of the forest close in around us.

We threaded the canoe through thickets of speckled alder, dodging the crooked rubbery branches as best we could. I ducked under a low hanging bush, swung the nose of the canoe to the right around a sharp bend and ran up against our first Waagansis log jam. I stashed my pole, lowered myself into the brook, waded around to the bow and pulled us over the tangle of fallen trees, some of them still rooted in the muddy bank. For the first hour, this became the routine, me poling for a minute or two, sliding in and out of the canoe, wading through water that would be knee deep one minute and chest deep the next, dragging us over and around obstacles.

I began to lose my sense of direction as the brook circled back toward the bridge, then wound back in the direction of the Little Main, splitting into channels that ran in opposite directions and then merged again farther downstream. All we could do was try to follow the channel that appeared to have the greatest flow. When we floated into a deep beaver pond, we faced our first real obstruction. From the moment we started down the brook we had been seeing cut trees with tell-tale tooth marks and peeled bark and beaver tracks in the mud, so we weren't surprised to reach the dam, a solid wall of muck mortar and sticks holding back the brook to create a pond with a trickle of water flowing out below. Beaver dams are inconvenient for human travellers but they create water storage networks that are a critical part of the forest ecosystem. The head of the dam was low enough for me to push the canoe up against it. Tommy stepped out onto the top of the dam and walked around to the base. I threw a rope down. He pulled and I pushed until the canoe slid over the top down across the mud into the brook below. We climbed back in the canoe, one major obstacle now behind us, with more to come.

There's a romantic side to outdoor adventures and running rivers. Those are the stories we tell when we return and eventually they become all we remember of a trip. But in moments of honesty we admit to a level of hardship on every canoe trip, especially if we are camping along the way. On Waagansis Brook, the hardships came upon us around every swampy bend. Along with the log jams, sloppy mud, alder thickets and beaver dams were the mosquitos, blackflies and the dreaded *ceratopogonidae*, also known as no-see-ums, or *brûlot* in French because of the burning sensation they leave behind. These tiny pests become especially thick at dusk or just before a rain. The rain started falling an hour into our trip down the brook, and we kept running into fallen trees. Our only choice was to go over or around them until eventually we reached the

river. I was wet to my shoulders and covered in muck. *Les brûlot* were the
least of my worries.

We pulled the canoe over two more beaver dams. Throughout all of
this, Tommy was entirely at ease, pointing out tracks of moose and deer
in the mud along the banks and small trout swimming in the beaver
ponds. Late in the afternoon we finally punched through to the mouth
of Waagansis Brook, where we floated into a deep pool and out into the
Little Main Restigouche. I turned the canoe back upstream and landed
on a muddy beach. Tommy announced that he had enjoyed every minute
of the trip down the brook, and we opened cans of beer to toast our
arrival at the river. I rested with the canoe while Tommy assembled his
fly rod and cast a fly over the trout we could see rising on the far-edge
pool beside the alders. Then we ate sandwiches and finished our beers.
The river at the mouth of Waagansis is a narrow strip of water divided by
a rocky, grass-covered island. The rain started to fall harder, so I pulled
waterproof rain pants and a jacket over my wet clothes, figuring there
would be more wading ahead. I would save my dry clothes for when we
stopped for the night. We stayed on the beach at the mouth of Waagansis
long enough to enjoy the moment, but soon we climbed back in the
canoe, anxious to explore the new waters that lay ahead and feel the pull
of the current as it carried us down through the valley.

We floated on the Little Main Restigouche through a steady rain, the
bands of storm clouds sweeping upstream as we followed slips of current
through a maze of rocks and trees that had fallen into the stream. In
the deep cuts along the bank red-and-grey-speckled brook trout darted
among clusters of stones. Through breaks in the trees on both sides of the
river, we could see the edges of clearcuts and spruce growing in rows on
the hillsides above the river. From time to time I had to step out to walk
the canoe around the edge of a log jam, but it was mostly clear running
for about an hour—until we ran into the first large tangle of trees. I
pushed the nose of the canoe onto a gravel beach above the jam. We had
no choice here but to make a full portage. We unloaded and I carried the
gear downstream, then turned the canoe over to pour out the water that

had accumulated in the bottom from the rain and runoff from my boots. I scraped out the leaves, branches and mud that we had taken in on the way down the Waagansis and washed the inside of the canoe with a sponge. Then we carried the canoe down below the jam and reloaded, making a few adjustments for balance, moving more weight to the front to give me better control with the pole in the back. We pushed off into the current again, agreeing it was time to start looking for a suitable place to camp.

We stopped about an hour later on a narrow strip of gravel beach with a flat stretch of ground behind it and an abundance of driftwood and old beaver cuttings strewn about that we could use for our fire. We set up the tent back from the beach on a strip of sand. The rain had stopped, so I changed into dry clothes while Tommy cast for trout in the run opposite the camp. Despite the rain, there was a ban on open fires until after eight p.m. because of dry conditions in the forest in recent weeks. As soon as we were legal, I started a fire in a makeshift stone firepit on the beach, feeding it with driftwood and handfuls of ferns and grasses to create a smoke smudge that I hoped would send a message to the no-see-ums that they were unwelcome in our camp. I filled the kettle in the river and put it on the fire to boil for washing later in the evening and rested with a drink of Scotch while Tommy cooked a dinner of sliced pork, potatoes and carrots over the gas stove that we had set up on a small folding table.

After we washed the dishes Tommy wandered upstream to fish. I was tending the fire when I heard him call out to tell me that a black bear was crossing the river just upstream. I walked upriver to have a look. The bear had crossed from our side of the river to the opposite bank and was standing frozen, looking directly at us. Tommy said it was a young male, judging by the narrowness of his head. He figured it was born the previous January and probably chased off by its mother a few weeks earlier to live on its own. The bear walked down the beach on the other side of the river and stopped about twenty-five metres upstream. We stared at each other for a few minutes until he turned and ambled back upstream along the bank and disappeared around the bend. I went back down to the fire.

When I heard Tommy call out to tell me that the bear had returned, I had to come clean about my unjustified fear of bears. I say unjustified because I've seen black bears many times in the wild and have never had an unpleasant encounter. But I've seen their grace and speed, and their awesome strength when they swim through heavy river currents, and I tend to imagine worst-case scenarios despite the fact that I know I would have a better chance of being mauled by a domesticated dog. I walked upstream to join Tommy, who was reading the apprehension on my face and now questioning the constitution of his travelling companion. I told myself that it was helpful to be travelling with a man who not only had killed bears but had skinned them and eaten bear sausage. For my sake, Tommy gave a shout and told the bear it was time to move on. The bear turned and stepped up into the woods opposite our campsite and disappeared into the forest. "We'll take the knives and hatchet into the tent," Tommy said with a reassuring smile. "Just remember, if he comes in, go for the eyes."

I shook off the second sighting and told myself the young bear was curious but uninterested in a closer encounter. I strung up my fly rod and walked down to cast in a pool below our camp just as the late evening sun started to break through the rain clouds. The early summer light lingered long in the sky. We sat by the fire and Tommy roasted marshmallows, squishing them between chocolate-covered cookies, a snack that we decided was as perfect as anything we had ever eaten. The temperature dropped and the dew fell heavy on the camp. I pulled on a down jacket and wool hat that I kept on when I slipped into my sleeping bag. Both of us were woken in the night by beavers swimming in front of our campsite and slapping their tails on the water to let us know that we were encroaching on their territory. From the tent we heard the rumble of the engines of mechanized wood harvesters working through the night, reminding us that we were travelling on this exquisite water through a narrow band of forest, a fragile barrier separating us from an industrial logging operation. One modern harvester, with one skilled operator, cuts one hundred trees an hour, one thousand trees a shift, one hundred thousand trees in a month, although the forest industry isn't counting trees; it uses a formula that measures cubic feet of wood per productive machine hour in dollars and cents.

15 I never met K.C. Irving, but I have met and worked for his sons, grandsons and great grandchildren. When K.C. Irving died in 1993 at the age of ninety-two, I was a reporter at the Irving-owned *Telegraph Journal* newspaper and helped prepare the coverage for the next day's newspaper. When he died, *Fortune* magazine reported that he was the eleventh wealthiest person in the world. Several days later my father presided over his memorial service at the Presbyterian church where Irving and his family had been members. K.C. Irving's biographers Douglas How and Ralph Costello recount a story my father told at the service about the day he was preparing for the funeral of K.C. Irving's first wife, Harriet, in 1976. My father was in the church hall in the basement, opening folding tables to set up for a reception after the service, when K.C. Irving, then close to eighty years old and a multi-billionaire, arrived with his three sons: James known as J.K., Arthur, and Jack. K.C. Irving asked my father, who was a much younger man, to step aside. "Reverend Lee, don't move that table," he said. "My sons and I are used to this kind of work."

The purchase of the Black Brook property was K.C. Irving's first big move into the forestry business in New Brunswick, and it came rather late in the game. J.D. Irving, K.C.'s father, had run a sawmill and owned a few thousand acres of woodland, but his was just one of many companies harvesting trees from the wilderness. Irving's biographers wrote that K.C. saw unlimited opportunity in New Brunswick, a place of "thin and scattered population," with 85 per cent of its lands forested, "split and sluiced by rivers." It was also a place of compliant government, where people voted the way their parents had, either Liberal or Conservative, "and no other creed of politics amounted to much."

If, at times, K.C. Irving could mistake what was good for him with what was good for New Brunswick, as his biographers concede in a moment of gentle criticism, the same could be said of New Brunswickers and their governments. The description of the province when K.C. Irving began to build his business empire could be repeated word for word seven decades later. The only difference in the narrative today is that K.C. Irving charted a course for his family's business that has grown into a network of more than two hundred fifty enterprises in Canada and the United States worth twelve billion dollars.

K.C. Irving entered the forestry business in 1933 when he bought a struggling company in Saint John called Canada Veneers. The company manufactured hardwood veneer plywood, a process that involved sawing thin layers of yellow birch and gluing them together to create a board that was harder and more stable than traditional sawed lumber. Veneer was used in the construction of buses and then, during the war, airplanes. The de Havilland Aircraft Company had designed a light, agile bomber called the Mosquito that was built of veneer panels, creating a huge demand for veneer that resulted in a recovery and expansion of Irving's new company. By the end of the war, Canada Veneers was the largest producer of hardwood veneer in the world, and K.C. Irving had become a wealthy man.

The demand for veneer turned K.C. Irving to the forests in search of a reliable supply of premium yellow birch logs. In 1943 he bought the d'Auteuil Lumber Company and its Quebec timberlands. Then he began shopping for available forestlands in New Brunswick at precisely the time when a huge tract of forest granted to the New Brunswick and Canada Railway and Land Company came up for sale.

The company had begun acquiring Crown land in the late 1870s through its contract to build a railway line from south to north to connect with the Intercolonial Railway. As part of the deal, the government of the day transferred to the company 650,000 hectares of Crown timberland that included the hunting and fishing territory of the Wolastoqiyik of the Tobique River and the Mi'gmaq of Gespe'gewa'gi. The railway venture was an economic failure, and by the time Irving was searching for real estate, the New Brunswick Railway Company had leased its railway line to the Canadian Pacific Railway and, to pay off its shareholders, was selling the grant of Crown forest. There was a brief debate in the New Brunswick Legislature about whether the railway grant should be returned to the Crown but the consensus was that if the land was to be used in support of industry, and by industry it meant sawmills and paper mills, it didn't matter who owned it.

In 1943 Irving purchased the railway land in the headwaters of the Restigouche River, the tract that is now called Black Brook. Two years later he bought what remained of the railway company and another 280,000 hectares. For the next five decades CPR would operate the "surface assets" but the land beneath the tracks had been sold. It was as simple as that. More than 400,000 hectares, public land that had been given away to support a public works project, was now the private property of one family.

From there, Irving's expansion in the forestry business was breathtakingly swift as he continued to buy hundreds of thousands of hectares in New England, along with lumber, paper and pulp mills on both sides of the border, at the same time securing long-term leases of Crown timberland.

When Irving entered the business, logs were still being moved from the forests by way of the traditional spring river drives, but a technological revolution was about to sweep through the industry ending the labour-intensive operations that had long sustained rural communities throughout the region. The agrarian-style harvesting system of handsaws and horses was replaced first by chainsaws and gas-powered skidders and then by mechanical wood harvesting.

These technological changes were revolutionizing the forestry industry around the world, but K.C. Irving's bold innovation was made in the lands around the headwaters of the Restigouche when in 1957 he began planting spruce seedlings. "He put black spruce in the hollows and planted white spruce higher up," his biographers wrote. "He cut down standing trees, tens of thousands a year, for pulp and lumber, cleared the ground with great, crushing machines that created a landscape like something from the barren reaches of the moon." On these newly plowed fields,

seedlings grew in straight rows and the mixed Acadian forest of old disappeared cut by cut.

In a ceremony held the same summer I set out for Waagansis Brook,
K.C. Irving's grandsons Jim and Robert, surrounded by a crowd of employees, celebrated their father J.K. on the occasion of the planting of
the company's billionth seedling. Jim Irving, now the co-chief executive
officer of J.D. Irving Ltd., dressed in khakis and an open-necked plaid
dress shirt, spoke of the legacy of his grandfather's tree planting program.
Jim Irving is a tall, powerful man like his grandfather, now grey-haired
and slightly stooped. Delivering staccato sentences in a deep baritone, he
praised the company's employees for all their hard work then thanked
his brother and co-CEO, Robert, for his leadership in the tissue business.
Looking up from his notes, he described the economic formula that drives
the family business. "We know the difference between a standing tree
and the box of tissue on the retailer's shelf: we add thirty-five times the
value of the tree. It's really important. That's the business." When the
speeches were over they pulled back a blanket made from green spruce
boughs to unveil the stone monument and planted the seedling with
shiny steel shovels.

16 We woke at first light. I made coffee for me and tea for Tommy
on the propane stove, lit a smudge fire and watched the sun rise to
the sound of drumming partridges on the other side of the river. The
morning mist rose in a cloud illuminated by the early morning light
reflecting off a stand of poplar trees and willows overhanging a sharp
meander downstream. We spent an hour casting for small trout in the
water around the camp as we waited for the sun to hit our tent and dry
it at least a little before we packed and pushed off. We left our camp at
about eight thirty, and a few minutes later, I fell out of the back of the
canoe. There was nothing graceful about it. I had nosed the canoe down
through a slim channel on the right bank, and the stern failed to make

the corner. The canoe bounced off a rock and I fell overboard, all the way in and under, wet from my boots to my hat. Tommy had a good laugh as I pulled out one more set of dry clothes from my pack. If I fell in again, I would be staying wet. I laid my wet clothes on top of the load in the canoe to dry.

The river grew wider and deeper and during breaks in the cloud cover the sunlight reflected off the stones on the bottom. Through the morning Tommy offered me a naturalist's commentary on all the life that lay before us. Trappers know more about wild spaces than anyone who spends time in nature, for they read the landscape with a view to not only what's happening now but also what's going to happen later. Traps must be set in places where the trapper anticipates an animal will travel, so Tommy has learned the habits of all species along the traplines: what they eat, where they live, how they interact, what routes they take — all discerned through careful observation of the subtle signs and disturbances they leave behind.

The writer John Rowan was also a trapper. He called the forest his perfect library. "There is a religion in the pine forest, which appeals most strongly to a man's best nature," he wrote. "Nowhere else does he feel so utterly and entirely dependent on the Giver of all good. Nowhere else can he so fully enter into the feelings of the writer of the beautiful 104th psalm." The psalm recalls how God sent springs into the valleys to run among the hills where birds nest in trees filled with sap and that we should all rejoice in the riches that the Earth provides. "There is hardly a day or night in which the student may not learn something new," Rowan wrote. "Signs invisible to the unpracticed eye are as legible as the large type to the old woodsman, who besides being a close and keen observer, must be a thinker too, for every day he has to match his reason against the wonderful instinct of the animals whose senses of hearing, smelling, and seeing are many times more acute than those of their two-legged hunter."

Rowan became a great admirer of the beaver. He recalled how on the Causapscal River, a high rocky tributary of the Matapédia, he helped to cut a breach in a beaver dam six feet wide, lowering the water level in the pond by a foot. It took two men with axes a couple of hours to breach the dam. The next morning, the dam had been repaired, and the water was back to the same level it had been. He noted that when a heavy freshet approaches, the beavers would cut a gap in the dam to allow the water through so the flow wouldn't destroy all their work, or they would design a weak spot in the dam that would release like a natural floodgate when the pressure rose.

He marvelled at their engineering, the way they regulated water, stored food and managed the size of the colonies and the supply of wood. "Their influence on the features of the country constitutes another parallel with man," Rowan wrote. "One half the lakes and nearly all the wild meadows are the work of past generations of beaver. First of all, the small brook is dammed; by-and-by this dam becomes solid and forest trees take root and grow on it; as other outlets of the water occur they are closed by these indefatigable workers, till at length the pond assumes the proportions of a lake, and remains for all time to attest to their powers. The meadows are formed by the draining of the lakes."

That afternoon on the Little Main, Tommy explained the difference in the appearance and habits of red-headed mergansers and American wood ducks. He pointed out where the swallows dig their nests in the mud on the riverbanks and where the woodcock hide in the tangles of brush along the shore. He taught me to recognize the shrill cry of a nighthawk, how we know they are approaching long before we see them: "When you hear them, they are still high in the air," he said. We saw nesting pairs of bald eagles gliding above the river and a great horned owl swoop down from the top of a towering balsam fir. We floated past a series of beaver lodges, some in use and some abandoned and now occupied by otters.

About mid-morning, as the sky cleared into a brilliant blue, we ran into another log jam where the river had meandered to the left around what had been an island but was now the right-hand bank with a long, dry gravel beach. The only way around the jam without a long canoe-carry over the dry riverbed was to pull directly up to the logs in the middle of the rush of current and find a way over. I stepped out into the river and walked us over as close as we could get to the left bank and, with Tommy holding the canoe in place, climbed over the logs. I found a patch of firm ground, and Tommy passed the gear from the canoe to me one piece at a time that I then carried to the shore below the jam. When the canoe was empty, we pulled it over the top, walked it down to the pile of gear and reloaded. The whole operation took the better part of an hour.

We paused for lunch on a spit of sand above a deep pool below the jam. Later in the afternoon, farther downstream, we stopped to inspect the remains of the old New Brunswick Railway Company fishing lodge. All that is left are three chimneys made of stones from the river mixed with some imported bricks, crumbling and covered in moss, surrounded by a young stand of fir and spruce. K.C. Irving inherited the lodge when he bought the railway land that became his Black Brook property. He abandoned the old camp and built a new one at the mouth of Boston Brook farther downstream. In time, these last traces of the old lodge will melt back into the forest.

We floated past sprawling elms, tall spruce laden with cones and towering mature yellow birch until we came to the mouth of the Gounamitz River, a fast, rocky stream that spills down from the north, the first major tributary that flows into the Little Main Restigouche. In the pool where the two currents meet, we saw schools of large trout cycling up and down in the current. As we dropped below the mouth of Gounamitz, we saw a tall man holding a canoe pole, standing on a wooden structure built on the side of the river. I pushed our canoe across the river and pulled up alongside him. We introduced ourselves and told him where we had been and where we were heading. He introduced himself as Bill Lee, the camp manager for J.D. Irving Ltd. at Boston Brook. After a short conversation, we remembered that he had guided my father on the Restigouche many years ago.

Lee explained that the structure he was standing on, large wooden boxes filled with rocks and covered with decking, had been designed to collect silt and sediment that had been filling in the pool. The structure had been damaged in the spring freshet and needed to be repaired or rebuilt. He was taking measurements to draw up a restoration plan. He told us that a few salmon had been seen in the pools around Boston Brook, which was good news. Although we had seen many trout, we had yet to see a salmon, and we had been looking. I asked about what we might expect on the river below Boston Brook, and he suggested we stop at the lodge to speak to the guides there who knew more about that stretch than he did.

We pushed off and left Bill Lee to his work, floating down toward the lodge past a row of angled stone walls that had been installed in the river to keep the current flowing on the right bank where it ran up against another wall built to protect the lawn in front of the lodge. Where Boston Brook flows into the river, both banks had been neatly rocked and a lawn planted and mowed to the edge of the water. K.C. Irving liked straight lines in nature and it appears his heirs have inherited the same aesthetic. It's a never-ending project. Wild spaces are messy and unpredictable, and as everyone knows, there's something in a river that doesn't love a wall.

I steered our canoe to the side of a floating wooden dock just downstream from the outflow of Boston Brook, left Tommy there and walked across the lawn to speak with the guides on the porch of the sprawling lodge. I introduced myself and told them we had been chatting upstream with Bill Lee, and he had directed me to them to ask about what to expect downstream, how far we had to travel and where they might suggest we camp for the night. One of the guides suggested that we stop at Eight Mile Pool that he remembered had a camping spot on the beach and good water to fish. I left them on the porch and walked back down over the lawn where Tommy was holding the canoe in the current alongside the dock.

K.C. Irving's biographers recount an incident on that lawn that took place in the summer of 1965 when Hubert Humphrey, then vice-president of the United States, had come to visit the industrialist and fish for salmon. Humphrey and his secret servicemen walked out of the lodge early in the morning to head out on the water when "a plane came roaring down the river, low, spewing mist." The bodyguards drew their guns and pulled Humphrey down into cover, fearing they were under attack from the air. "In fact, the pilot had designs only on the insects that might spoil the vice-president's day, but no one had remembered to tell either Humphrey or his bodyguards," they wrote.

Six years after the gathering with the vice-president at Boston Brook, K.C. Irving quietly moved to Bermuda to establish a new base for his empire outside the reach of new estate and capital gains taxes. He issued a brief statement: "I am no longer residing in New Brunswick. My sons are carrying on the various businesses. As far as anything else goes, I do not choose to discuss the matter further."

A decade after his visit, Hubert Humphrey, who had returned to the United States Senate after an unsuccessful presidential run against Richard Nixon, sponsored the first act to protect public forests in the United States. "The days have ended when the forest may be viewed as trees and trees viewed only as timber," Humphrey said. "The soil and water, the grasses and the shrubs, the fish and wildlife, and the beauty that is the forest must become integral parts of resource managers' thinking and actions."

According to my family's history, Hubert Humphrey's failure to defeat Richard Nixon in 1968 was what brought us to Canada. My father had made a pact with his university friends that if Nixon were elected president, they would all leave the country. The pact may have been more bravado than commitment, but there was no question that my parents were searching for a new beginning for their children in the north. My father ended up being the only one of his friends who left, and it gave him bragging rights during the years of the Watergate scandal. Their decision to move to Canada changed the course of my life, which decades later directed me to the river, and in the mysterious ways of fate was why I was standing on the lawn beside the mouth of Boston Brook that July afternoon so many years later.

17 Below Boston Brook, the Little Main, now carrying the waters of the Gounamitz, became a different river with stronger currents, deeper pools and long sweeping meanders, creating a new rhythm for the canoe. I love working a canoe through the obstacles of a small stream but there everything is immediate; my focus remains a couple of canoe lengths ahead at best and most of the time a lot closer than that. But now I was able to navigate the river with a longer view, searching far ahead for the subtle ripples and lines on the water that show the primary band of current, for if I could keep the canoe in that flow, then we were running with the river, not against it. Staying in the flow without hitting any big rocks along the way is really all there is to running a river in a canoe, although sometimes that's easier said than done.

For the first time we were making choices about which side of small islands we would choose as the best passage. Later in the afternoon a large bull moose loped across the river just downstream from us, stepping up onto a small grassy island as we slipped down the other side. About five p.m. we reached Nine Mile Pool, a circle of deep water shaded by high banks at the end of a long bend to the left. A spring gushes in on the far shore across from a sandy beach. When we dropped over a ledge into the deep water we contemplated stopping and then decided to continue on to Eight Mile, where we planned to set up camp. As we were floating over the lower end of the pool that we call the tail-out, I saw two large salmon and two grilse (the name for small salmon that have spent only one winter at sea) swimming into the pool. I pushed the canoe toward the shore below, stopped, and after a short discussion we decided to spend the night there and see if we could hook one of those fish. I walked the canoe back up to the beach. We set up the tent on the sand, unloaded all our gear, turned the canoe over and hung up our wet clothes to dry on a makeshift clothesline.

There are libraries written about the sport of fly fishing for Atlantic salmon for those who are interested. I have nothing to add to these volumes but these few words for those who have never experienced the sport. I've spent a lot of time trying to catch fish, and I've had many species of fish on the end of my line, but this I can say with certainty: there's fly fishing, and there's Atlantic salmon fishing. They are two different activities. In the first place, Atlantic salmon don't feed in fresh water when they return to their home waters to spawn. So why they will eat a tiny fly at all remains a mystery. Those who say they understand the habits of the salmon are full of baloney, to put it kindly. Salmon flies are more art than insect because they don't look like anything in nature, unlike a trout fly that is designed to look like something a trout wants to eat. The names of salmon flies reflect this: the Rusty Rat, a Restigouche favourite, doesn't look anything like a rat; the Green Highlander looks nothing like a Scotsman; the famous Same Thing Murray was named not for its designer but for his friend, who asked what fly he had used to catch a salmon. The designer replied: "The same thing, Murray." Salmon fishing is about trying to convince a fish that is not feeding to eat something that would never be part of its diet. That's why, in the first place and the last, they are hard to hook. But the miracle of the whole enterprise is that when the stars align, when your fly passes over the right salmon at the right time in the right place, they will eat a fly in a burst of power that explodes from the water. The fly rod in your hand bends hard and the fish rips line off your reel. That's the whole game right there, and I know my words are underselling it.

For many years now in New Brunswick, all salmon anglers must release their fish back into the river after hooking them, known as catch and release. It's a conservation measure and from an ethical standpoint is more problematic than catching a fish, killing it and eating it. Even though we know that a salmon carefully handled and released quickly will survive the experience, there is no question that the fish would have been better off had it avoided the episode altogether. There's been a lot written about the spiritual connection we have with a fish after it's been hooked on a fly rod, lifted out of the water, photographed and then let go to return to the wild, as if we have become participants in its grand migration and so on. I have no intention of trying to sell that bill of goods. My rule is that if I am going to continue to fly fish for salmon in the time of catch and release, once I hook one, I get it off my line as soon as possible and I never take it out of the water. In my case, the good thing for the salmon is that I'm not a particularly skilled angler; most salmon have nothing to fear when I'm on the river.

We fished the pool that evening. Tommy started at the top and I started down at the tail-out, casting out across the river at a downstream angle and letting the fly swing down at the speed of the current. I soon hooked a fish, which likely was a grilse. I say likely a grilse because I never saw it. It bent my rod, stripped some line and then I lost it before I could bring it in to the shore. We call this an "early release." All evening the salmon were jumping and splashing in the pool. When a big fish jumps, it sounds like someone is standing up on a high bank above the river dropping boulders into the pool. We fished until dark, then Tommy grilled tender strips of moose meat over the fire on the beach for dinner.

We rose at dawn and fished for a couple of hours and hooked nothing then broke down the campsite and floated to the Eight Mile Pool where Tommy hooked a salmon and lost it before he could bring it to shore. On a stretch of water below Eight Mile we turned a corner and almost ran over an American black duck and a parade of ducklings. The mother flew out in front of the canoe, splashing and weaving to divert attention away from the ducklings. "There's seven little ones," Tommy said. "There's six in that bunch and one loner." He asked me to push the canoe to the right bank so the little loner who was frantically swimming downstream to avoid us could turn back upstream and rejoin its mother. I kept us close to the opposite bank, at which point the mother flew back upstream to rejoin the group of six, and the little loner paddled in under some brush near the shore crying for its mother to return.

The river was widening and flattening around every turn. The wind began to blow downriver, and on a long straight stretch I turned the canoe sideways to catch the breeze. I sat down with my pole across my lap and we enjoyed the ride, both of us keeping an eye out for hidden rocks that might cause us trouble if we hit them broadside to the current. On the lower end of the Little Main there are logging roads that run into the river, including one at the Four Mile Pool, a popular landing for anglers and family picnics. We floated past a family swimming there, girls and boys splashing in the shimmering flat water.

Some writers have noted that it is strange that this river is called the Little Main Restigouche when the Kedgwick is the larger of the two major headwater tributaries. When we reached this lower part of the Little Main, I realized why it carries the name of the main river. Here the Little Main takes on the character of the main river in a way that the Kedgwick never does, wide and purposeful with high cliffs rising above vast holding pools. The Little Main is more Restigouche in character than the Kedgwick that is narrower and swifter from its headwaters to the mouth.

We arrived at a camping site at a place called Micmac Pool late in the afternoon. This was the site of an old fishing lodge that has been demolished, the stone fireplace and hearth now integrated into a cooking shelter, the tin from the camp roof still attached at the top of the chimney. The campsite was immaculate, maintained by a crew hired by David LeBlanc's watershed council. There's a high bank opposite the campsite, a pool in front, a long swift run above and below the deep water. I bathed in the river in the evening, changing into the last of my clean clothes. Occasionally, motor canoes passed by from downriver, many of them run by new jet outboards that allow them to travel over shallow water without fear of hitting rocks with propellers. That evening, a young moose walked out of the forest to drink in the river just below our camp, raising his hackles when he smelled our presence in the downriver breeze.

The rain returned on our final morning on the Little Main. Tommy grilled trout for breakfast that we had caught upstream the previous afternoon, then we packed up and put on our rain gear. We floated over the final miles of the Little Main, noting places we would like to return to fish on another trip. In some of the pools, fly fishermen were casting from anchored canoes. We passed by the mouth of Five Finger Brook and through a promising-looking pool below it and then slipped downstream beneath the Montgomery Bridge. A few minutes later we landed the canoe on the beach below Arpin Canoe Restigouche headquarters.

We took some photographs on the beach, and I left Tommy at the canoe and walked up the hill to the office. It was early afternoon. André Arpin was up on his staging still working on the roof project, despite the spitting rain. It seemed as if nothing had changed here since we left, and I had my usual moment of vertigo that comes over me when I step out of a river trip. Every time I go to the Restigouche I feel as if I've spent time on another planet, and it takes time to acclimatize when I return. I stopped and gave André a brief account of our trip. Marie-Christine was out on business. Her office manager, Louise Poirier, told me that she had received calls from Fredericton wondering if we had made it out. I returned the satellite phone, picked up my car keys and drove down to the beach. We loaded the wet gear in the back, tied the Tripper on the top, and drove up to the top of Broderick's Hill, where we had cell service. We placed calls home to say we were back safely and on our way. On the drive home I recalled the old saying that there's nothing more that can be said of good friends than that they are the kind of people you'd run a river with. I told Tommy that he had been all of that and more.

Water

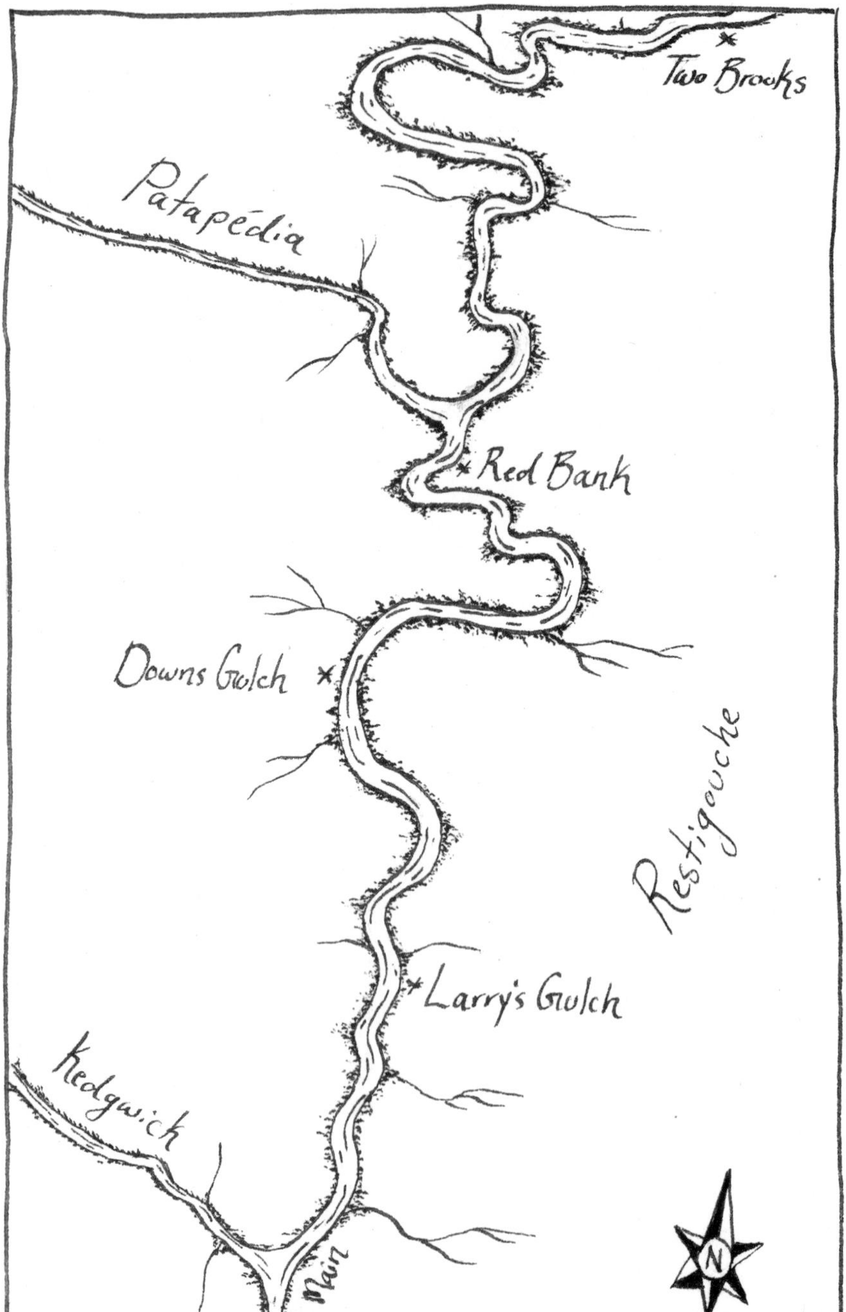
Two Brooks
Patapédia
Red Bank
Downs Gulch
Restigouche
Larry's Gulch
Kedgwick
Little Main
N

The way up and the way down is one and the same.

—Heraclitus

1 The French chemist who discovered that water was not one thing but a chemical compound containing hydrogen and oxygen was guillotined during the French Revolution. In 1811 an Italian scientist confirmed that a single molecule of water is two atoms of hydrogen and one atom of oxygen. Years later we came to understand how a cloud of electrons bind the atoms together. But, as the poet D.H. Lawrence reminded us, "there is also a third thing that makes it water, and nobody knows what that is." The extraordinary properties of water remain one of life's enduring mysteries.

Water is the only substance on Earth that in its natural state exists as a liquid, solid and gas. Its transformative motion on Earth and through the atmosphere makes life possible. The energy of sunlight and wind converts water in rivers, lakes and seas into an invisible gas called vapour. Plants and trees draw water from the Earth through their roots and expel vapour through their leaves. Scientists call this cycle of vapour production evapotranspiration. We glimpse this cycle on the river when the cool night air sometimes converts vapour back into tiny droplets of water that we see as morning mist, suspended over the flow and swirling up along the hillsides. Vapour returns from the atmosphere to the Earth when it is converted into its liquid or solid form and falls from the sky as rain or snow.

These movements we understand. But what makes liquid water so stable that it covers more than 70 per cent of the surface of the Earth? What gives water the ability to absorb great amounts of heat and cold and remain a liquid? Why does water transform itself into a lattice of crystals when it cools so that it floats in its solid form, and why is it the only liquid that behaves in this way? One pragmatic answer is that so fish can live through the winter. But that leaves us searching for the third thing that makes it water, and we don't know what that is. Why is it that water takes up nutrients essential for the sustenance of life yet repels those that destroy life? Why is the density of water such that it allows a canoe to float on its surface while fish and beaver swim through it just below?

We know that the Earth doesn't produce water, although flowing rivers and bubbling springs create the illusion that it does. What we have now is all we've ever had and all we ever will have. So where did water come from in the beginning? For a long time, the prevailing theory was that 3.8 billion years ago, frozen asteroids crashed into the Earth, releasing ice that melted, flowed into rivers and lakes and filled the oceans. More recently, a Dutch scientist advanced a theory that crystals of ice were attached to particles of cosmic dust during the Big Bang fourteen billion years ago.

This theory suggests that all the water on Earth has been in the stream of creation from the beginning, and through the molecules of water in our own bodies each of us is intimately connected to the long story of the Earth itself.

2 A wave of heat settled in the river valley the morning after I returned from the Little Main Restigouche. I spent the weekend at home in Fredericton drying and repacking camping gear for the second stage of the trip, from the confluence of the Little Main and the Kedgwick, fifty-seven kilometres down the main river to the Two Brooks landing. Early Saturday afternoon I returned Marty's Old Town Tripper along with an offering of my deepest gratitude and a bottle of whiskey. When I returned, I pulled my long boat trailer into the driveway and rolled the tarp off the canoe that would carry me the rest of the way down the Restigouche to the tidewater.

Every old river canoe has a story. These stories are part of an oral tradition and have both long and short versions depending on the circumstances of the telling. The short version of my canoe's story goes something like this. In the early 1900s a guide named Burton Moore designed a canoe for poling his guests and supplies up and down the Tobique River. He called it the Guide Special. In 1925 a craftsman named Vic Miller started building canoes for sale in a Tobique river town called Nictau, and a couple of decades later bought the Moore Guide Special mould for one hundred dollars. In 1960 Vic's grandson Bill spent the summer learning how to make canoes and, in the years that followed, took over the family business. In the early 1990s, Bill Miller built a twenty-two-foot Guide Special for a man who had a fishing camp a few kilometres downriver from the Miller homestead. Four summers ago, I bought that canoe from that man's son. Since then I've made a few repairs to the gunwales, transom and fibreglass finish, and added a Restigouche-style anchor system on the bow. My Tobique River canoe is an outlier among the larger, more muscular Restigouche canoes. People I meet on the river sometimes ask about its origins. In river culture this is an invitation to stop and strike up a conversation. This we do when we're running on river time.

When British writer John Rowan travelled through the Restigouche valley before the arrival of the Intercolonial Railway, he warned the tourists who came after him not to be in a hurry, for if they were, they'd lose their tempers or perhaps their minds. The mail driver would stop for an hour on the road to have a chat with the driver of your carriage. Or the ferry operator would lend a hand to someone struggling with a timber barge and stay as long as it took to solve the problem. "Expostulation is useless, and haste is worse than useless; you may just do in Restigouche as Restigouche does," Rowan wrote. "It is different from the rest of the continent."

The summer the Miller canoe became part of our river trips, our youngest daughter, Lucy, had turned ten, and we were gearing up for her first season of camping on the Restigouche. We were searching for a new canoe that could carry a load of supplies, Lucy and a friend, and a small dog. The search took us into the valley of the Tobique, and into a summer in which I rediscovered river time. In mid-July I bought a canoe trailer from a boat dealer in Fredericton and drove north with Lucy to pick up the Miller canoe from the seller's home in Bathurst. We arrived late in the afternoon, loaded the canoe on the trailer and camped that night on a hill above the bay. The next morning we drove west through the forest across a ribbon of patched blacktop toward Mount Carleton and then south down into the Tobique valley to meet Bill Miller.

The evening before we left Fredericton, Bill sent a note with directions to his home that I handed to Lucy to read aloud while I drove: "It looks like a fine day for a drive to Bathurst. Mount Carleton is a delightful place to spend the night too, and you are welcome to stay here as well. My truck is in Grand Falls getting the 100,000-mile maintenance check, and it should be ready to pick up by noon. I should be here no later than five p.m. tonight, and I will be here all day tomorrow as well. It might be nice to dip your new canoe in the Tobique and sail to Riley Brook. From Bathurst take Route 180 and head west about 60 miles to Route 385 that leads to Mount Carleton and Plaster Rock. For about five miles that road turns to a dirt road before you get to the Park. From the Park to Nictau is about 22 miles and it is all paved. Within a mile of Nictau you will cross a concrete bridge across the Campbell River that is sometimes called the Right-Hand Branch. The first house you will see is a white one with a blue roof, then a couple of camps, then a white house with a black roof, and in behind that one is a large house with a red roof. Looking downriver from that is my farm that has a new log house with a green roof, a huge barn, and my Mom's house. The number is 4160, Route 385, but since our mail comes from Plaster Rock that number can only be seen when going north on Route 385, and the number is on the post for my mailbox, which has my name on it too. Oh, the farm is on your left when coming from the Park. The shop's a large red building with an aluminum roof, and there will be a few canoes out in the yard. It will be great to meet you."

After we crossed the concrete bridge and the Right-Hand Branch, Lucy picked out all the landmarks that were not Bill's farm before we reached the log home that was, which we found without seeing the number on the post because we were driving south on Route 385. By the time we parked and stepped out of the car, Bill had come out his back door to greet us. He's a tall, heavyset man with a soft round face, grey hair and beard, a shining smile and the strong, creased hands of a craftsman. He was making strawberry jam that morning, and we could see he had dripped samples on his beard and shirt. He walked around the trailer, running his hands along the gunwales of the canoe, and said it had a long life ahead of it. Then he took us up the hill to his shop, where there were canoes stacked outside waiting for repair and two new ones with polished bottoms ready for delivery. Dry rough-sawn wood was stacked beneath a sloped lean-to shelter, and the wall beside the door was decorated with a collage of old license plates. The shop was infused with the smell of cedar and decades of canoe-building clutter: sawdust and shavings; strips of various kinds of wood; partly finished paddles; wooden canoe seats; a bench covered with containers of brass nails, planes, chisels in various sizes, knives, hammers and saws. In the centre of the shop floor was the heavy Guide Special mould resting on a wheeled trolley. A mould looks like an unfinished upside-down canoe made of aged white pine and galvanized steel bands.

Bill cuts, planes and steams Eastern white cedar for the ribs that are bent across the mould to form the shape of the canoe, with half ribs nailed in between to strengthen the floor. He nails thin cedar planking over the ribs and fashions gunwales from white spruce, the stem and thwarts from ash, maple or beech. On my canoe, he had added a square stern with an oak transom and a hard fibreglass finish, a practical improvement over traditional canvas covering. The square stern, added after it was taken off the mould, allows it to be run by a small outboard motor with the waterlines unchanged, so the Guide Special responds to the push of a pole just like its original V-stern design was meant to do, without the drag of most square-stern motor canoes.

Bill Miller's work is a continuation of an art that began on these rivers with the work of the Mi'gmaq and Wolastoqiyik. The oldest surviving birchbark canoe in the world, known as the Grandfather Akwiten Canoe, was made by Wolastoqey craftsmen on the banks of the the Wolastoq, the Saint John River, in the early 1820s. A British army captain stationed in Fredericton shipped the canoe and two others to his family estate in Galway County, Ireland, when he returned home in 1825. He died in 1847 during the potato famine. After his death, one of the canoes found its way to the National University of Ireland in Galway, where it hung from a ceiling in a stairwell for a century and a half until a geology professor traced its origins to New Brunswick and sent it to the Canadian Museum of Civilization to be restored. In 2009 it was returned to the valley of the Wolastoq, where it is now on display in the Beaverbrook Art Gallery in Fredericton. I visit it from time to time. Its lines are still straight, the birchbark bound and sewn with thin black spruce roots. It is decorated with images of flowers and fiddleheads, the edible ferns that push their heads up through the rich floodplains of these northern rivers after the freshet retreats in the spring.

John Rowan wrote of the difference in the designs of the Mi'gmaw and Wolastoqey canoes he encountered during his travels through New Brunswick in the mid-1800s. The Mi'gmaw canoes had high bows and sterns and sloping tall gunwales in the centre to throw off the waves in the Restigouche and Miramichi estuaries. They were about twenty-two feet long, three feet across the beam and weighed 115 pounds. The Wolastoqey canoes were as long but narrower with low gunwales and light enough to be carried by one person on long portages. Both were made of birchbark, peeled in a sheet from a large tree, with gunwales of cedar, a lining of cedar strips and hardwood thwarts to keep the canoe stiff so it holds its shape. A pitch made of resin and grease was used to seal the seams and a pitch pot was essential equipment in every canoe. My Miller Guide Special is a combination of Mi'gmaw and Wolastoqey design with the wide, flat bottom of the Restigouche canoe and the finer lines of those made in the valley of the Wolastoq.

After we had finished touring the shop, Bill invited us in to taste his jam and suggested we christen the canoe in the Tobique that afternoon.

He said we could put in at the Forks Pool just upriver from his home and I could pole down to the community of Riley Brook, which happens to be the perfect length of river run to fill a summer afternoon. He would drop us in the river, drive to Riley Brook and leave our car and trailer there for us. I asked him how he would get back home after he dropped off our car and he said he would hitchhike. I decided this was too great an imposition to ask of a man who was stirring a kettle of strawberry jam. We thanked him for the tour and the jam, promised to stay in touch and drove down to Riley Brook where we stopped beside the river to have lunch at a motel and restaurant called the Bear's Lair.

Over lunch we struck up a conversation with the owners, Don and Evelyn McAskill, who were sharing the cooking and serving duties. Don asked about the canoe parked outside and we told him the story of where we had been. He said he agreed with Bill Miller that the canoe needed to be dipped in the Tobique River, that this was the right and proper thing to do, and he offered to drive us back up to the Forks and then return to his place, where he would leave our car and trailer beside the river. The sun had just burned through the early afternoon clouds. Lucy and I decided we couldn't refuse this second offer, so after lunch we headed back upriver with Don at the wheel and launched the canoe at the Forks where the Little Tobique and the Right-Hand Branch meet.

I pushed us out into the pool where the two little rivers become the Tobique proper, and as we dropped down into the current below, Lucy turned in her seat and announced that we had just given away our car and trailer to a stranger. I agreed that we had. We thought about that for a few minutes, and then we decided that if we never saw them again, it would have been worth it to be where we were at that moment. We had been given the gift of an afternoon on the river and we accepted all of it, just the two of us and the canoe and the rippling waters. Late in the afternoon, when we rode the current under the stone bridge and ran down into the village of Riley Brook, the car was waiting as promised on the shore by the Bear's Lair.

3 The only thing missing on that summer afternoon on the Tobique was fish. In 1953 the government built a hydroelectric dam at the mouth of the river, in the heart of the Wolastoqey community there, creating a lake behind it and flooding a gorge called the Narrows through which canoes and fish had passed for thousands of years. Five years later the government built a second power dam seventy kilometres downstream on the main stem of the Saint John River at Beechwood. When the Saint John River Board reported on its proposal to build a third dam farther downstream just north of Fredericton, it concluded: "Special measures will have to be taken to counteract any adverse effects arising from certain changes brought about by power developments. Such steps would enhance the value of the Saint John River as an asset to the Province of New Brunswick."

More specifically, "certain changes" included flooding a ten-thousand-acre river valley where there were Wolastoqey fishing, hunting and gathering grounds and archaeological sites, displacing more than five hundred families, destroying homes, farms, schools, churches and cemeteries. In response to the proposal, a dentist, naturalist and writer named George Frederick Clarke helped to create the Association for the Preservation and Development of the Saint John River in its Natural State. "The word beauty seems to have fallen into disrepute for a time in this scientific age," Clarke said, telling the people of the valley: "These farms are yours; these homes are yours; the graves are the graves of your ancestors—fight for them."

Clarke's campaign was dismissed as sentimental and emotional, which of course it was. His campaign was also political, but that aspect of his appeal was never addressed. Clarke's objection was that the government of New Brunswick was exercising the power of the state to expropriate and flood an ancient river valley in the name of economic progress. The government had taken measure of ends and means, choosing "power for progress" over what was the most beautiful stretch of the river valley, where riverside towns nestled among a series of snowshoe-shaped islands that Wolastoqey legends called the footsteps of *Glusgap*. The islands, fertilized with silt from the spring freshets, were for many generations a source of fiddleheads, medicinal plants, wild grapes and sweet grasses for the Wolastoqiyik, and later farmed by European settlers and their descendants. George Frederick Clarke took to telling these farmers in public meetings to "meet them with your muskets."

In the fall of 1963 Premier Louis Robichaud embarked on a "power tour" of hydroelectric developments along the Columbia River in Washington State and rivers managed by the Tennessee Valley Authority before proceeding with the construction of the $113 million Mactaquac dam whose purpose was "to attract power intensive industries to New Brunswick." Robichaud promoted the dam as "the economic salvation of our province," an example of how a society might plan for a better future, taking "full advantage of modern scientific and technological progress applicable to the rural economy." In June 1968 the Mactaquac dam began holding back water and the valley flooded and the snowshoe islands disappeared.

Before the construction of the dams, the Saint John River was the most prolific habitat for migratory fish in eastern North America. In designing its "special measures" to counteract the effects of the dam, the government was mainly concerned about only one species, the Atlantic salmon, that supported both a commercial fishery in the estuary and a sport fishing industry upstream, particularly on the Tobique, an international destination for anglers. To mitigate for the disruption in salmon migration, engineers built a hatchery at the base of the Mactaquac dam. Returning salmon were captured, loaded in tanks, trucked upstream and released above the barriers. Thousands of hatchery-reared juvenile salmon were released below the dam to compensate for the loss of natural reproduction above. Meanwhile, millions of other migratory fish continued to arrive at the base of the dam. Striped bass, sturgeon, shad, eels and smelt that came to the dam searching for their lost spawning grounds were turned away. No one was measuring those losses.

The government was counting salmon and its own records document the spectacular failure of the mitigation program. For salmon populations on a river that had already been stressed by the forest industry and log drives and two dams upstream, the third dam was just too much for any kind of mitigation program to counteract. The offspring of the fish that spawned in the Tobique after being trucked around the dams couldn't find their way back to the sea, and the hatchery-reared salmon didn't survive well in the wild without the natal stream-imprinting of juveniles hatched in the headwaters. No provision was made for the downstream passage of salmon that attempted to return to the sea after spawning. For two decades the salmon migration gradually declined then dropped off the charts, following the predictable pattern of extirpation events. The fishing lodges in the upper reaches of the river around Bill Miller's shop in Nictau closed, as did the Wolastoqey fishery, the famous salmon pools on the outskirts of Fredericton and eventually all angling above the head of tide.

The Tobique Salmon Club that had operated at the Forks where Lucy and I launched the Miller that afternoon sued the New Brunswick Electric Power Commission for damages. It took a $400,000 settlement to the Restigouche valley where the club bought property on the Matapédia River and still operates there under its original name. Meanwhile, the mitigation failure flowed downstream. Atlantic salmon began to disappear from all the Saint John River tributaries below the dams and more than thirty rivers that flow into the Bay of Fundy, none of which are dammed. During the past decade, sixteen genetic strains of salmon that originated in what are known as the inner Bay of Fundy rivers have been listed as endangered under the Canadian Species at Risk Act and show no signs of recovery. Even George Frederick Clarke wouldn't have seen that one coming.

During this time, the salmon in about twenty rivers in the outer Bay of Fundy, including the Saint John River system that runs through my home city, have been designated a threatened species, one step removed from endangered. This triggers a government investigation, a kind of environmental forensic reconstruction of a major accident. The outer Bay of Fundy salmon report released in 2014 is an account of a relentless

industrial assault on the river and surrounding aquatic systems. The report concludes that a series of hydroelectric dams were a catastrophe for
the river, but in addition to the big dams, two hundred smaller obstructions were built on various rivers and tributaries. Then there were the
chemical, toxic and deoxygenating wastes deposited in the river from pulp
and paper and lumber mills, forest spraying, farms, fish hatcheries, food
processing plants, and waste- and rock-handling facilities, and the leach-
ates from salt piles and the acid drainage from abandoned mines. There
were sewage outflows from cities and fine silt runoff from roads, farms,
forestry operations and a military training base. There were changes in
river flow caused by the dams and the introduction of invasive species. As
a final insult, the already stressed river began to experience fluctuations
in water temperature caused by a warming climate.

A similar report has been written about the rivers of the inner Bay of
Fundy. These rivers suffered many of the same assaults, without the main
stem dams. And they were subjected to a giant pipe from a potash mine
that pumped brine into the inner bay in the area of their outflow. Finally,
both the inner and outer bay salmon suffered from what scientists call
"depressed population phenomena," a condition in which a population no
longer has sufficient numbers to school or find suitable genetic partners.
It is the condition of a species on the road to extirpation.

Half a century after the construction of the dams, the forest industry
in New Brunswick collapsed. Twenty-five sawmills and three pulp
and paper mills closed after the construction of the dams, and now a
crumbling Mactaquac dam powerhouse needs to be rebuilt or removed,
a project with a price tag in the billions of dollars. The dams are no
longer promoted as instruments of progress but as indispensable links in
the provincial power grid. The multi-million-dollar mitigation program
at Mactaquac is now mainly working to preserve the salmon gene pool.
The dam that was designed to transform this great river into an asset has
become a liability for an already highly leveraged power utility.

I hope I live long enough to see the day when the dams are removed,
so I can watch the river begin to heal itself. Even if I do, I know that

much of what has happened is irrevocable, the consequences of a series of decisions made by a few men during a period of about fifteen years during the life of a fifteen-thousand-year-old river.

As my river companion Tommy Colwell says, "Once something is lost in nature, it's hard to get it back."

4 A couple of weeks after Lucy and I returned from the Tobique with the Miller, my wife, Deb, and I set out for the Restigouche with Lucy, her friend Ruth, and our West Highland terrier, Cody. We rented a second canoe from Marie-Christine Arpin, loaded our gear into her truck and she drove us into the headwater hills of the Kedgwick River, pulling the Miller on the trailer. She followed dusty logging roads for two-and-a-half hours, speaking in French on her radio every few minutes to the drivers of logging trucks to alert them of our position and give them time to slow down when they passed. We drove down toward the river along a road through a clearcut then a band of buffer forest into a clearing beside the Kedgwick Forks where the North and South branches meet. We unloaded and set up camp in a clearing on the bank of the river beside the Forks Pool. From there we would run downstream fifty-two kilometres to the confluence of the Kedgwick and Little Main.

The next morning we loaded the canoes, floated through the Forks Pool and dropped into a roller coaster ride of tight meanders and rapids that wound through the high mountain valley. I found out that first morning just how much I still had to learn about poling. For one thing, I learned the hard way that when I was launching from the shore into the current, I needed to pull the anchor and push upstream first then swing the bow into the current and allow the flow to spin me downstream. If I pushed the stern out first, the current caught the canoe broadside and it was difficult to turn the bow downstream. Poling is all about working with the river, not against it. The Kedgwick taught me that.

The Kedgwick is the most important spawning tributary in the

Restigouche system. There the salmon spend the summer season, holding in deep pools fed by cold-water brooks, waiting to spawn in the fall. All day long we saw fish in pools and pockets of deep water, darting away from the shadows of our canoes. We pitched our tent that evening in a makeshift campsite Marie-Christine had cleared for her clients just above a rock-filled stretch of river and the warden's cabin at Rapid's Depot, where there was once a small village built as a staging ground for lumber companies in the days before mechanization. Throughout the night we heard the sounds of the new logging industry at work, graders smoothing the gravel road and trucks rumbling down from the clearcuts in the hills. I remember thinking as I lay awake in the tent that these hills, this valley and this river are now hard under siege by the modern industrial world.

We know that logging activity in the headwaters is already causing flow disruptions in the Restigouche. We don't know all the implications of these disruptions, because this is an experiment still in its early stages, and research into its long-term effects is limited. But we can well imagine the consequences will not be easy to undo. The bulk of forestry research in this part of the world has focused on how to maximize the harvest and how to grow trees straighter and faster so they can be taken to the mill sooner and produce more board feet of lumber and tonnes of fibre.

What we don't consider often enough is the intimate and complex connection between the land and the water. We can't argue that we didn't know that this connection exists and that we haven't been issued a warning. A century ago the forester and natural philosopher Aldo Leopold began documenting how water and the land around it operate as one unified organic system. He called this understanding of the complexity of "the land organism" the greatest scientific discovery of the twentieth century. From that discovery he developed what he called the land ethic: "A thing is right when it tends to preserve the integrity, stability, and beauty of the biotic community. It is wrong when it tends otherwise."

On a wild river, when water falls from the sky in rain or snow, some of it falls back into the flow, and some falls on the hills and in the valley.

There water is filtered through trees and the low canopy and mosses on the forest floor, gradually returning to the river in springs and streams that sustain the flow in dry periods. During the filtering process, water absorbs life-sustaining nutrients such as nitrogen. "All land represents a downhill flow of nutrients from the hills to the sea," Leopold wrote. Therefore, when we measure the health of a river system, we must consider the health of the watershed through which the water flows. The health of the Restigouche watershed influences not only its patterns of flow but also the chemical composition of the water and the flow of nutrients that it deposits on its run to the sea.

5 After our first run down the Kedgwick, our group has come together on the river at least once each season. Deb and I sometimes call our group the Restigouche Expeditionary Force, a name we adopted from a charcoal graffiti scrawl we found on the ceiling of a campsite shelter. We've all grown on these trips: Lucy and Ruth moving from the passenger seats in the Miller to navigate the river in their own canoe, our terrier learning how terrifying it can be to spend the night alone in the dark woods after chasing a squirrel too far from our campsite, Deb and I learning how to stand back to allow all of them to go where they will, trusting that they will return to us.

For the second stage of my Restigouche trip, I had recruited the members of the Restigouche Expeditionary Force, along with Deb's childhood friend Michelle, her husband, Will, and their eight-year-old daughter, Charlotte. My weekend task was to gather the gear we needed to support the larger group and be ready to leave for the river first thing Monday morning. Over the years we've learned, in theory, that the most important lesson of packing for a river camping trip is to bring what's needed and nothing more. Everything that goes into the canoes at the start must be portaged or carried to each campsite and reloaded along the way. The challenge for us is our definition of what's needed. For the Expeditionary Force, essentials include: folding chairs and two small folding tables; a complete camp kitchen including a portable gas stove, a large cast-iron kettle and oversized cast-iron frying pan; tents and sleeping mats; books to read; notebooks and pencils; a deck of cards; head lamps and lanterns; bottles of wine and glasses; a foldable saw and hatchet; a canoe repair kit, extra rope and a first aid kit; life jackets; a large tarp to make a cooking shelter in case of rain; smaller tarps to cover our gear at night; dry kindling in case we need to start a fire in the rain; and a dry bag for each of us filled with clothes, rain pants and a jacket.

Then there's the food. When Deb and I started running rivers together a couple of decades ago, she taught me how to cook well in the outdoors, and over time even her river menus have evolved into more ambitious enterprises. Long ago I left behind my Presbyterian habit of stuffing a sleeve of crackers and a can of sardines in my pocket and calling it a meal. To prepare for this trip we had two large coolers, one for perishable food and another for cold drinks, jugs of drinking water and a waterproof box filled with dry food items. We also had the ingredients to bake a chocolate cake with pecans in the cast-iron kettle, a project planned by Lucy and Ruth. All this was being gathered the afternoon before we left.

I was consumed with my usual worry over packing lists as I loaded the trailer, the Miller on the bottom and Deb's canoe on a rack above it. Her canoe, called the Prospecteur, is an agile sixteen-footer made of Royalex by Esquif in Quebec. It's the canoe we rented on our first Kedgwick trip that Deb eventually purchased from Marie-Christine. I filled the Miller with paddles, poles and camping equipment, pulled the tarp over the top, strapped down both canoes and helped Deb finish packing the remaining dry bags and coolers of food.

We left Fredericton early Monday, July 2, 2018, and drove north back into the valley of the Restigouche. We arrived at Arpin Canoe Restigouche just after noon and checked in with Louise in the office to confirm that her driver would pick us up at Two Brooks mid-morning on Thursday. I drove down to the beach, unloaded the Miller and the Prospecteur and piled the gear on the shore while Michelle and Will rented a canoe for themselves and Deb rented one for Lucy and Ruth. I left the canoes and the gear on the beach, drove back up into the yard, parked and left my keys with Louise. I walked back down to the beach, settled the canoes in the river and began distributing the load, all of us anxious to get out of the heat and flies into the cooling breezes on the water.

We pushed off from the beach shortly before two p.m., Lucy and Ruth in the lead, followed by Michelle and Will and Deb paddling the Prospecteur with Charlotte riding on the front seat. I took up the rear in the Miller, carrying most of the gear and Cody, who was standing on top of one of the coolers. I allowed the current to carry me, resting the pole in the water as a tiller, and watched Lucy and Ruth slip past the whirpool at the mouth of the Kedgwick then alongside the ledges at Campbell's Pool, following the flow from one side of the river to the other. Lucy's now a fearless paddler who has learned the art of pausing above a rapid to give herself the time she needs to choose a line. When she drops in, she's all in, no second guessing.

My companions had scattered far ahead of me by the time I passed the floating dock in front of the Kedgwick Lodge just above Fence Pool on the left and the outflow of a cold-water brook on the right. I pushed into the languid Looking Glass Pool that carried me down over a gravel bar and scattering of boulders and ledges into the swirling waters of Jimmy's Hole. There the flow collides with the right-hand bank where a cliff as tall as a three-storey building rises from the river bottom. The water meets this rock wall at an angle that causes it to spin down at the same time that it is bending left around a ledge, creating a sharp, irregular meander and a pool of tremendous depth and stability. There were no anglers casting at Jimmy's in the heat of the afternoon, so I made a slow pass through the heart of the pool, looking down into the water, waiting until the salmon appeared, hundreds of them sweeping upstream through the current, the sunlight reflecting off their silver sides as they slashed through the water beneath my canoe.

I've been told many times that the pool was named for a boy named Jimmy who drowned here long ago but it may have been simply named after James Gillis, the man who sold the river frontage to Archie Rogers in 1882. Whatever its origins, it has always seemed to me to be a modest name for a pool that holds anywhere from three hundred to three thousand salmon depending on the time of the year. Danny Bird hires a warden to stay in a cabin on the shore and watch over Jimmy's all season long. All the human-generated technology and money in the world couldn't create a Jimmy's. Nature's formula for its creation would be something like this: push a glacier through a valley of ancient rock formations for a few thousand years; add a flow of water with the perfect temperature, velocity and chemical composition that suits a species of fish with genetic coding that has evolved since the Devonian age; and wait ten thousand years. Then you might have a Jimmy's.

By the time I dropped out of Jimmy's into Moffat's Pool below the cliff, the other canoes in our party had disappeared around the bend and Cody had moved up to his favourite position, lying on his stomach across the bow staring down into the water, which is a precarious position for a little dog with a habit of falling overboard. That's why he wears a red life jacket with a looped handle on the top. I have retrieved him from the river enough times to suspect that this may be a game. I allow it as a concession to the tempestuous mind of a terrier.

I took a few deep breaths to release the last of the worries of packing and organization I had carried with me to the river and turned all my attention to what lay ahead. I chose the left-hand channel where the river funnels into a heavy rip around a long gravel island, turned the nose of the canoe into the current line, felt the pull and leaned into the steady push of the pole.

I stayed close to the left shore until I passed the high bank at Cedar Ledge Pool where I steered into the centre of the river through a swirling pool that passes over a sheet of submerged rock called Flying Eddy. The river then divides around a grassy island, and I chose the left passage down into a grand sweep of a pool called Soldiers. There I allowed the canoe to drift in the downriver breeze into the faster water below. I had come to a stretch of water, known as Cheyne, about four kilometres downstream from the mouth of the Kedgwick. The water I had just passed through and the pools in the valley that lay ahead are connected to two exclusive salmon-angling lodges: Larry's Gulch that is owned and operated by the New Brunswick government, and Downs Gulch that belongs to the Irving family. All of the river frontage here is public land but fishing is private, reserved for the exclusive use of the guests of the lodges.

Over the years I've often wondered how it happened that the government and the wealthiest and most influential family in the province came to have lodges on this stretch of the Restigouche. So, early in the spring, before I left for the river, I composed some questions and made a request for government documents and after months of back and forth with the Department of Natural Resources, I received a large package of letters and internal communications. Those documents raised more questions that sent me to the provincial archives where I searched through boxes of old government files, gathering the scattered pieces of the story.

What happened here, elite ownership of exclusive licenses, emerged from a system of river management on the Restigouche that dates back to the late 1800s. This irregular management system, the only one of its kind in the world, determined the course of the river's history and continues to dominate the economic, political and social life of the valley today. I've spent many days pulling apart the strands of the tangled narrative of how this happened. When I finally began to see how it all came to be, it marked a turning point in my inquiry, as if the landscapes of the river at long last came into focus and new and unexpected stories were rising around every bend.

At the heart of the story is the question of property rights on a wild river, defined in a single sentence by Tommy Colwell during our trip down the Little Main when he said, "I never understood how you could own something that moves." I didn't have a satisfactory answer then but what I would tell him now is that on the Restigouche you can own and lease private fishing rights, even though water and fish are always in motion. What I would also tell him is though this is how it is and has been, it was not always so.

6 The Mi'gmaq who met the European fishermen, explorers and settlers in the valley of the Restigouche had a long-established system of government within a defined territory that they considered not a possession but a sacred order. "Within this land, a widely shared, coherent and interrelated world view existed," writes James (Sa'ke'j) Youngblood Henderson, research fellow at the Native Law Centre of Canada. "It was a place where the life-forces or *manitu* of stones, trees, rivers, coast, oceans, animals and people resided in harmony and where the Mi'kmaq maintained an awareness of these life-forces (*manitu'k*). To put it simply, the world view of *Mi'kma'ki* had an order that a respectful human could participate in but not presume to possess or own. The Mi'kmaq had an obligation to protect this order and a right to share its uses; however, only the unborn children in the invisible sacred realm had any ultimate ownership of the land." Within Mi'gmaq territory, some hunting and fishing grounds were assigned to extended families after generations of continuous use, but most of the lands and waters were shared by all, allowing families to move with the seasons, hunting and gathering on the land and fishing in the rivers and the sea.

The European settlers who came to the river valley carried with them a fundamentally different understanding of territory and property that originated in medieval Europe and feudalism. The feudal system of government developed with remarkable uniformity in hundreds of small states after the collapse of the Roman Empire. In this way, both the French who came to the valley and the British who assumed sovereignty after them shared a similar history and understanding of their relationship to the land and water. In the feudal order, all land in a state was owned by a monarch who leased estates to an aristocracy. The estates were protected by knights and farmed by indentured serfs. It was a system organized around obligations up and down the hierarchical order, all leading back to the Crown. As the feudal system collapsed, ownership of property became associated with freedom and the dismantling of social hierarchies.

Still, elements of feudalism persisted under British Common Law, which became the new law of the land in Mi'gma'gi. Under common law, all land is still ultimately owned by the Crown, but citizens can hold what is called land tenure. The law regarding rivers has also retained elements of feudalism. After the arrival of William the Conqueror in England in 1066, rivers were fenced off to create private fishing preserves for the Norman kings. The Magna Carta of 1215 placed limits on the power of the monarchy and, among other things, opened rivers for common navigation. But title to the *ripa* or bank of a stream included private rights that extended along the river bottom to the midway point of the flow, including the right to restrict fishing. That's what the common law allows, though there is no requirement to exercise these rights. In the nineteenth century, the New Brunswick government adopted this system of riparian rights on its salmon rivers. This became the legal foundation for the creation of a series of private wilderness preserves for a new aristocracy on the Restigouche.

The first to recognize and seize the opportunity to lease and purchase fishing rights on the Restigouche were the railway men, Sandford Fleming and his partner and sometime rival Charles Brydges, the railway developer. In 1871, during the construction of the Intercolonial Railway, Fleming and Brydges negotiated a lease for the entire Restigouche River for ten years for an annual fee of $20 (about $400 today). They divided the river between them at a pool called Indian House, below the mouth of the Patapédia River. Four years later Fleming started buying real estate. In March 1875, he paid $250 (about $5,000 today) for a Crown land grant of fifty acres on the New Brunswick shore of the Restigouche opposite the mouth of the Patapédia, giving him riparian rights on the most productive salmon pool on the river. I found the handwritten deed in the archives. It had first been written as a sale to Brydges, but that name is crossed out and replaced with Fleming's own signature. Fleming purchased another Crown lot with riparian rights downriver at the big bend at Cross Point, for $279, again striking out Brydges's name and replacing it with his own.

During this time Americans came to the valley and began purchasing riverfront land, including Archie Rogers and his uncle William Neyle Habersham of Savannah, Georgia, a wealthy merchant and collector of fine wines who secured lots around the Kedgwick Lodge. Land grants with riparian rights were secured at other pools that have remained among the most productive on the river, including the Junction Pool, Tom's Brook and Brandy Brook, where a cold stream flows into the river above a vast holding pool.

In 1882 the Supreme Court of Canada referred a case involving a dispute over private fishing rights in New Brunswick to the Judicial Committee of the Privy Council in London, England, then the highest court in the land. The referral asked two questions: did riparian rights apply to rivers in the new Dominion of Canada, and if so, who was to manage these rights on Crown land, the provinces or the federal government? The Privy Council ruled that riparian rights could be applied in Canada and that the provinces should be the manager of fishing rights on Crown land. The next year, the New Brunswick government passed legislation stating that riparian rights would remain with all land titles secured before the 1882 decision, but riparian rights would be excluded from all future land grants and remain with the Crown. And it authorized the provincial government to begin leasing Crown fishing rights on salmon rivers.

The new American aristocrats of the Gilded Age, their deep pockets filled with the riches of the great industrial and urban expansion after the Civil War, enthusiastically bought into the opportunity to lease private fishing rights on the Restigouche, not only because the river offered the finest angling opportunities on the continent but also because these rights were unavailable in their own country. When the United States won its independence from the British monarchy in the American Revolution, it established property laws based on an understanding of natural law where rivers were a resource to be shared by all citizens. The American system was modelled after Roman law, which divided the things of the world as being either the property of someone or no one. The things owned by no one include air, running water, the sea and wild animals. Under Roman law and in the new land of the free, rivers and the fish that swam in them were a shared resource. On the Restigouche, the Americans were more than willing to become the new lords of the river and join the system the New Brunswick government had designed just for them.

7 As I began to collect old records of these events, I found that the happenings on the Restigouche were more thoroughly reported in New York City than in the river valley. On June 8, 1880, the *New York Times* announced the creation of a fishing club on the Restigouche under the headline "A Sportsmen's Paradise: The New Home of the Restigouche Salmon Club." The article reported that forty gentlemen from the city had organized themselves into an association to create a private fishing and shooting preserve in the Acadian wilderness of New Brunswick on the Restigouche River. The club had purchased the lands and river holdings of Daniel Fraser, who had been providing outfitting services for anglers beside the Matapédia River. The club paid $32,000 (about $700,000 today) for sixteen hundred acres, including the Fraser homestead, a store, a private cottage, a post office and two buildings used as quarters for guides. The new Intercolonial Railway station and telegraph office were a hundred metres away. The club purchased additional land on the north bank of the river "in order to control the scenery and the exclusiveness of the neighbourhood of their headquarters." The club members shipped in bed linens, table cutlery, china, carpets and furniture and hired a staff of cooks and servants.

"The waters of the Restigouche River are deliciously clear and cool and swift in their flow, and the bed of the river is of stone, almost as

regular in its surface as a street well paved with cobblestone," the reporter
wrote. "The banks are well wooded to the margin of the river, and, at
intervals, are pleasingly diversified with rocks and lofty bluffs, over
which hundreds of small forest streams, fairly alive with trout, find their
way into the main channel. The chief glory of the river, however, is the
abundance and magnificent quality of its salmon."

The founding club members were the super elite of the New York
business and social order. Once these rail cars of money and power and
political influence began streaming into the Restigouche valley, they
never stopped. Among the founders of the club was Chester Arthur,
who had served in the New York militia during the Civil War and who
became the collector of the Port of New York and a Republican politician
after the war. William Kissam Vanderbilt moved downriver from the
Kedgwick Lodge to become a member, as did William Habersham, who
helped to expand the club's river holdings by negotiating leases on the
Kedgwick and Upsalquitch Rivers. Other founding members included
William Earl Dodge Jr., a mining and railway magnate; Charles Lewis
Tiffany, the jewellery merchant; Pierre Lorillard, a tobacco, cigar and
snuff merchant and owner of thoroughbred horses who bought sterling
silver horseshoes from Tiffany's; John Lambert Cadwalader, a wealthy
lawyer who was president of the New York Public Library; and R.G. Dun
of Dun & Bradstreet.

In the fall of the year the club was founded, Chester Arthur was
elected vice-president of the United States on the ticket with James
Garfield. President Garfield was shot by an assassin on July 2, 1881, and
died seventy-nine days later. Arthur became the twenty-first president
of the United States, serving from 1881 to 1885. Throughout his years
in office, he continued to visit his new wilderness clubhouse beside the
Restigouche River.

The happenings on the Restigouche became the subject of regular
stories in the *New York Times*, its reporters typing dispatches about
those of consequence who had been seen at the railway station packed
for an adventure in the northern wilderness. On December 23, 1884, the

Times reported on a meeting of the Restigouche Salmon Club (RSC) in New York City. The club's representatives had been to Fredericton and purchased a three-year lease for twenty-two miles of the upper Restigouche and a one-year lease for the Patapédia River. It had also arranged for leases above and below the Matapédia clubhouse for terms of three to five years and declared its interest in securing all the rights for the pool at the mouth of the Patapédia. "If this negotiation is successful the board is of the opinion that there will be waters for angling for all members who visit the river next season," the newspaper reported. At that meeting, Chester Arthur, the president of the United States, was elected president of the Restigouche Salmon Club.

The following August the *Times* published a story under the headline "The Angler's Paradise" that reported on the "great crowd of Americans" who had travelled to the river that season. Chester Arthur had caught ninety-eight salmon, averaging twenty-four pounds each, in one week. In July 1892 the *Times* reported on those who were "whipping" the famous salmon waters of New Brunswick and eastern Quebec. They were all owners of riparian rights, leaseholders or members of the club. The reporter noted that there were about 150 more boxes of salmon shipped from the Matapédia Station than the previous year. Manhattan real estate heir Robert Goelet and architect Stanford White were fishing at the famous Red Bank Pool where Goelet had landed eight salmon in one day, each averaging more than twenty-five pounds. Harry Hollins, identified as "Mr. Vanderbilt's broker," had caught thirteen fish in two days downriver at Brandy Brook.

At the same time as the club was establishing itself in Matapédia, Dean Sage of Albany, New York, was putting down roots upstream. Sage was born into wealth and took over his father's lumber business and forest real estate holdings. He was a philanthropist with a special interest in the development of Cornell University and a collector of rare books. Known to his friends as Fierce Dean, he was also more or less a professional sportsman: an angler, an author of books and articles on sport fishing, a boxer and the owner of trotting horses.

Sage had bought land on a rocky bluff at the confluence of the Restigouche and Upsalquitch, and for several seasons he camped there in tents. He then built a rough cabin that he used until Stanford White designed him a proper lodge at about the same time he was creating Vanderbilt's lodge upstream. White, who would become a member of the club, was creating his own Restigouche style of rustic elegance, lodges with a central gathering room and bedrooms off to the sides, with sloped shingled roofs and wide, covered porches supported by raw cedar posts.

In August 1897 White took a tour of his new Restigouche designs to attend to some construction details, travelling down through the Waagansis portage to Archie Rogers's Kedgwick Lodge. Downriver he visited Camp Albany, another one of his lodges near Toad Brook, arriving just in time to stop the construction crew from putting a second coat of red paint on the roof. "The first coat of paint was such a brilliant red that as you turned the corner a mile off at the Chain of Rocks it hit you in the eye just like a cannon ball," White wrote in a letter to Robert Goelet.

Dean Sage named the Stanford White lodge "Camp Harmony" after Julia Harmony Twichell, the wife of his long-time fishing companion Joseph Twichell, a Congregationalist clergyman from Hartford, Connecticut. Twichell was an abolitionist who, soon after the outbreak of the Civil War, left his studies at Union Theological Seminary to enlist in the Union army as a chaplain. Throughout his life he was one of the writer Mark Twain's closest friends.

In 1888 Sage published *The Ristigouche and Its Salmon Fishing*, gold-embossed and expansively illustrated by his artist friends. He had 105 copies printed in Edinburgh. Sage wrote that the opportunity to lease Crown water was enormously attractive to the American sportsmen who were securing exclusive fishing rights throughout the valley and working with the government to regulate the river. Clearly, Sage had been following political and legal developments. "Since the establishment of the rights of the riparian owners to the water, the Ristigouche Club has acquired a large portion of the best fishing on the river and has put up on the upper waters several small houses for the temporary accommodation of its members," he wrote. "There are also six or eight individual owners of pieces of water; some of the settlers have refused to sell out their fishing rights, preferring to rent them from year to year, and the Provincial Government still owns a good deal of land along the river which it does not grant without excepting the riparian right."

His book is a combination of fishing stories, practical advice for the gentleman salmon angler and lavish and detailed descriptions of every pool and bend in the river. "It is a noble stream, with no falls or rapids in its whole course that a canoe cannot surmount," he wrote. "Its numerous windings and abrupt turns, so favourable for forming good salmon pools, also gives a variety and choice of beautiful scenery which is rare to find on any river. There is no mile of the Ristigouche above Matapedia which has not some peculiar charm of its own, outside of the wonderful clearness of its waters and the different forms they assume in their rapid journey to the great Gulf of St. Lawrence, from the long flat, where they move with a glassy and tranquil smoothness, but a swiftness that has to be felt to be recognized, to the pools, with their thousand little ripples dancing in the sunlight, the white-crested rapid with its waves of might, and the swirling eddies rushing over the rock-strewn bottom, where the great salmon rest on their upward way."

8 Among these various stories of money and privilege, I discovered a Mi'gmaw guide named Larry Vicaire, the namesake of Larry's Gulch. As I pieced together a picture of the man, I discovered a lost world of grand Restigouche adventures and the story of a river guide who had navigated a radical social and economic transformation in the river valley, the consequences of which still reverberate today.

In the mid-nineteenth century Larry Vicaire began appearing as a character in magazine articles about wilderness fishing on the Restigouche. I found him in 1853 accompanying a British military officer and writer named Campbell Hardy, stationed in the colonies for fifteen years and an avid fisherman and hunter. Hardy was the first sporting author to describe his adventures on the Restigouche in detail in a two-volume work, *Sporting Adventures in the New World*, published in London.

Hardy arrived in Bathurst on August 19, 1853. He soon visited "the Mission" across the river from Campbellton where he found a community of two hundred Mi'gmaw families living in log houses and farming. There he hired two Mi'gmaw guides who had a newly constructed bark canoe; one of them was Larry Vicaire and the other a man named Francis. Hardy wrote that Larry had a long discussion with his wife before he left. It seems that this may have been one of his first guiding trips that sought to push far upriver and overland into Wolastoqey territory, and she didn't want him to go for fear he wouldn't return. Larry prevailed, and the men left early on the morning of August 21, poling, wading and dragging the canoe up through the labyrinth of islands on the lower part of the river. That night, they slept at Daniel Fraser's farm in Matapédia.

In the morning Larry and his crew loaded the canoe with fresh butter, potatoes and salt pork and the group pushed upstream. The river was low after weeks of little rain and they often had to get out and walk. They camped that night beside a long meander below the mouth of the Upsalquitch that the lumbermen called the Rafting Grounds for this was the place where the white pine masts floating in the freshet would run against the bank and be rafted together for the remainder of the passage to the sea. The next morning, when they were ascending through a heavy rapid above the Rafting Grounds, Larry's pole snapped in half. He dropped to his knees and guided the canoe back down to the base of the run. They beached the canoe while he cut and carved a new pole. Then Hardy and his companion walked upriver on the shore while Larry poled the lighter canoe up through the rapid.

They passed the mouth of the Patapédia and camped at Devil's Half Acre where a rugged cliff forces the river through a narrow cut, churning and boiling as it drops into a deep pool below. They caught a number of salmon there that Larry cooked on a forked stick over the fire, finishing the meal with biscuits and molasses. The next morning, soon after they departed, they ran over a rock and cut a gash in the canoe. Larry reassured Hardy that he would put a wooden bottom over the bark if the water dropped any lower. He patched the gash, sealed it with the pitch pot and pushed on.

Hardy wrote of passing through the gulch that years later would be named for his guide. "The banks were lower and shaded by a pleasing mixture of evergreen and deciduous foliage," Hardy wrote. "Occasional islands, densely wooded with maples, birches, and elms, and fringed with tangled thickets of dogwood, moose-bushes, and berry-yielding shrubs of every variety, expanded, though lessened the depth of the river, and entailed a general disembarkation, and a splashing walk by the side of the canoe."

Later that afternoon they reached the rough home of a man Hardy called Chain, whose name was more properly spelled Cheyne. His was the last house on the upper Restigouche, built on the shore opposite a sharp cliff and deep salmon pool, serving as a resting place and store for the lumber crews and, later, parties of anglers. More than four decades later, Archie Rogers wrote in his logbook at the Kedgwick Lodge that on Monday, June 25, 1906, he and his companion L.S. Thompson beached their scow at Cheyne's to feed the horses. While they were there, Thompson took his fly rod out on the water and hooked and landed eight salmon, two of them weighing more than thirty pounds. "A fool for luck that man," Rogers wrote.

Larry had never been above Cheyne but they met a group of lumbermen who had, and they told them how to find the route up the Little Main Restigouche to the Waagansis Brook portage. Six kilometres upstream they passed the mouth of the Kedgwick, where the Arpin headquarters is now located, and camped on an island farther up the Little Main, just below where Tommy and I had spent our final night on the first stage of our trip. They waded and pulled the canoes most of the day until they passed Boston Brook and reached the mouth of the Gounamitz where Larry cut a series of long cedar strips and lashed them to the bottom of the canoe to protect it from the rocks. He pulled the canoe upstream the next day, portaging over a log jam, until they found the mouth of the Waagansis, marked with a wooden sign. They camped there and in morning pushed into the brook, which "surpassed our worse expectations," Hardy wrote. "Dense thickets overhung the channel, generally at the height of three feet only from the surface of the water, and sometimes almost excluding the day-light. The stream itself, so narrow in places, as scarcely to allow of the passage of the canoe, sometimes deepened into six or eight feet of water; obliging us to re-embark in a dripping state, though only for a few yards." It was reassuring for me to read that the Waagansis has maintained its essential character during the last century and a half. When they arrived at the portage road they feasted on blueberries and raspberries and shot a partridge that they roasted and shared.

On September 3 they reached the Wolastoq. It was Larry's first time coming this far and as he looked out over the valley, he commented, "Guess he's a pretty big river." He turned the canoe over and removed the cedar strips, resealed the seams with the pitch pot and exchanged the poles for paddles. They floated downriver and arrived in Fredericton on September 10. "Larry and Francis appeared quite bewildered at the size of the town, and the dress of the military quartered there," Hardy wrote. "Through our long absence from the abodes of civilization, we felt strange in walking the crowded streets, and in speaking to our old friends. We were known at first by few, for our clothes were in such a dilapidated state, and our beards so wild-looking." Hardy paid Larry and Francis two dollars (about sixty dollars today) for each day of their grand adventure and they returned home overland by coach.

During their time on the river, Larry had made such an impression on Hardy that he composed a long passage to correct what he called "the universal lies" told about the Mi'gmaq People. "It is the white man who has kept aloof from the Indian, oppressed him, deprived him of his natural means of supporting existence; and in the first instance, obtaining a sure footing on his soil by courtesy and conciliation, has gradually, by increasing might, laid hold of his whole territory," Hardy wrote. "Go into his wigwam, and gain his confidence; and when you shall have heard his tale, delivered with a degree of impassioned eloquence which would become a finished orator, if you leave not his tent ashamed of your own callous and oppressing race, you have not the heart of a Christian.

"It is owing to their habitual reserve and caution, and their patient endurance of hardship, that the character of the Indians has been so little known and appreciated. The consciousness of primary wrong to his race of long-continued neglect, and of tissues of violated promises, both personal and national, is still vividly and constantly impressed on his mind, and occupies his thoughts. Such is really the truth. The Micmac Indians are still an unconquered race, the forest lands, daily doled out to the inflowing tide of emigration, are still theirs by right, and though they say they are 'great friends of Queen Victoria,' not one of them would designate himself her subject."

9 Thirteen years after this adventure, Larry Vicaire embarked on another, this one recorded by an American journalist who wrote under the name Penman. The article, simply titled "The Restigouche," was published in 1868 in *Harper's New Monthly* magazine and illustrated with a series of pen-and-ink sketches. Penman was the pseudonym of Charles Hallock, one of the leading sporting writers of his time, a graduate of Yale University and Amherst College, the founder of *Forest and Stream* magazine and author of many books about fishing and hunting throughout North America. "The Restigouche" is an illuminating and unsettling document, filled with rich descriptions of the landscape and communities Penman encountered on his 1866 trip — and an exuberant intolerance. Penman wrote in the language of a committed white supremacist and his article was published without reservation in a respected magazine widely read throughout North America and Europe.

Charles Hallock was a supporter of the Confederacy during the Civil War and worked as a runner around the naval blockade between Halifax and Bermuda. He was the editor of a newspaper in Augusta, Georgia, and lived for a time in Saint John, New Brunswick, where he edited the forerunner to my old newspaper, the *Telegraph*. Writing as Penman, he made a point of the fact that he despised African Americans and Acadians and feared the savage Indians. I suspect the fear of his Mi'gmaw guide was feigned for dramatic effect for his audience at home. Throughout Penman's account, he contradicts himself by presenting Larry Vicaire as a river guide and woodsman of great ability who showed nothing but an abiding "good-will and kindness" to the author at every moment of their trip together.

In 1866 Hallock boarded a steamer in Boston, landed in Saint John, then travelled by train to the Acadian village of Shediac on the Northumberland Strait, where he boarded another steamer north. He noted that the Acadians on the coast, the "Jeans and Jeanettes," were remarkable for the tenacity with which they clung to what he called their "old habits and associations." This included speaking their native language. "Few understand English or care to," he wrote. The steamer was populated by French priests and nuns, schoolmasters, members of the legislature, militia officers, and Mi'gmaq, sixty passengers in all sharing a dozen berths. "The ladies took the berths, the priests and schoolmasters kept in a knot by themselves, the nuns retired with their dismal hoods and conventual character, the Indians maintained their habitual exclusiveness, and the legislators drank beer and discussed Confederation."

He landed at Dalhousie and travelled overland to the Mi'gmaq village beside the Restigouche. He arrived on St. Anne's Day to find the people celebrating a Mass and a community feast with foot races and dances and the shooting of rifles into the air. He engaged two guides from the community to take him upriver, one of them Larry Vicaire. They travelled together to the house of Daniel Fraser, a "monarch of no small realm," who had more than one hundred employees engaged in lumbering, trapping, hunting, farming, salmon fishing and road building. Hallock admired Fraser, a forceful Scotsman and member of "Nature's nobility," who stood six feet four inches tall. At Fraser's,

Hallock enlisted a travelling companion he found sitting on the porch assembling rods and reels. In his article the man is known simply as the Captain.

That night a thunderstorm and hard rain swept through the valley. They sat outside on the porch where they were joined by Daniel Fraser's brother Aleck, who gave a long and colourful lecture about the Battle of Restigouche that was later no doubt shaded in Penman's prose. In the article, Aleck's story included a fanciful tale of a love affair between an Acadian woman named Marie and a captive British army officer who betrayed her and swam to safety, saving the day during the battle and leaving her dead with a "musket-ball through her beautiful brain."

In the morning, Hallock, the Captain and their guides set out in two canoes with provisions of pork and molasses, hard bread, tea, salt beef, flour, whiskey, cooking utensils and blankets. They poled eighteen miles upstream on the first day, and Larry made a camp by cutting spruce boughs for a bed and lighting a fire to keep the swarms of blackflies and mosquitos at bay. The following afternoon they came to the mouth of the Patapédia, where they camped and the Captain landed their first large salmon. The next morning's fishing landed more salmon. Larry grilled strips of salmon in pork scraps over the fire and made tea. The river upstream was alive with fish.

They passed the mouth of the Kedgwick and continued up the Little Main to Boston Brook where a torrential rain began to fall. Larry cut sheets of birchbark to cover his guests and stopped periodically to bail out the canoe. When they decided to make camp, Larry turned the canoe over and placed Hallock underneath. Then he cut logs, laid them out on the beach, pulled the bark off a birch tree and made a fire on top of the logs. He lashed the paddles to the gunwales of the canoe to prop it up and used the long setting poles to build a lean-to over the campfire. He laid sheets of birchbark and spruce boughs across the poles to make a watertight roof then dried the softest boughs by the fire to make a bed. Larry boiled the kettle and cooked salmon and trout over the fire. "Never was a pipe more fully enjoyed, or a noggin of brandy drank with greater relish, than after that meal," Hallock wrote.

The rain fell through the night and the river had risen up almost into their campsite by morning. Still, they pushed on in the rain to the mouth of the Waagansis. When they reached the mouth of the stream and the portage route, Hallock thought he was being pushed straight into an alder thicket. He lay flat in the bottom of the canoe while Larry pulled and cut their way through, losing his hat and tearing his shirt. By the time they had reached the head of the brook the rain had stopped. Larry cached all the food and equipment they didn't need to take with them, spread their clothing out in the sun to dry, then carried the packs, paddles and poles halfway across the three-mile portage. Next he came back for the canoe, completing the portage in about four hours. After camping that night on the road to La Grande Rivière, they floated down to a village where Hallock and the Captain travelled by wagon to Grand Falls and from there by steamer down to Saint John. Larry and his fellow guide returned the way they came, back through the Waagansis portage, down the Restigouche to the sea.

10 Larry Vicaire also worked for Dean Sage at Camp Harmony and was mentioned in his book, in particular for his sense of humour and prowess as a storyteller at gatherings around the campfires. But Larry's most famous client was Princess Louise, Queen Victoria's daughter, who had married Ian Campbell, the Marquis of Lorne. When Lorne was appointed governor general of Canada in 1878, it was hoped that the posting in Ottawa might prove to be a healing change for a troubled marriage.

In the spring of 1879 a vice-regal party headed east to visit the most famous angling destination in the country, the Restigouche River, with permission to fish the private waters leased by the railway men. They departed on a steamer from Quebec City upon which they were joined by Charles Hallock, who was on his way to the river and offered to brief the party on how to fish the Restigouche. He later wrote of encountering the princess on the rail. She was wearing an alpaca dress and seaside hat. He left the vice-regal party with some angling wisdom and a few of his salmon flies. The party boarded the Intercolonial Railway in Rivière-du-Loup, slept in the railway car at Matapédia and had breakfast at the Fraser homestead. Charles Brydges was waiting there with a luxury houseboat designed like a private railway car with a dining area and sleeping quarters built on a scow that could be pulled by a team of horses. The boat was nicknamed *Great Caesar's Ghost*.

The party left Matapédia on June 18 aboard the *Ghost* with an entourage that included Lorne's father (the Duke of Argyll), brother Archibald, sisters Mary and Elizabeth, his secretary and aide-de-camp, and a lady-in-waiting for the princess. A government fisheries officer acted as head guide, but the serious work on the river was entrusted to Mi'gmaw guides. For the princess they had recruited the most experienced and skilled guide on the river, Larry Vicaire. The party stopped for one night at the mouth of Brandy Brook then proceeded upriver to Indian House Pool where they set up camp for a longer stay.

The Toronto *Globe* dispatched a correspondent from Matapédia with Mi'gmaw guides to find the princess and her party. The correspondent, writing without a byline, described the journey in exquisite detail. He wrote of the grandeur of the mountains covered in rich Acadian forest. He wrote of the effect of the late-day sunlight when the trees glow on the hills, "the soft, delicate effluence of the sunbeams streaming through the outer leaves and resting on the inner ones." He wrote at length of the clarity of the water, how "each little green island" appeared "like an emerald set in crystal." He camped the first night near Brandy Brook and noted that it had a flow so clear he could see the stones on the bottom as if no water was running over them at all.

He slept on a bed of spruce boughs beside the brook and woke before first light to warm himself by the fire. At sunrise clouds of mist rolled

WATER   139

up from the river onto the sides of the mountain ridges. As sunlight
streamed into the gorge, the mists dissolved and the river was suddenly
"clothed in myriads of gilded ripples." He camped the next night at Red
Pine Mountain Brook where in the morning he was met by a fisheries
department officer who delivered a letter stating that the governor general
had asked that the newspaperman not approach the vice-regal party.
The correspondent, who had a letter of permission in hand from Lorne's
secretary, dismissed this "pretentious" document as an annoyance, serving
only "to show how easy it is for meddlesome and officious people to
misrepresent the Governor General."

Above the long meander at Cross Point, he found a sign swinging
from a tree on the bank pointing the way to the "Silver Grill" and a
Colonel McNeil hailing him from the shore. There he found that McNeil
and a Scottish Conservative politician named Lord William Buller
Fullerton Elphinstone had set up dining and cooking tents with a staff
of attendants as a kind of temporary shoreside respite for the princess and
her entourage. McNeil and Elphinstone had been fishing the pool and
had killed more than a thousand pounds of salmon in ten days of fishing.

Continuing upstream, the correspondent approached a large gravel
bar where the river splits into three channels below the expanse of the
lake-like Indian House Pool and saw the princess with Larry and another
guide floating downstream, Louise "wearing that same inimitable look
of unobtrusive, but fearless, self-possession, as she drifted down the swift
current in her frail bark canoe." A log structure on the shore beside the
pool was being used as a cooking house and the *Ghost*, moored by the
beach, was serving as a dining room and sleeping compartment for the
Duke of Argyll. A footbridge had been built over the brook near a row
of blue-and-white striped tents, the floors covered with spruce boughs
overlaid with a strip of carpet in front of the cots. The princess's tent had
a "dark Brussels carpet" and a "dainty little dresser" with a mirror. Beside
hers were the tents of Lady Mary, Lady Elizabeth and the attendants,
complete with a washbasin, pitcher and mosquito netting. A nearby clearing had been cleaned up and a gravel path installed to offer a promenade

for the ladies to take their exercise because the meadows that became wet with dew in the morning and evening "would be anything but tolerable."

The princess had hooked and landed several salmon, including a particularly large fish in the pool at Indian House. The next day she and the ladies canoed down to the "Silver Grill" while Lorne and some of the men travelled upriver to fish the pool at the mouth of the Patapédia.

The correspondent had all that he needed and floated back downstream to file his story. The vice-regal party stayed at Indian House until the end of the month. Princess Louise drew a stylized portrait of herself seated in the centre of a shortened Mi'gmaw canoe with its distinctive curved gunwales. She is wearing an ankle-length dress with long sleeves and a broad-brimmed hat with a bow draped in mosquito netting. There are two guides in the canoe: the bowman seated by the anchor line smoking a pipe, and the head guide, who we can assume is Larry seated in the stern and leaning on a paddle to hold the canoe steady in the current.

Larry Vicaire worked the final seasons of his life at Camp Albany, a lodge upstream from Camp Harmony owned by Americans Abraham Lansing, a lawyer and politician from Albany, and Dudley Olcott, president of the Merchant and Farmers' Bank of Albany. Lansing wrote of Larry's death in his *Recollections*, in a passage dated June 11, 1885. "Larry is dead and with him dies much special and valuable knowledge of these woods and the Restigouche. A connecting link between the present and the past is now gone." In 1884, Larry's wife had died, and though he joked he was looking for another he had been in mourning and drinking heavily. At Listuguj, he had been causing such an uproar that he had become alienated from his friends and even his daughter and her husband, who also worked as a guide for Lansing. According to Lansing, Larry had gone out into the cold on a winter night and died of exposure.

There are several stories of the interactions between Larry and the princess that may be more local legend than fact. The one reported by Sage is the most plausible. He wrote that the princess insisted on standing up in the canoe when she was casting and Larry, breaking protocol, placed his hands on her shoulders and pushed her back down in her seat. That one I believe to be true, because in a Restigouche canoe, the guide is the king. The other stories — one about him jumping into the river to keep the canoe from upsetting and another of him dismissing a portrait she painted of him as ugly — may or may not have happened. An even more implausible story is that the princess became so annoyed with Larry's firm orders in the canoe that she said something like, "If you think you're so important, maybe they should name this place after you." That one, I like to imagine to be true.

The naming of Larry's Gulch is a modest memorial for a man who made such a large impression on all who travelled with him and benefitted from his knowledge and expertise and deep generosity. I have given the story of Larry's life, such as we know it, so much attention because in it I understood for the first time the consequences of the transformation of the wild river into Paradise Restigouche. The historian Peter Thomas wrote that when Larry died "the river was rapidly closing" to the Mi'gmaq, who for thousands of years had travelled freely on these waters, "unless they became camp servants to rich men from afar, whose only journeying was from pool to pool or camp to camp." And in his death, alone and exposed on a winter's night, I saw the great tragedy that was unfolding for his people in the years when the new angling aristocracy pursued its seasons of sport.

11 As the *Globe* correspondent chased the story of the vice-regal fishing expedition upriver, there was a different kind of story unfolding downriver from the Matapédia train station that he missed altogether: the Mi'gmaq were fighting for their survival. The leasing of the fishing rights on the Restigouche combined with new fishing regulations, had turned the ancient order of the Mi'gmaw world on its head. The Peace and Friendship treaties the Mi'kmaq had signed with the British a century earlier had confirmed their right to fish and hunt in their traditional territory as they always had. But the terms of the treaties were not honoured on the Restigouche. For the British had brought to the Restigouche the common law tradition of private fishing rights and a history of regulation that gave priority to angling over harvesting for food with nets or spears.

By the time Sir Edmund Head arrived in the colony of New Brunswick with his fly-fishing kit to be the next lieutenant-governor, the government had already established seasons for fishing on the Restigouche that limited the use of nets or spears above the tidewater. Soon after he arrived in Fredericton, Head had seen to it that the legislature passed new laws that banned fishing by any method other than angling with a fly above the head of tide and created a licensing system for nets at fishing stations in the estuary.

The rules were loosely enforced in the early days. Dean Sage wrote about white settlers drifting nets in the river, an activity he described as "harmless law-breaking." Spearing was another matter, and Sage explored this issue in a passage in his book that could have been written by Hallock. "Until about fifteen years since, the Mic-Macs at the Mission depended for a large part of their subsistence on the salmon, which they got entirely with the spear; and when they were suddenly prohibited from exercising this immemorial right, they felt it to be the worst blow that the dominant race had ever inflicted. The poor creatures could not at first believe that the river was no longer theirs to fish, and that after a certain day it would be a crime to take their food from the waters which had always been free to them. After a few sad experiences from their violation of which they could not but consider a most unjust and cruel law, they submitted, and addressed themselves to the impossible task of extorting a living from the sterile farms they have at the Mission. Under the influences of whiskey, natural improvidence, and the deprivation of their chief means of support, their extinction seems a matter of not a very long time."

For Sage, the preservation of the salmon for the angler was a moral imperative, while the extinction of the people who had lived in the valley for thousands of years before he came to vacation there was simple inevitability, unrelated to the American acquisition of river rights in a foreign land. The sport of angling was a refinement of a civilized people, the taking of fish for food with the spear a practice of a lesser race from a distant past. And as a river guide observed years later, anglers were harvesting fish in large numbers; only the method of their dispatch had changed. The fly and the gaff had replaced the spear. The gaff was a long stick with a large hook on the end that the guides used to capture the salmon when the angler reeled the fish to the side of the canoe or into the shallows by the beach. The new upstream harvest was largely shipped out of the valley in boxes filled with river ice collected in winter and stored beneath layers of sawdust in ice houses at the lodges. The Restigouche salmon were served at fancy dinner parties in New York and Boston and during Chester Arthur's time no doubt cooked in the kitchen of the White House in Washington, DC.

How could Dean Sage have written such a passage? Sage on the face of it was no Charles Hallock. He admired Camp Harmony's Mi'gmaw guides and visited their homes in the community of Listuguj. He was a highly educated man, a devout Episcopalian with a social conscience. His constant angling companion was the abolitionist Joe Twichell. The truth was that even opponents of slavery in the United States believed in the superiority of the white race, including those like Abraham Lincoln, who came to see the Civil War as the terrible price willed by divine providence upon his country for the sin of slavery.

Americans like Sage were well versed in the tragedy that had already befallen Indigenous peoples in the United States. In 1831 the young French nobleman Alexis de Tocqueville and his friend Gustave de Beaumont spent nine months travelling in America. De Tocqueville kept a journal and returned to France to write with extraordinary precision and insight what remains the definitive study of the nature of democratic society, *Democracy in America*. De Tocqueville described a scene late in 1831 on the banks of the Mississippi River near Memphis where a group of Choctow people were removed from their lands and pushed west on a forced migration into what was then considered Indian territory, part of the "Great Removal," also known as the "Trail of Tears." It was the heart of winter and there was snow on the ground and ice chunks floating in the river currents. Some of the people were wounded or sick. There were infants in arms and elders so infirm that they soon would die. They had no tents, no carts, only what they could carry in their arms and on their backs. "I saw them embark to cross the great river, and this solemn spectacle will never leave my memory," de Tocqueville wrote. "One heard neither tears nor complaints among this assembled crowd; they were silent. Their misfortunes were old and they felt them to be irreparable." When they climbed into the boats that would ferry them across the river, they left their dogs on the shore. When the dogs realized they were being left behind, they let out a great howl and threw themselves into the icy water in an attempt to follow their people through the currents to the other side.

"One cannot imagine the frightful evils that accompany these forced migrations," wrote de Tocqueville, who was well versed in evils, his family having lived through the terrors of the French Revolution and the violence that played out on the blood-soaked streets of Paris. On the banks of the Mississippi, he recognized that he was witnessing human suffering of another kind. "At the moment when the Indians left their paternal fields, they were already exhausted and worn down," he wrote. "Behind them is hunger, before them is war, everywhere is misery.... I would not want a reader to be able to believe that my picture here is overcharged. I saw with my own eyes several of the miseries that I have just described; I contemplated evils that would be impossible for me to recount."

Sage quoted Longfellow's *Hiawatha* in his writing and recorded the stories told by Mi'gmaw guides in a formulaic broken dialect of a kind that I recognize from the stories told of my family's history in the southern United States. My ancestors were slaveowners in Tidewater, Virginia, before the Civil War, and after the war engaged in mythologizing the past, creating a fiction of gentle aristocrats living in harmony with their devoted African American slaves, who were not only treated with kindness and compassion but in fact loved their life on the plantation in service of their masters. Slavery of course was always supported by chains and the lash, and no dressing up of the past by future generations could erase the sins of my ancestors.

In 1884 a distant relative of mine named Thomas Nelson Page published a popular novel called *Marse Chan*, set on a fictional plantation modelled after a Tidewater estate that was owned by my great-great-grandparents before the war. Page's novel was written almost entirely in an imagined African American dialect that bears a startling resemblance to the dialogue in Sage's account of Mi'gmaw storytellers. Both Page and Sage were acquaintances of Mark Twain, who published *Huckleberry Finn* the same year as *Marse Chan*.

Twain's work was of a different kind. In his account, when a boy and a runaway slave found freedom on the river, they also found each other in friendship, a deep connection that confused and confounded Huck Finn, who had been raised in a society that taught him the lessons of white superiority. In Twain's account, redemption was made possible by the liberating currents of a great and beautiful river that flowed through the violence of a dark and broken society. We all might keep this in mind as we seek reconciliation with the Mi'gmaq on the Restigouche that can only begin with an honest accounting of the past.

In the new Dominion of Canada, the fortunes of the Mi'gmaq went from bad to worse. The Indian Act of 1876 created reserve land for them, where they were to be treated as wards of the state and trained for assimilation into a "higher" form of civilization. Their lack of citizenship was expressed most clearly in the fact that while the Mi'gmaq were prohibited from owning property on the reserves, those lands could still be expropriated and granted to property-owning white settlers as needed. But the heart of the assimilation program for the Restigouche Mi'gmaq was on the river, where the government first limited salmon spearing to a small area below the tidewater before granting them a license for a fishing stage for nets. The following year, when fisheries officers and missionaries arrived to set up the stage and offer instruction in this new way of fishing, Mi'gmaw fishermen resisted, took to the river in canoes and continued to spear salmon, some of them destroying the nets. The government's response was to arrest them and lease the net station to non-Indigenous fishermen who were to share the paltry proceeds with the Mi'gmaq.

John Rowan recognized that the new federal government's policies had been particularly destructive for the Mi'gmaq of the Restigouche. "They have not prevented greedy settlers from robbing them of their land, and latterly they have prohibited them from spearing salmon," he wrote. "For hundreds, or perhaps thousands of years, these Indians have lived upon the salmon in the summer, and if it was thought advisable in the interests of the fisheries to prohibit spearing altogether, the Government should have given them some equivalent. What they did give them was one net which brings in about a dollar per annum to each family." Rowan noted that the Mi'gmaq had been told that a large number of anglers would visit Chaleur Bay and employ them at high wages, along with giving them the salmon they caught. While some found work as guides at the lodges upriver, the jobs were scarce and provided a subsistence living for only a handful of families. Meanwhile, during the first two decades of its operation, the Restigouche Salmon Club members harvested more than 195,000 pounds of salmon from its waters alone — and shipped most of their catch out of the valley to the big cities of the Eastern Seaboard.

"Under the present system of leasing them, not one Indian in a hundred is employed, and I am told that some lessees endeavour to recoup themselves for the rent by salting and carrying off the salmon," Rowan wrote. "The laws are enforced against the Indian, but not against the white man; the former requires a torch which makes him conspicuous, the latter uses his net quietly but effectually in the dark."

Charles Akroyd, a British sportsman of moderate wealth and fierce independence, was one who tested the unspoken disparity in the application of the Restigouche fishing laws. Akroyd moved into a room above a pub in Campbellton in the spring of 1881, planning to fish on the Restigouche for six weeks; he ended up staying for three years. Akroyd was as rough as Dean Sage was refined and later told of his adventures in his book *A Veteran Sportman's Diary*. Akroyd hunted in the winter and fished in the summer, one year leaving Campbellton in August in canoes with a group of Mi'gmaw guides, poling upstream more than two hundred kilometres into the headwaters of the Kedgwick River, then hauling the canoes overland to the source of the Rimouski River, which they descended, arriving in the Gulf of St. Lawrence in October. That arduous trip was not for the faint of heart.

Dean Sage, who referred to his river neighbour as Mr. A, tells the story of a day when Akroyd was on the riverbank beside the water he was leasing at Grog Island and a canoe floated down through the pool sweeping a net behind. Akroyd launched his canoe and chased the netsmen downriver, confronted them then laid a complaint with the magistrate in Matapédia. When the case was heard, the charges against the netsmen were dismissed and the judge ordered Akroyd to pay the court costs. It seems even the courts for a time expressed sympathy for the traditional rights of settlers to fish.

While the Mi'gmaq were being administered off their river and the anglers were pursuing their sport upriver, the settler commercial fishery continued to expand in the bay. During the 1894 season, the commercial net fishery in Chaleur Bay harvested an estimated 1.5 million pounds of salmon. In the years following the death of Larry Vicaire, the lodges began turning away from the Mi'gmaq and hiring new generations of guides from among the white settler community, until the only lodge owner on the river who continued to employ the Mi'gmaq was Archie Rogers at the Kedgwick Lodge.

12 In response to resentment among the settlers over the leasing system on the Restigouche, the government opened a stretch of the Upsalquitch River in 1894 and sold day passes to anglers for three dollars a day. A government memo justified the continued leasing system, expressing surprise that there should be any objections to the restricted access "when the object in doing so is chiefly to establish a system of effective guardianship, the cost of which, if made a charge upon the provincial revenue, would be very considerable. Experience has demonstrated that fishing rivers even moderately easy of access, when freely opened to the public, have never long remained attractive to the angler."

In the beginning the leasing of fishing rights on the Restigouche was seen as a source of government revenue and a way to develop a sport fishing industry in the province. Later the leases were integrated into a management regime that the government justified as a way to preserve the salmon resource: private interests would protect their property; a river left open to the public would be overfished and the salmon would disappear. The exclusion of the Mi'gmaq and the non-property-owning citizen in the valley was based on the assumption that it was by necessity one or the other: private fishing rights or a rampage of destruction.

The relationship between ownership and responsibility and care for the Earth is a long-standing philosophical debate. Is environmental stewardship a political or private responsibility? Are we better off holding lands and waters in common or placing them in private hands? These questions have divided the conservation movement into those who argue for collective political action and those who dedicate themselves to creating private land trusts. In recent years we've even taken to privatizing pollution, allowing for the trading and purchasing of emissions and taxing the release of carbon into the atmosphere, creating economic incentives for responsible action.

Long ago, the Greek philosopher Plato argued that common ownership of property makes collective action possible and recommended the abolition of private property. Conversely, Aristotle contended that private interests were related to virtuous activity. Writing in the wake of the Industrial Revolution, Karl Marx argued that private property rights were an obstacle to collective action, that the interest of individuals in a world of equality would be best protected by common property controlled by citizen collectives. While Marx was writing in response to the destructive nature of bourgeois capitalism without limitations, the communist agenda was one of rapid industrialization for the benefit of the working class. This in the end proved as destructive of natural systems as any form of government in history. On the Restigouche, questions about the relationship of ownership to care remain at the heart of a river management system that has persisted for more than a century.

Soon after the club settled in Matapédia, it helped to create, along with the other lodge owners on the river, the Restigouche Riparian Association, incorporated in 1911, and for decades it became the primary regulator of fishing on the river. The Riparian Association hired wardens and pressured the Restigouche Log Driving and Boom Company to keep river passages open for migrating fish during the annual log drives. Dues from the lodges financed the association, and it used its resources to buy riparian lots from commercial fishermen on the lower end of the river so it could permanently retire the nets. By 1928, the association had seventy-five wardens working on the river, living in small cabins at three-mile intervals. In 2005, Wilfred Carter, the founder of the conservation organization the Atlantic Salmon Federation, praised the Riparian Association as having been the best defense against salmon poaching on the Restigouche for more than a century. "Governments that are responsible for safeguarding renewable resources like valuable Atlantic salmon have never taken their responsibility seriously and government wardens have been too few for the huge areas that have to be protected," he wrote. "That is why private groups, like the Restigouche Riparian Association have been created and without them salmon stocks in the Restigouche and many other rivers would have been destroyed by poachers long ago."

The one thing no one wanted to talk about, then or now, was whether the creation of a private aristocracy on the river was the only viable system to conserve salmon and protect the river, especially when it created and perpetuated such deep divisions in the river valley. Apart from the argument about whether it was effective, was it just? The Roman Institutes of Justinian define justice as "the constant and perpetual wish to render everyone his due." There is a carving of the emperor Justinian proclaiming the Institutes on the doors of the entrance to the Supreme Court of the United States. On the Restigouche, it was hard to see how this would be possible when so much had fallen into the hands of so few.

13 Four decades after the government began leasing the waters of the Restigouche, it cautiously responded to public demands for change. In 1927 the government removed waters—now part of the Larry's Gulch and Downs Gulch holdings—from the river-lease auctions. According to a statement by the minister of lands and mines at the time, the new "government open water" was set aside "so that fishing would be available for the largest number of people in the most equitable way," a hyperbolic description of a fissure in the wall of a system that had been designed to make fishing available for the fewest number of people in the least equitable way. For residents of New Brunswick, the fee on the new open water would be $5 a day ($75 today), and for non-residents $25 a day ($380 today). Those who wanted to fish had to make an application to the ministry, a process that created another kind of exclusive club in which reservations were granted to those in alignment with the government of the day.

That same year the government increased the upset price for all the leases in the Restigouche auction from $16,815 to $51,250. The leases would be renewed at public auction every ten years. On March 27, 1927, the *New York Times* reported that the price increase on the Restigouche was causing concern among all leaseholders, in particular among the members of the Restigouche Salmon Club. "In the past this group has been able to regard its salmon fishing privileges along the Restigouche as assured," the reporter wrote. "Consequently, they were a good deal upset by the recent announcement from Fredericton N.B. through *The Royal Gazette*, that the policy had been changed." Despite the complaints about the pricing, the club planned to be there to bid at the spring auction. The next month, the *Times* reported again on the increase in the price of the Restigouche leases, noting that the auction is "the only event of its kind in the world and the competition is expected to be much more keen than on former occasions."

The new "government open water" policy created a conflict between a family of veteran New Brunswick guides named Ogilvy, who set up a rough camp on the north side of the river, and an outfitter named Jack Russell, who had built a permanent camp high on the south bank of the river above the mouth of Larry's Gulch Brook. Russell had retired from an international business career with the Chrysler Corporation to pursue his dream of running a wilderness fishing lodge, and he did not know that he had waded into a political soup. The government had given him a mandate to operate an outfitting business on the river, but all requests for fishing dates flowed through the minister's office. David Ogilvy was unhappy with the competition from Russell and wrote to the government in the spring of 1933 to complain: "I cannot but feel that a very unfair advantage has been taken. If this policy is to be persisted in, I fear a bunch of our old and reliable guides will be driven to the bread lines."

At the same time H.A. Carr, a New Brunswick lawyer who had served as the representative of the Restigouche Salmon Club at the lease auctions, began writing letters to the government complaining about the "open water" and the conduct of the guides who, among other things, were fishing on Sundays. He was also concerned that Jack Russell was planning to build a road into his new lodge on the south bank, expressing a remarkable disdain for the citizens of the province that he called settlers. "In my opinion that would be a grave mistake," Carr wrote. "It would bring those undesirable settlers that much closer to the river. They are, as you know, a desperately destructive people. We have always been fighting against this and believe that the value of the Restigouche River is due largely to its privacy."

He wrote again later with further objections to the road, stating that it would create a fire hazard, because fires were generally caused by the settlers. "They would simply encroach along that right-of-way, gradually through politics and everything else, get a Grant here and a Grant there, burn up the green country and finally come through on to the river itself." He said the river should be held "strictly for sport" and preserved for that purpose. Carr may have been writing to express his own views and not as an official representative of the club, but the resentment toward anyone other than guests of the angling clubs using the river was not his alone and is still alive in some quarters today.

In 1936 the tension between the Ogilvy family and Jack Russell was broken by a new government that chose sides. It bought out Russell and turned the operation and camps over to David, Hendry, and Jock Ogilvy, who ran it for the next eighteen years. The Ogilvy operation offered angling opportunities for residents and non-residents who could both afford it and find an open date among the parade of businessmen and special guests of government ministers. In 1953 the operation was passed on to an astute local businessman named Allie Murray. He repaired the Ogilvy camps and built new ones that became the forerunner to the present-day Larry's Gulch Lodge. In 1962 he bought another lodge just downriver from the Restigouche Salmon Club and took over that lease. A decade later he retired, sold Larry's Gulch Lodge back to the government, and the second lodge to J.D. Irving Ltd., with its Downs Gulch fishing rights to be leased at auction every ten years.

When the news spread through the valley that Allie Murray had sold Larry's Gulch Lodge to the government, a few dozen local residents came to the river in 1974 to stage a protest about the lack of public fishing access. This incident is sometimes called the Battle of Larry's Gulch, although it was apparently a rather peaceful affair, and the crowd dispersed when the RCMP arrived. The government was aware of the frustrations among the citizens of the Restigouche valley well before the protest. A 1971 internal government "Report on a Study of the Control of Angling Waters in New Brunswick" recommended reorganizing and removing the lease of a stretch of water below Downs Gulch from future auctions. This led to the creation of three new Crown Reserve stretches for New Brunswick anglers through a system that allows residents to

apply for fishing dates in a lottery draw. The government also opened
the lower twelve kilometres of the Little Main Restigouche for New
Brunswick resident fishing only.

When the government assumed the operation of Larry's Gulch, it
became largely inaccessible to citizens of the province. "Top priorities will
be given to V.I.P.'s and guests of the province associated with industrial
and social development," stated the government policy of 1975. "Citizens
of the Province may apply for the remaining fishing dates, but they
must be sponsored by a Cabinet Minster or an elected member of the
Government who will submit their name to the Minister of Natural
Resources in writing. Reservations may be cancelled at any time if
the facilities are needed by the province." When the river leases were
auctioned in 1979, there was a reassignment of the waters, allowing the
lease at Downs Gulch to expand upstream because it had been "too small
for Irving's requirements." J.D. Irving Ltd. won the lease at auction, the
upset price increasing from $15,100 to $25,700 to reflect the additional
pools. The Larry's Gulch stretch expanded upstream to compensate for
the pools now attached to the Irving lodge.

Not much has changed since then, except for one more backroom
development that I would discover in the stack of documents released to
me by the Department of Natural Resources.

14 In all of the political machinations upriver, the Mi'gmaq downriver
were all but forgotten. Between April and November of 1961, a young
doctoral student in anthropology from New Mexico named Philip Bock
came to the Restigouche River to interview the Mi'gmaq as part of his
thesis research. By then the Mi'gmaq were confined to an ever-shrinking
tract of reserve lands still referred to as the Mission near the mouth of the
river. Bock reported that the priests played a central role in all aspects of
life on the reserve, including the running of local schools. He found that
the priests minimized the Mi'gmaq's historic claims rather than trying

to understand their history and connection to their traditional lands. The priests considered them "simple and childlike," warning them in a sermon, spoken in English, "Do not think of the priest as just another man." Bock reported: "The Indians, though protesting their faithfulness to their religion, make a sharp distinction between the Church and its priest, whose authoritarian attitudes, meddling, and demands for money they strongly resent."

Bock found a tourist pamphlet, poorly translated from French, distributed at the Ste-Anne mission church with the title *Restriction of This Territory Since 200 Years*: "With the coming of the Europeans, it was necessary to give limits to the Indian liberty. By slow steps, the authorities established the system of Reservation. What compensations the Indians have received by being placed in Reservation, would you ask? Land, free schools for their children, free doctors and hospitals or Sanatorium for their sick people. They actually received also from the agents, other help for urgent necessities. In fact, they have more opportunities than their neighbours, to earn money and obtain their independence."

What had originally been a reserve of about two thousand square kilometres had been reduced to about fifty square kilometres along three kilometres of river frontage downstream from the mouth of the Matapédia. What Bock found was a people of great kindness, hospitality and dignity, beset by deep poverty, who were not equal legally or socially to other members of Canadian society. The First People of the river had preserved their language but were losing the threads of their own story.

"The conditions of life have changed so drastically at Restigouche during the last sixty years that almost all sense of cultural community has been lost," Bock wrote. When he showed young people accounts of early Mi'gmaw life on the river, they either said that it was "all made up," or if they accepted it to be true, they told him it was "like reading about another world," which of course it was. "Of all the questions asked during my time on the Reserve, the one most often repeated—sometimes defensively, sometimes pleadingly—was: *Can you tell me where the Indians come from?* Though it must occasionally have represented a request for historical enlightenment, in nearly every case I sensed the latent content: *Can you tell me who I am?* I answered the historical question with some mumbled phrases about land bridges and Bering Strait, but for the latent question I had no answer."

What Bock didn't see coming was the renaissance at Listuguj that would begin just two decades later. The Mi'gmaq were a people badly bent but not broken and they would have to engage in a final season of resistance before turning back to the river for salvation.

15 Below Cheyne on that July afternoon, I rode the current that sweeps past Larry's Gulch Lodge, built on the edge of a high bluff, surrounded by neatly mowed lawns and gardens above a fleet of canoes anchored in a row on the beach below. A few kilometres downstream I floated into the Irving waters and past the lodge at Downs Gulch on the left bank. It is a modest operation by multi-billionaire standards, with one main dining room, a sitting room with a stone fireplace and a covered front porch connected to a series of motel-style rooms facing the river. The diesel generator rumbled in the distance and seven motor canoes were anchored in formation on the beach beside a floating dock. The road access is on the right bank, where there is a small dock and a canoe for ferrying guests across. What you can't see from the river is the Downs Gulch Aerodrome just up the hill that can accommodate small jets.

In the years that followed K.C. Irving's death I continued to work for the family's newspaper. In the spring of 1995, I convinced my editor to allow me to write a series of stories about Atlantic salmon conservation. After the publication of the series, I worked for a time as the editor of the *Atlantic Salmon Journal* magazine before returning as editor-in-chief of the newspaper. During this time I was invited, along with my father, my mother, and my son, on several fishing trips to Downs Gulch. We flew into the valley on Irving planes and were driven in a van from the airstrip to the river, then poled across by staff, our luggage following in another canoe and delivered to our rooms. Servers in white uniforms brought us three meals a day and we fished with a personal guide through the morning and evenings. In the afternoons we napped or read in chairs on the deck.

On one trip home from the river with my father, the pilot told us he had to make a detour. We landed on an airstrip near Moose Lake in a remote corner of northern Maine, where we waited until a mud-splattered SUV drove out of the forest and parked beside the plane. Jim Irving, accompanied by his chief forester, emerged from the SUV wearing work boots and a plaid shirt. On the flight to Saint John Jim Irving was unfailingly polite but all business, asking me questions about the newspaper operation, which was then going through a technological upheaval and the closing of an old press in Saint John.

Later we would have conversations in his office about the editorial character of the newspaper. He told me he preferred his newspaper to be "spicy but not hot," a publication that wouldn't cause him discomfort as he went about conducting his other business. I was young and had an inclination toward heat, but I understood that he was the owner and had the right to have the publication he wanted. I eventually stepped down as editor and moved on to professional pursuits outside the influence of the family—and to more modest fishing adventures on the Restigouche with my friends.

What I didn't know until I opened my package of documents from the Department of Natural Resources was that during the years I was visiting Downs Gulch, Jim Irving was privately negotiating a deal so that the Downs Gulch Crown waters would no longer be part of the ten-year auction. In August 1996, J.D. Irving Ltd. made a proposition to the government to trade the Restigouche lease for one with twenty-one kilometres of riverfront land it owned on the upper reaches of the Main Southwest Miramichi River, as well as the lease of eleven kilometres of land the government wanted to use as part of a new park development in southeastern New Brunswick called the Fundy Trail. Anyone who knew anything about salmon rivers in New Brunswick would recognize that this proposal leaned heavily in Irving's favour. The Downs Gulch stretch included a series of productive pools and was exclusive and highly prized Restigouche water. The Miramichi water was far up in the system and had long been considered open water for anyone to use. Legally, the Irving company had riparian rights, but it had never been considered valuable enough to post and protect as exclusive fishing.

In February 1996, at the request of the minister, the Crown Lands Branch provided the government with a rationale for the lease exchange. An analysis based on the number of weeks of fishing, the quality of the fishing and the size of the fish, among other things, reached the lukewarm conclusion: "These two stretches of river have somewhat similar attributes." When that opinion was circulated among bureaucrats who knew the territory, the analysis was different. The director of the Fish and Wildlife Branch wrote a note on July 4, 1997, stating the obvious: "In respect to angling waters, the proposed exchange is not equitable. The Crown is offering much more valuable angling waters on the Restigouche River for Irving waters on the Main Southwest Miramichi River. The Irving waters have essentially been publicly available for the past number of years." His recommendation was: "Advise Mr. Irving that unfortunately the Department of Natural Resources and Energy finds his offer unacceptable." Alternatively, he suggested that the government ask that more Miramichi river frontage "of greater recreational value" be included in the deal. Another senior Natural Resources official weighed in: "From an angling perspective, the Crown Restigouche waters are more valuable than the Irving Miramichi Waters, even with the additional waters that Fish and Wildlife Branch has requested. I assume that the fairness of the deal, including the Fundy Trail component, has been addressed by Crown Lands Branch."

In March 1997 the minister of natural resources wrote to Irving confirming government's intention to proceed with the deal as proposed. As the details of the deal were being drafted, an alert bureaucrat warned that the arrangement would violate the provincial Fisheries Act, which laid out specific rules for leasing salmon waters. The act stated that all angling leases were to be for a term of not more than ten years from the date of issue and must be made to the highest bidder at auction after being advertised publicly, and that the bid must be at or above any upset price set for the lease. The minister of natural resources solved the problem with the stroke of a pen on June 17, 1998, changing the designation of the Downs Gulch "angling lease" to "river lease lands" that fell under the Crown Lands and Forests Act, taking the Fisheries Act out of play.

As the final contract was being drafted, Jim Irving had a further request. On August 13, 1998, he wrote to the deputy minister of natural resources, George Bouchard, asking that the clause in the Downs Gulch "angling lease" that required the hiring of four assistant game wardens from June 1 to November 1 and two full-time cleanup people from June 1 to August 31 be removed to reflect the change from an "angling lease" to a "river lease." He didn't think it was fair that he had to hire people in connection with his lease and that the government didn't have the same terms on its new acquisition on the Miramichi.

"It seems to me what is fair for one is fair for the other," Irving wrote. "However, in the interest of resolving this matter, and in anticipation that your Department will properly police and maintain the section of the Miramichi River which we are leasing to you, we are prepared to provide equivalent employment for an equal number of persons in our Salmon Conservation Program so that there would not be any reduction in employment but that we would have the opportunity to more meaningfully employ those individuals. If you can agree to this point, we will delete from the river lease for Downs Gulch the standard angling lease clauses which you have currently included in that lease." The government agreed to his request.

In a submission to government in 1998, the Irving camp reported that the buildings, canoes and motors at Downs Gulch were worth about $600,000. The lodge employed one manager, six guides, four wardens, two members of a cleanup crew, and three others. The budget for salaries was about $171,000, maintenance and supplies about $25,000. The cost of the angling lease fee was $61,600. On March 24, 1999, the contract was signed: In exchange of mutually beneficial leases no rent was to be paid. "The sole purpose of this lease is to give the lessee exclusive fishing privileges," the contract states. The deal was for a ten-year term and automatically renewed for another ten years unless otherwise terminated before the renewal date. "It is the intent and commitment of lessor and lessee that the lease will be renewed," the contract states.

I've thought a lot about this deal, perhaps given it more of my time than it's worth. Maybe it's just another episode in the irregular history of management on this river and I should have just turned it over and left it in my stack of papers. But I kept returning to the fact that what made it legal was an order from the minister that substituted the word "angling" with "river." If that makes it technically legal, does it also make it right? And how did we come to this, that a great river, a miracle of nature, became just another object to be traded? In the end, the whole affair felt shabby, another backroom deal that closed with a petty wrangle with one of the wealthiest families on the continent over small change. In 1876 John Rowan had observed that the Restigouche leases were not in fact put up to public competition and sold to the highest bidder; "they go by private favour and by backstairs influence." There is a remedy for this way of doing business that I learned from my old friend the newspaperman. That is, that the kind of influence that flourishes on the backstairs wilts when drawn into the clear light of day. So, in the end, that's what I have decided to do.

16 I caught up to Deb and Charlotte and Michelle and Will just below the Downs Gulch lodge. Lucy and Ruth were somewhere farther ahead, and I knew they would wait for us downstream. We floated through a channel on the right side of a long island where the river is cutting hard into the bank, dropping trees into the river and changing the course of the flow that for years had been running on the left side. At some point soon, maybe next season, the river will decide which way it wants to go. We stopped to swim and cool off at the Trotting Grounds, named for the wide gravel bar where teams of horses pulling river scows had the footing and space to pick up the pace. At the lower end of the Irving lease waters, we passed the mouth of Tracy Brook, a strong stream that flows in from the left and spills a long band of cold water down the shoreline. In all the historical salmon angling literature, Tracy Brook is described as a prized cold-water pool, and when I first came here a couple of decades ago I often saw schools of salmon and trout resting in the outflow. In recent years the pool has been filling in with gravel and sediment washed down from the brook.

Below Tracy Brook the river runs wide at the upper end of three Crown reserve angling stretches that I have often visited. We followed the lazy lines of current across a long shallow flat until we came to a campsite on the right-hand bank called Hafford, where there are picnic tables, fire pits and two shelters in a clearing beside a stream. One of the shelters has a stone fireplace attached that once kept the Expeditionary Force warm through a long driving rainstorm. We planned on camping there that evening and found Lucy and Ruth waiting for us in their canoe by the beach flanked by a fleet of canoes and two dozen Boy Scouts swimming, splashing and shouting in the river while their leaders set up tents in the clearing.

The Scout leaders offered to make space for us, but after a brief huddle we decided to continue on downstream to find a quieter place to camp. We pushed back into the current and floated around the bend to a small campsite beside the mouth of Stillwater Brook. The brook cascades down through a deep gorge and below it, the river bends in a long meander where it runs flat like a mirror and salmon can be found in trenches of deep water. On the right shore there's an almost perpendicular hillside of mixed hardwood and softwood forest through which bands of shale were glowing in the light of early evening. Far down on the meander, we saw two canoes and a group of four anglers spending the summer evening on the Crown reserve waters. One was sitting in a lawn chair, the others standing in the river in waders casting flylines into the swing of the current.

Will and I carried the picnic table and the steel fire ring from the clearing down to the beach to make room for three tents up on the grass beside the brook and then we unloaded and set up camp. Lucy and Ruth took a swim, and I started a driftwood fire on the beach, balancing on the ring a large cast-iron pan in which Deb created a chicken, shrimp and chorizo paella as the sun set over the river. The heat of the day held late into the evening, and after dinner we sat out until dark watching the fireflies dart in the tall grasses around us before dousing the fire and heading for the tents.

In the morning I made coffee and Deb cooked sausages, potatoes and eggs over the fire. We were in no hurry to push off. I took a walk down the shoreline below the brook as the fleet of Scout canoes came downriver and disappeared around the bend. The anglers were back, one wading along the beach and two fishing from their canoe. An occasional cluster of white clouds blew across the big sky. The anglers in the canoe slowly worked their way upriver, one running the outboard motor while standing on the rear seat, the other standing on the front seat holding a canoe pole, both looking down into the water, searching for salmon that might be lying in the colder flow below the brook. It was early but already it felt too hot to be fishing. Deb had settled in the wooden chair in the Miller reading with Cody at her feet. The teenagers had retreated to their tent for more sleep. We were falling hard into river time.

17 On the river the buffer of forest created the illusion that we were deep in wild country, the hills here appearing as the Acadian forest should, a mix of spruce, pine, fir, poplar, elm, birch, ash, maple, willow and alder. The concept of leaving a buffer of forest along the course of a river is a relatively recent forest management tool first applied across Canada and the United States in the 1960s and 1970s. Most jurisdictions, including New Brunswick, chose a width of thirty metres to be a sufficient buffer for most watercourses with the recognition that a wider buffer may be necessary if the shoreline is steep, as much of it is in the Restigouche valley. More recently scientists have been addressing the many questions that arise from the use of buffers. How effective are they in controlling siltation, nutrient loss and water temperature and in protecting animal habitat?

The consensus is that buffers do help to protect rivers, and the most current research is pointing to the need for the development of integrated watershed management plans tailored to the needs of each river valley, taking into account its topography, climate, soil content and water chemistry. In a river valley with steep hillsides, ecologists recommend that the buffer begin not at the river's edge but at the crest of the hillsides. The suggestion that a thirty-metre buffer with modifications for slope is what's needed in every river valley is a convenient measure for forest managers, but we shouldn't operate under the illusion that it is anything more than that.

Long-term scientific studies into the effects of clearcutting and buffers on rivers and streams remain in their infancy, with some exceptions. One of these is the Hubbard Brook Experimental Forest in the White Mountains of New Hampshire. Established in the 1960s, it has become one of the most intensively studied forest landscapes on the planet. In the valley north of Boston through which Hubbard Brook runs, various sections of forest were clearcut in the 1960s and 1970s, in some areas leaving the logs on the ground and in other areas removing the logs. Some areas were sprayed with herbicides and others were left to regenerate naturally.

As the scientists expected, stream flows in the spring started earlier and were greater in volume after the cutting. What surprised them were changes in the chemical composition of the water. They did not expect that the cutting would block the cycle of nitrogen production, an essential step in the life cycle of plants and trees. After clearcutting, the nitrogen in dead plants on the forest floor decomposed, producing increased amounts of ammonium and nitrates that washed into the water. Nitrate concentrations ranging from 60 to 80 milligrams per litre were recorded after the cuts, exceeding health guidelines of 40 milligrams per litre. The retention of vital nutrients, such as nitrogen, was "greatly diminished" following a cut. The studies suggest that reducing the size of cuts, protecting stream channels and avoiding the logging of steep slopes can minimize the long-term environmental effects.

Still, there is much we don't know about the ecological consequences of modern forestry operations, especially regarding forest plants and trees that have no commercial value. A University of New Brunswick research team has studied the impact of intensive logging and herbicide spraying on a group of tiny plants called bryophytes, the mosses, liverworts and hornworts that often carpet a forest floor. Most of the bryophytes are less than a centimetre tall, and several hundred species are found in a natural Acadian forest. The many species of bryophytes intermingle and form a spongy turf on a shaded and moist forest floor. They have no deep root systems and are particularly sensitive to loss of shade and water. Once bryophytes disappear, they are slow to return, if they return at all.

"While it is easy to recognize catastrophic negative effects, experience has taught us that the accumulation of small effects can be just as serious, and can be difficult or impossible to reverse," the researchers wrote. "While our knowledge about their details is fairly limited, there is ample evidence that bryophytes are ecologically important components of the forest. In some forests, there may be as much carbon tied up in the bryophytes as in the trees. They provide habitat for numerous invertebrates, and nesting material for a variety of rodents and birds.... At a broader scale, their extensive mats harbor nitrogen-fixing bacteria and absorb water, slowly releasing it to the feeder roots of trees and other rooted plants, thereby influencing water and nutrient cycles as well as soil temperature."

The work of bryophytes as nitrogen fixers is one of the most import-ant chemical processes in the natural world, and relatively few plants and trees can do it. A nitrogen fixer contains bacteria that convert nitrogen from the atmosphere into organic matter stored in nodules in their roots. Nitrogen is an essential ingredient in the process that creates the proteins and genetic coding systems that sustain life in plants and animals. When plants die and decompose, nitrogen is both released back into the atmosphere and converted by bacteria in soil into ammonium and nitrates, which are absorbed by new plant growth. Nitrogen fixers bypass this second step in the nitrogen cycle, which is why farmers learned to plant nitrogen-fixing legumes such as alfalfa and clover in crop rotations.

New Brunswick has been one of the most reluctant jurisdictions in Canada to protect natural spaces. In the early 1970s, conservationists and scientists who were watching industrial development consume natural spaces began urging the government to protect areas to maintain biodiversity, provide witness areas to measure environmental changes and preserve old forests for scientific research. Such a program was a long time coming. The first protected natural areas legislation was passed in 2003 after a series of contentious public hearings across the province. The forest industry organized and intervened in the process, appearing at all the meetings to express its unanimous opposition to the plan to create protected areas, warning of job losses and economic catastrophe in rural communities. By the end of the process, consultants were measuring the precise number of jobs that would be saved or lost under various proposals and how many millions of dollars were at stake in stumpage fees and tax revenues, as if we were controlling not only nature itself but also the global economy. In 2003, proposed protected natural areas in the Restigouche watershed were left out of a New Brunswick wide plan that set aside 3.5 per cent of Crown land.

Since 2003, several other small sections of forest have been designated protected natural areas. In 2014, the same year that the government signed new forest management agreements that allowed for more wood to be harvested from Crown forests, it also selected new areas on the Restigouche for protection. Local environmentalists, including André Arpin, had long been advocating to have the entire Stillwater Gorge set aside to create a witness area similar to Hubbard Brook that would allow scientists to study the life of a cold-water brook as it evolved through an uncut forest. J.D. Irving Ltd. objected to the Stillwater designation, because it would block access to stands of "overmature" balsam fir that could be cut and trucked to the nearby Kedgwick sawmill and interfere with roads needed for other harvesting operations in the area. So the government decided to protect a smaller section of the forest around Stillwater Brook and another area just upriver that happened to be the block of forest surrounding the Irving Downs Gulch fishing lodge.

For years, the Canadian Parks and Wilderness Society has been advocating for more protected natural areas in the Restigouche valley, with particular attention paid to the protection of riverbanks, slopes, streams and old-growth forest. Two decades ago, André Arpin invited the society to visit the river. He began meeting with Roberta Clowater, the executive director of the New Brunswick chapter, to discuss ways they might create more protected spaces throughout the watershed. Eventually their discussions turned to the idea of creating a new linear corridor park along the Restigouche River and its tributaries that would extend forest buffer zones on Crown lands to create a large protected area. André Arpin wasn't buying the argument that the only way to create jobs in the valley was by cutting more trees.

"He was determined that there needed to be more conservation around the river and a nature tourism sector," Clowater recalls. "They need to have a destination they can count on, that they can reliably promote to customers around the world as a nature destination. He was constantly trying to figure out how to not drive them through clearcuts to get to the river. That's where the idea of the Restigouche Wilderness Waterway came from. We started thinking about a park that would put some boundaries around how close industrial activities could come to the Restigouche, the Kedgwick, the Patapédia, the Upsalquitch on Crown land."

Over a number of years the society circulated the plan in communities through the valley, recognizing that a change such as this would only come with the support of the people of the river. The Restigouche River Watershed Management Council developed a feasibility study and held public meetings about the proposed park. The vision is to create the Restigouche Wilderness Waterway, a protected corridor with a buffer forest on either side of the river and all its tributaries. In addition to the ecological imperative, the park would also preserve the wild nature of the river, enhancing the quality of the Restigouche as a wilderness tourism destination, returning to a vision that years ago vanished in the rush to bring industry to the northern reaches of the province. The Canadian Parks and Wilderness Society recommended that the park create a five-hundred-metre buffer zone on each side of the river, including the tributaries. In 2019, when the government began public hearings for the park and meeting with Mi'gmaq communities, local residents, conservation groups and camp owners, it proposed a buffer of two hundred metres so that the new park would have little impact on the logging operations in the valley. There is a lot of work ahead before the park is realized, but at least the discussions have begun. After years of work that began with André Arpin asking his customers to sign a petition asking for the river valley to be protected from industry, the Restigouche Wilderness Waterway is starting to take shape.

18 We packed up late in the morning and dropped down through Stillwater Pool. I slipped Cody into his life jacket as I approached the heavy rapid above Devil's Half Acre, then found a line through the whitecaps and the flow between the rocks down through the churning gut into the pool below. There are two small cabins at the base of Devil's where the Crown reserve anglers stay, one group fishing above and one below on a stretch known as Three Sisters, named for three boulders clustered together at the head of a pool. Below Three Sisters is the Red Bank Crown reserve I have visited many times.

About a decade ago I began making an annual spring angling pilgrimage to the river with Marty Stewart and Butch Dalton, my light-hearted long-time friend. Both are skilled canoe captains and fishing and hunting guides. Butch always reminds me that there are no measures of success or failure on these trips and that no matter what happens, "the Restigouche never disappoints."

Red Bank is named for the deep pool below a high sandstone bank where the Restigouche Salmon Club once had a traditional Stanford White–style lodge. The club transferred the lodge to the government when the lease was taken out of the auction. The lodge housed Crown reserve anglers for several years until the government destroyed the building because it didn't want to maintain it. The cabin for New Brunswick anglers that replaced it is a Spartan structure. It includes a main living space with a table and two benches, a wood stove, a kitchen counter and sink, two bedrooms with two single beds each, and a bathroom with a sink held up by a crooked tree branch and a toilet that flushes, slowly. Gravity pipes cold water from a spring on the hill in back of the cabin to feed the toilet and sinks.

We make our annual trips to Red Bank in twenty-six-foot Sharpe motor canoes loaded with coolers of food and drink, waterproof barrels of bedding and clothes, all manner of fishing gear, kitchen supplies, a portable barbecue, gas stove and lanterns, beer on ice, bottles of red wine, mosquito nets to hang over our sheets, and pillows and sleeping bags. Marty always packs proper wine glasses wrapped in newspapers so we can drink in a civilized fashion. We anchor the canoes in a small backwater in front of the cabin, lug our gear up the bank, pour drinks while we assemble our fly rods, then push back out into the river and spend the next three days following a series of pools that extend down through the valley.

On one trip years ago, Marty brought along a wooden box that contained the ashes of his friend Bill Page, an artist and angler who had come to Red Bank so many times that we still refer to a section of the Red Bank Pool as "Billy's Corner." Before he died, Page asked that some of his ashes be poured in the Red Bank Pool. On the afternoon of the second day we anchored the two canoes together in the centre of the pool and drank a toast to Bill Page. Marty emptied the box of ashes over the water and we watched the cloud slip down into the depths of the pool. Then Marty stood up and announced that he was going to catch a salmon for Billy, so Butch and I motored off to the side to give him room and a few minutes later Marty hooked a large salmon, the first of the trip. I still have the photograph I took of Marty with that fish on his line and his fly rod bent double, or I might have come to believe I had imagined the whole thing.

Shortly after noon the Expeditionary Force floated past the Red Bank cabin and stopped at the rocky beach on the lower end of the Red Bank Pool. Everyone cooled off in the river and then with the teenagers and Michelle and Charlotte still swimming, I made a beach fire and grilled sausages. We pulled the lawn chairs out of the canoe, Will retrieved cold cans of beer from the cooler and we sat in the downriver breeze until everyone was tired of swimming and ready to push on.

Below Red Bank there's a long, wide downhill run until the river narrows and sweeps left into a pool call Wishart's. One evening years ago, when I was fishing with Butch Dalton, we anchored on the shore here and waded alongside the pool casting over a run of large salmon fresh from the ocean that came to the fly almost every time we passed through the pool. Through it all the rain was falling hard, splashing on the river. That evening on the beach at Wishart's I felt as far from that other world out there as I have ever felt in my life. I remember Butch turning to me and saying, "You know that we will be talking about this night for the rest of our lives." We stayed as long as we could before motoring back upstream in the rain. We arrived at the cabin just before dark where Marty was waiting with the wine glasses set out, a bottle of wine open and steaks ready to go on the grill.

The Expeditionary Force canoes slipped below Wishart's and a short run later turned into the beach at White Brook Island. This is my favourite place on the river to camp. The island is open and breezy and has lots of room in the soft grass to set up tents. There are long views up and downriver, illuminated in the evening by the magic light of the setting sun on the far shore. We lugged the gear up into the meadow, pushed the coolers into the shade and set up the tents. It was still hot, so we all walked up to the head of the run and let the current carry us down to the campsite, then did it all over again. Later we barbecued chicken over the fire and ate dinner, holding plates on our laps in a circle of lawn chairs in the shallows beside the canoes. In the evening Lucy and Ruth baked their chocolate cake in the cast-iron Dutch oven, a delicate process that requires laying coals on the lid and strategically turning it for even heating. When the cake was finished we poured the kettle on the coals and called it a night.

19 We swam again in the morning and slowly broke down the camp and packed. As we were loading the canoes a broad, flat-bottomed aluminum boat with a large jet outboard, centre console and steering wheel sped through the pool, pushing its wake up on either shore. The arrival of these jet boats is a new development on the river. They are propelled by powerful outboard motors without propellers that run like air boats, their design demanding that they travel at high speeds over the shallows. Those of us who are concerned about the impact of this activity on fragile juvenile fish habitat and advocate for restraint and caution don't yet have comprehensive data to support our contention that there should be restrictions on their use. In time, researchers will turn their attention to the ecological impact of these large jet boats, but for now another new technology is once again running ahead of us on the wild river.

Below White Brook Island we picked our way through a long rocky run to the mouth of the Patapédia. The river narrows just above, where the cold flow runs in from the left shore and merges with the main flow that churns into a cliff that is part of the Sandford Fleming lot. The Patapédia is a sweet mountain river that I have canoed and fished many times with Deb and my father and brother. Here at the mouth of the Patapédia, the currents have created a deep tank of cold water above a hard-right turn below that is protected by a long ledge. A small warden's cabin is on the corner. The Patapédia Pool has become known as the Million Dollar Pool, the name suggesting that someone paid a million dollars for it, but this is not the case. The *New York Times* reported in 1927 that the Restigouche Salmon Club members coined the nickname because "they have had a million dollars-worth of sport by fishing it." The riparian rights to the pool come in part from the Fleming lot that cost him $250 and was part of "an outright gift" of all of his Restigouche land and fishing rights to the club. In addition, the club has a New Brunswick Crown lease extending from the Fleming lot downriver that most recently cost $87,300 a year, a modest fee for a "million dollars-worth" of sport.

The club's many celebrity guests have all fished here. The *New York Times* published a brief report on July 10, 1945, that the Duke and Duchess of Windsor had landed five Atlantic salmon at the Million Dollar Pool. They had flown in from New York as guests of Izaak Walton Killam, the Montreal financier. Their largest fish weighed twenty-three pounds and the duchess caught three of the five. Nelson Bryant, the former outdoors editor of the *New York Times*, has written accounts of fishing this pool as a guest of his long-time friend, member Joseph Cullman III, the former chairman of the Philip Morris tobacco company.

When we entered the pool that morning in July, two canoes from the club were anchored below the mouth of the Patapédia. A guide wearing a green RSC uniform sat in the rear watching over a woman in a broad-brimmed hat and sunglasses who was standing and casting a fly into the current while a man in a ball cap was sitting in the chair in the centre waiting his turn. We passed carefully behind them, keeping our distance so as not to disturb their fishing.

We floated into the deep water in the corner, which is like canoeing through an aquarium. I stayed there for a while to watch the salmon glide through the spill of water that washes down from the outflow of the Patapédia. The current along the ledge is slow and flat, and grasses and wildflowers grow in crevasses along the waterline.

The river now carrying the water of the Patapédia divided and grew swifter as we dropped out of the Million Dollar Pool and approached the expanse of Indian House Pool, where Princess Louise and her entourage had camped long ago. Since then the Restigouche Club has built a lodge high on the hill where there is a commanding view of the valley. This Standford White design resembles the Kedgwick Lodge but is larger. There was a Canadian flag flying in front as the Expeditionary Force approached and guides were on the beach cleaning the canoes. Three men who had been fishing were walking up the path carrying their rods on their way to lunch and their afternoon siesta. It was shortly after one p.m. Atlantic standard time, but the Restigouche lodges, regardless of their physical location, run on eastern standard time so the guests don't have to change time zones when they fly in from the cities on the eastern seaboard or central Canada. The lodges have created an informal Restigouche angling time zone; I'm certain Sandford Fleming is rolling over in his grave.

A couple of years before this trip, the Expeditionary Force arrived at Indian House Pool on an afternoon in late June during a four-day trip from the mouth of Kedgwick to the Rafting Grounds. After camping two nights in warm weather, we realized we were getting desperately low on ice. Deb and I decided that we would stop at Indian House and ask if we could buy a small piece of ice either from the ice house or the well-equipped kitchen. We stopped at the beach, left Lucy and Ruth with the dog in the canoes, walked up onto the lawn and spoke with a young woman who said she would inquire about ice. She disappeared into one of the staff cabins. Before she could return, an older man in an RSC uniform arrived. He appeared to be unhappy that we were there, so I apologized for intruding and asked if it would be possible to buy some ice. I also asked about the fishing. He said the fishing was poor, made disparaging remarks about the Mi'gmaw nets in the estuary as the cause, and then walked away and disappeared into a cabin. He reappeared only to signal at a distance for us to leave the property.

I was surprised, but I should have expected it. For decades the club and other lodges have been complaining about the presence of canoes on the river. In the mid-1990s I visited the club headquarters in Matapédia and met the former manager Al Carter, who told me the greatest threat to the river was unregulated canoe camping. Carter and his brother Wilfred, of the Atlantic Salmon Federation, grew up fishing on the rivers of the Gaspé Peninsula. Both of them were towering, forceful men, but where Wilfred was gentle and politically astute, his brother was blunt and stern. After a long career in the oil business, Al Carter managed the club for twenty years. In those days, as part of the lease agreement with the New Brunswick government, the club was required to create and maintain campgrounds on the river, a job that has since been contracted to David LeBlanc's Restigouche River Watershed Management Council.

"We bid with our eyes wide open," Al Carter told me. "We supply picnic tables, toilets, fireplaces, and firewood. There's a regulation for us that says we have to supply a campground. But there's no regulation that says you have to go there. And there should be. What the hell's the use of telling us we have to build a campground if you can go down and camp across the river from it? The canoes are not regulated at all. And we have said for years that unless the canoes are regulated, we cannot fish. Everybody who is a non-New Brunswick resident is a damn American. It's all, 'Go home, damn Americans. Leave the river to us. It's our river.' I've fished salmon all my life. I'm glad I've got fifty years of fishing behind me and not ahead of me. Many things concern us. And all we're trying to do is have a little fun and go fishing."

It was a memorable encounter. What he was expressing that day was born from the management system that created a Restigouche hierarchy that excluded everyone but the leaseholders and those who worked for them from a sense of ownership and belonging on their own river. Carter wasn't making it up when he reported bad behaviour from some parties of canoe campers on the weekends, who drank too much and left litter behind. But why should they care when they were told the river wasn't theirs, when they were treated like intruders in the valley in which they lived? Why wouldn't you drop your shorts and show your ass to moneyed guests on the porches of the lodges when you'd be run off the manicured lawns like a criminal trespasser if you stopped to strike up a conversation? And why should the Mi'gmaq even begin a dialogue with the lodge owners and club members who regularly disparaged them and minimized their long history on the river?

What I do know is that the divide is not what it once was. David LeBlanc's watershed management group is changing the culture on the river, and the new manager of the club is not of the same generation or temperament as Al Carter. That's why when I returned from the trip after our unpleasant encounter at Indian House, I wrote to the manager, Todd Kennedy, to tell him what had happened. Years ago I probably would have shrugged it off as just the way it is on the Restigouche, but this time I decided if we remained silent nothing would change. To his credit, the new manager replied in the following way: "I am sorry to hear about your experiences on the river this past week. The last thing we want is for people leaving the river with any sort of negative experience, let alone a negative experience having to do with the Club. I appreciate your feedback, and I am not going to try and make excuses for what went on. I have discussed this email with my staff at Indian House, who obviously have their side of the story and did not mean to make you feel unwelcome. Staff are instructed to help out when and where possible, and to respect other users if they want respect themselves. Please accept my apologies."

At the bottom end of Indian House Pool is the large gravel island where the *Globe* correspondent first encountered Princess Louise and Larry Vicaire. The river splits into three channels here and Lucy and Ruth turned into the narrow, dangerous-looking channel on the far right because they wanted the challenge. I let them go and took the long way around on the far-left side. Where the three channels converge, we all met on the gravel beach and swam in the current while Cody had a long nap on the hot sand.

Later that afternoon we passed the long meander at Cross Point, where the river turns in a ninety-degree loop beneath a towering bank. We stopped on the beach on the corner to gather driftwood for our fire later in the evening and made one more stop below the Restigouche

Salmon Club's smaller lodge at Pine Island to cool off before the final run down to Two Brooks where we planned to spend the night and be collected in the morning. We stopped at the foot of the landing where the Restigouche Salmon Club has a warden's cabin on the hill beside the road. There is a campground just below. We saw that the jet boat that had passed us earlier in the morning was anchored there along with a couple of other canoes. Deb walked up the landing road and asked the warden if we could camp that evening on his lawn. He said he would love the company, so we spent our last evening sharing a campfire with this generous man and his old Golden Retriever. Late in the evening when darkness began to fall in the valley, Cody decided to spend some time inside the warden's cabin with them.

20 I woke at first light to find the temperature had not fallen much overnight. I took a mug of coffee down the rocky landing road to the beach and launched the Miller, lighter now without the load, poled upstream above the brooks and from there allowed the current to pull me down through the pool to the corner. The morning sun streamed through breaks in the trees and illuminated the river bottom in bands across the current and I watched salmon startled by the long shadow in the low water scatter under the canoe on the way down.

I heard the motor canoe downstream before I saw it, a guide and an angler from the Restigouche Salmon Club's Red Pine Mountain Lodge pushing upstream around the corner on the way to the Two Brooks Pool. Red Pine Mountain was one of the original Restigouche Salmon Club lodges. It has changed hands a few times over the years, first sold to a New Brunswick businessman and politician and then to an American millionaire and his wife. From 1994 to 2010 it was owned by an outfitter, Red Pine Mountain Lodge Inc., that offered Restigouche angling for those who could afford it. In 2009 it was charging $5,400 per person per week for a shared room, guide and canoe. The Restigouche Salmon Club reacquired the lodge and the lease in 2010 then bought the ten-year lease in 2013 for $42,000 a year. I've heard that there's been some grumbling among club members that this was a mistake because the fishing on this stretch has been poor in the summer in low water, and everyone wants to fish the Million Dollar Pool where a hookup is almost a sure thing.

More than a century ago John Rowan watched the development of the river leases with alarm and wrote at length about his concerns. He was skeptical of both the economic and conservation arguments. "The inhabitants of those districts in which there are salmon rivers are universally opposed to the leasing system; they say, and say with truth, that if the angling were open, ten anglers would visit them for one that comes now, and ten times as much money would be spent."

When the Department of Fisheries built a salmon hatchery on the lower end of the river paid for by the leaseholders, Rowan wasn't impressed by the new science of fish breeding in captivity and the release of the fingerlings in the river. "They are turned into the river when little more than half an inch in length, poor little, helpless, artificially reared creatures," he wrote. "But, of course, it is a great thing when brought to task for jobbing away the rivers of Canada for a tenth of their value, to be able to reply, 'We hatch so many millions of young salmon in these rivers every year.' They get credit with the outside world, and the toys to amuse themselves."

Everything in Canada was "saturated with politics," Rowan wrote, even the angling, so much so that he wondered whether a Conservative salmon would rise at a Liberal fly. The Restigouche was a magnificent river, he said, the finest salmon river in the world, and now with the Intercolonial Railway certainly one of the most accessible in the Dominion. If divided into sections and leased by fair competition, the river "would alone bring in as much revenue as all the rivers in Canada at present."

"I do not blame the fortunate owners of the rivers—no doubt many of us would be glad to get them on the same terms if we had the chance; but I do blame the Government for creating a monopoly not only injurious to anglers, but prejudicial to the interests of the Dominion," he continued. Leaseholders in many instances stayed a week or two on the river and then left for the rest of the season. Some seasons they never visited at all. "The casual angler cannot get a day's fishing, even when the river is deserted; that is to say the sportsman cannot for this dog-in-the-manger system is a harvest to the poacher. It is a case of absentee landlordism.... It is a monstrous injustice."

In the 1920s, the Restigouche Salmon Club's groceries were shipped into Matapédia by train from Stanford's Limited in Montreal, a specialty supplier of imported tropical fruits and out-of-season vegetables. The grocery menu Stanford's designed for the club in the spring of 1925 included asparagus, pineapples, eggplants, leeks, mint, mushrooms, seven varieties of onions and lettuces, strawberries, three kinds of raspberries, blueberries, gooseberries, cantaloupes, cherries, seven varieties of grapes, grapefruits from Florida or Mexico, eight kinds of oranges, seedless lemons and limes, California peaches and pears, watermelons, five varieties of tomatoes, nectarines, plums and pomegranates. The main course of the midday meal might have included prime rib of beef, sirloin steaks, legs of lamb, hams, pork chops or chickens. The meal ended with pies and ice cream, puddings and cakes and cheeses, followed by a fine cigar on the porch with a glass of whiskey and a long afternoon nap.

It was a river valley populated by people living as if they were on different planets. In the 1920s, decades before electricity came to the communities in the valley, the lodges were running gas-powered generators. Meanwhile, downriver at Listuguj, many Mi'gmaw families lived in homes without running water or electricity into the 1980s. In 1925, during a time when the Mi'gmaq were told it was forbidden to fish the river above the head of tide, the Restigouche Club alone harvested almost two thousand salmon from the river and shipped 32,376 pounds of fish in iced wooden boxes from the Matapédia rail station to homes in the big cities of the United States and Canada. A similar harvest from the club's waters continued for the next three decades until catches began to decline in the mid-1950s.

The reporter Ian Sclaners came to the river in the spring of 1947 and filed a story for *Maclean's* magazine that was published under the headline "Rich Man's River." "The Restigouche is where international bankers, merchant princes and industrial tycoons let down their dignity and wander around in clothes that they hope look old," he wrote. "It's where front-page celebrities fry their own ham and eggs—when the spirit happens to move them. It's where elder statesmen act like schoolboys. And it's where the angler's dreams come true if his bank roll can stand the strain. But most of us might as well dream of harpooning whales in the Antarctic. Except for a few miles, it's all owned or rented by the sort of folks who have town and country estates, butlers and chauffeurs, custom-built limousines and streamlined yachts, swimming pools and opera boxes. They aren't very hospitable to uninvited guests especially uninvited guests with fishing rods. The reception accorded intruders may be described as hot, not warm, and there's quite a difference. The signs posted on the trees say 'No Trespassing' and your chances of slipping by them are about equal to your chances of breaking into the vaults of the Bank of Canada."

In 1970 *Sports Illustrated* published a feature about Restigouche River salmon angling. "A River Running out of Eden" was written by Pat Ryan, a secretary turned reporter who would later become the first female editor of *People* and *Life* magazines. Ryan found in the moneyed man's world on the Restigouche a treasure trove for a feature writer of her talents. "Ninety years ago, in bowlers and knickers, the biggest of America's new-money men with names that still shake the halls of finance—Belmont, Whitney, Lorillard, Vanderbilt—went north to fish the Restigouche. Ham and bacon hung from the rafters of their sod-sealed cabins and whiskey was on the shelves," she wrote.

She visited the club's old Matapédia clubhouse that was then the modified Fraser homestead before it burned in the summer of 1983 and was rebuilt. In 1970 it remained "a strange exclusive meeting place for sporting millionaires," she wrote. "The plank floors now lurch with age, some pitching at 30-degree angles. A heavy-headed moose presides over a bare refectory-style dining room. Plaster buckles through the wallpaper, doors hang crooked on their hinges and drafts whistle up the stairs. A Victorian fringed shawl covers a parlor table and on it is a framed photograph of a royal couple on a throne. Only in the oak-dark members' lounge is there a sense of warmth and comfort. A *Wall Street Journal* and gin-rummy scorepads lie on a burnished table and the conversation is of Phippses and Mellons." She found "photographs of waist-coated gentlemen and veiled wasp-waisted women" hanging on the walls alongside an inscribed portrait of Winston Churchill and paintings left as gifts by artists who came as guests. There was an old sundial on the lawn and listing green rockers and ladderback chairs on the porch.

Ten years after Ryan's visit to the river, the Restigouche Salmon Club celebrated its centennial in high style. Members from the United States and Canada gathered at a suite in the Queen Elizabeth Hotel in Montreal for a catered reception before travelling to Matapédia on a special train with a separate luggage car following their private compartments. From June 14 to 22 the club was reserved for male members, no guests or wives allowed. The week opened with a meal of prime rib, Yorkshire pudding, Matapédia fiddleheads, potatoes, baby beets and broccoli. There were messages sent by telegram from former members and those who could not attend, speeches and tributes. Brinkley Smithers, an investment banker and long-time member, melted a portion of his personal gold collection to make all the members lapel pins for the occasion that featured a salmon leaping through suspended maple leaves, and New York business executive Walter Teagle III presented everyone with club centennial ties. "A souvenir book was printed, circulated and closely guarded by all members as a record of the event," wrote manager Al Carter. "The week was a resounding success."

That morning at Two Brooks Landing, I was at the end of our passage through the heart of the grand old angling culture on the river. Another ten-year lease auction is scheduled for 2023. In the old days the Restigouche auctions drew crowds to the legislature, including the lieutenant-governor, the premier and his cabinet, and lawyers from

New York, the galleries above packed with spectators, the auctioneer conducting the bidding from the Speaker's chair, as if what was happening was among the most important acts of state. More recently, the auctions have become more subdued affairs, with most stretches sold to the long-established lodges at upset prices, the event held in a sterile auditorium in a government office building and over in a few minutes.

A report on the economic value of the Restigouche sport fishery has calculated that the river supports 535 seasonal jobs, mostly guides, cooks and maintenance people at the lodges. Seasonal on the river usually means about twenty weeks of work followed by the filing of an Employment Insurance claim or the pursuit of various off-season jobs. I've spent a lot of time thinking about the river leases and the jobs they create because I have more than admiration for the artistry and skill of the Restigouche guides and staff at the lodges. Still I wonder why we should just accept that the leases on the Restigouche always were and continue to be for the greater good and roll them over for decades on into the future, when other management regimes may emerge from the creation of a Restigouche Wilderness Waterway that would support the jobs we now have on the river and quite possibly more. In all our deliberations we should remember that the river supports a tapestry of life, quite apart from this one species of fish to which we have attached such great value, and its reason for being is more than entertainment for a group of salmon anglers who have enjoyed more than their share of sport.

And there is the question of the "monstrous injustice" that John Rowan described. That morning at Two Brooks, I pushed the Miller into the shore to clear the way for the club canoe that had come up from Red Pine, dropped anchor and watched the guide and his guest fish. In that moment I felt the exclusion, not for the first time. No one had to tell me to leave the pool for it was assumed I knew the unspoken rule, that I could be on the river so long as I didn't disrupt a good day of fishing for the members of the club, and now that they were here the only right and proper thing to do was retreat. Once I had moved to the shore they carried on with their sport as if I were invisible.

Every time I feel it, I know my exclusion is nothing of the sort experienced by the people who live in the valley. Their stories are not those of the Restigouche aristocracy, the ones published privately in limited editions and circulated among themselves, or documented by fly-in magazine writers, who treat the social order here as a curiosity and create articles cut from the same well-worn cloth, dropping the same names, repeating the same anecdotes of the rich and famous and a Million Dollar Pool.

One afternoon in his office in the natural resources building at Listuguj, Fred Metallic told me about a conversation he had with a wealthy angler at a meeting in New York City. The man told him how his family had been coming to the Restigouche for decades, how much he values what the river has offered to him and how he experiences a kind of spiritual transformation when he is on the water. Fred replied yes, he understood all of this. Then he asked the man to imagine the depth of the connection of the Mi'gmaw people to the river and the land to which they have been inexorably bound for countless generations, a place that holds the archive of his people's history.

"We've buried our songs here," Fred Metallic said.

That morning at Two Brooks, I had travelled far enough to see that the story of the creation of Paradise Restigouche, and how it has been a blessing for the salmon and the people of the valley, and a necessary check on their destructive ways, was in need of correction. What happened here was the story of a privilege that had been bestowed on a few because they, by their own enterprise or often by the chance of inheritance, worked in big city offices instead of being descendants of those who have lived here since time immemorial or those who worked the hard lumber camps in the Kedgwick hills. To suggest it has been anything more than that would be to disrespect the story of the river and the history of the people of the valley. What I also knew was that the life of the river is long, and the chapter about the creation of a river flowing from Eden will someday, like all the marks on this shoreline, fade in the wash that flows down from the Appalachian hills.

I had all of this on my mind as I cleared the last of the gear out of the canoe, wiped it dry with a sponge, then walked up the hill to join my river companions, who had started a fire to chase the flies away before they cooked breakfast and began packing up the campsite. Marie-Christine's trucks would be arriving soon, and I had inquiries and arrangements to make before I set out on the last stage of my river trip. I had more of the story assembled than I had when I set out, but I knew I still had much to see and learn.

Flow

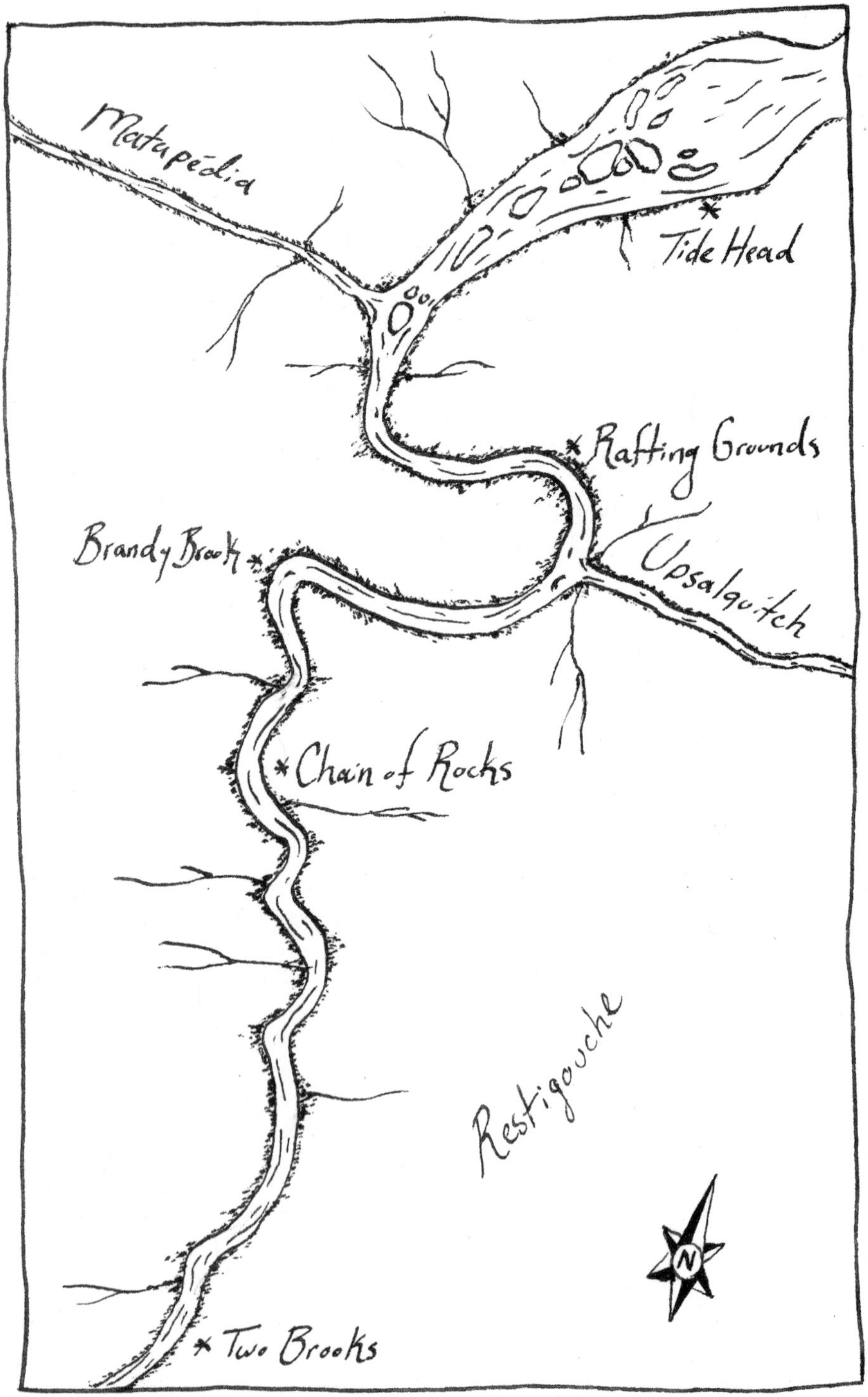
Matapédia
Tide Head
Rafting Grounds
Brandy Brook
Upsalquitch
Chain of Rocks
Restigouche
N
Two Brooks

Upon those who step into the same rivers other and other waters flow.

—Heraclitus

1 No two rivers are the same, yet all rivers flow through similar patterns of riffles, pools and meanders. Hydrologists have developed mathematical formulas that explain the shape and size of meanders based on the volume and velocity of a river's flow and the effect of current colliding against the shoreline.

When a river bends, the current rolls down and back on itself, scouring out a pool. When the flow of a tributary meets the current of the main river, the water rolls down and spins, excavating even larger pools than those found at meanders. The shape of meanders depends on the width and depth of the river, which is determined by the volume of the flow, which is determined by the size of the watershed that drains into the river. The shape of a meander is determined by the width of the river when its banks are full.

The hydrologist Robert Newbury describes the descent of rivers in this way: "In the steep headwaters, the steps of pools and riffles are closely spaced in the narrow channel. Further downstream as the drainage area and discharge increase, the steps grow longer and the pools and riffles more pronounced. In the low reaches, where water from all of the tributary branches has gathered, the river is widest and often meanders across the lower gradient of the valley floor. The pattern of the river's connected stairways leading into the continent is known by insects and fish, and by people living closely on the land."

How much sediment a river carries, and what kind, is determined by the material on the bed of the river and its banks, and by what hydrologists call the critical tractive force, which is a combination of velocity and depth of flow. All of these moving parts are influenced by changes in weather and climate and irregular variations in geography. Yet rivers throughout the world with similar-sized watersheds develop meandering patterns that are remarkably the same.

What remains a mystery is why a river's flow has a tendency to meander in the first place. In 1860 an Estonian scientist developed a theory that the sinuosity of rivers was influenced by the turning of the Earth on its axis, and this explained why rivers in the northern hemisphere tended to erode on the right side and rivers in the southern hemisphere on the left. In 1926, Albert Einstein dismissed this theory in a short paper in which he used the stirring of tea leaves in a cup to illustrate the hydrodynamics of velocity and friction that produce this effect without the turning of the Earth as part of the equation.

What scientists can't explain is why streams that flow across the surface of glaciers have a tendency to meander, or why ocean currents and water poured across a sheet of glass also move in the shape of rivers.

"Have you ever noticed how God's rivers never run straight?" my father once asked when he was preaching on the subject of ecology.

Perhaps that's all the explanation we need when we watch a river that has been artificially straightened begin to rebuild banks and curvatures, as if longing to return to its meandering ways.

2 I planned to complete the final stage of my Restigouche trip in early September after Lucy returned to school in the fall, leaving us weeks of summer for other adventures. During the last week of July, Lucy, Cody and I drove north into Mount Carleton Park to spend a night in a cabin beside Nictau Lake, the largest in a chain of narrow lakes in the valley connected by a network of streams, swamps and forest paths. Nictau was the hub of the ancient portage routes to the rivers to the north, east and south, and some of them are now being restored and maintained, including the 147-kilometre Nepisiquit Mi'gmaq Trail that runs from the park north to Chaleur Bay.

It was raining hard when we arrived in the park. We took shelter in our cabin and spent the evening playing cards at the kitchen table and reading in our bunks. In the morning the sky was clearing so we decided it was a good day to climb Mount Carleton. We followed the trail that winds up through the old Acadian forest and for a time alongside a stream that flows beneath the high canopy of mixed summer greens.

As we neared the top of the trail, we emerged from the forest and had to lift Cody up over a succession of rock ledges too steep for the short legs of a terrier. On the summit we came to the wooden hut that had once been a lookout tower staffed by a warden, who spent long days here during the fire season and slept in a one-room cabin halfway down the mountain. We rested on a wide flat rock, admiring the view of the network of lakes in the valley below. Beyond the boundaries of the park, we could see blocks of clearcut forest that extended out to the horizon in all directions like great wounds torn in the landscape, some of them patched but not healed by the squared off rows of new spruce plantations.

A couple of weeks later Deb and Lucy took a trip to Maine to visit a friend and I headed back north with Cody to the river valley. I checked into a room at Chalets Restigouche and launched the Miller in the Little Main, this time with the outboard motor on the back. The river had risen after a couple of days of rain and I planned to take advantage of the higher water to explore some of the pools above the bridge. The next morning I motored upstream to Micmac Pool where Tommy and I had camped weeks earlier. Although it's nothing like the physical experience of working the Miller with a pole, I enjoy the challenge of running the canoe with a small outboard motor, searching for small slips of water just deep enough to allow me to creep up over shallow gravel bars. The motor also gives me the freedom to travel upstream and back down to where I started without arranging for pickups and shuttles. I fished a series of drops through Micmac Pool, then worked my way back downstream, stopping to cast over some of the lower pools. Late in the morning

I anchored the canoe above the Montgomery Bridge, left it there and drove back up Broderick's Hill into the village of Kedgwick.

I had seen a sign for the Kedgwick Forestry Museum that appeared to be little more than a small cabin with a storefront reception connected to a small campground. I was curious to see what was inside. I paid the entry fee and took a short walk back through the trees where I discovered a replica of a winter logging camp from the years before the mechanization of the industry. In this patch of forest across the highway from the modern Irving sawmill where the yard is filled with rectangular stacks of dried lumber wrapped in plastic sheets, a group of retired loggers built one last winter camp with their saws and axes just as they had each year far off in the hills above the river.

They built a traditional low-roofed bunkhouse (because a low camp was warmer) out of unpeeled logs held in place with wooden pegs and dovetailed at the corners, a teamster's cabin (because the teamsters smelled of horses and needed their own space), the supply store, blacksmith shop, a visiting hunter's cabin (with a back door to escape unannounced visits from the warden), a cookhouse with a flat-top wood stove and a sign hanging over the tables calling for silence to encourage eating not talking, and a firemen's storeroom with hoses and pumps and fire maps — all to scale and just as it was in the woods of their youth. Inside the bunkhouse they built rows of bunks out of spruce saplings covered with a layer of boughs and rough wool blankets. During the winter cuts, the boughs would have been replaced every Sunday. There was a large oil-drum wood stove in the centre that had to be constantly tended in winter. In the store old ledgers recorded both the timber harvest, the distribution of supplies and the number of industrial accidents each season, of which there were many.

The loggers and teamsters advanced into the forest in the upper Restigouche in the 1830s. Theirs was a life of extreme physical labour from daylight to dusk in heavy snow, a job where hard men depended on each other in every push and pull of the saw. The cook and the teamsters were the first to rise in the darkness of the cold early mornings to prepare breakfast for the crews and feed and water the horses. The crews ate huge meals of potatoes with boiled beef, pork or fish. They sweetened their tea with molasses and drank their rum straight up. After breakfast they divided into three gangs: one that felled the trees, a second that limbed them and the teamsters who hauled the logs with their horses to the banks of the river or a nearby stream.

At the end of the cutting season the men abandoned the camps, "watered" the logs and rode the dangerous freshet on scows and rafts down to the mills. They wore nail-studded boots and used hooks and picaroons to keep the mass moving around tight bends and to break up log jams. Every year there were drownings. Cooks moved their kitchens onto scows and followed the river drive. The Restigouche Log and Boom Company maintained a network of floating timbers and fixed structures on the river to guide and control the speed of the drive and collect logs that had gone astray. It was an industry that ran on individual strength and collective courage.

Inside a display room were old photographs of the scows in the river, teams of three horses up to their chests in the river rapids, one from November 1943, the last year before the truck roads were opened in the valley. There were photographs of the horses riding the scow on the run downriver and of the kitchen scow with a white-aproned cook standing on the bow. There were oiled leather hobnailed boots, two-man cross-cut saws, large cast-iron cooking pots and the construction diagram for a thirty-foot scow called a Flanger that was designed to navigate the tight turns on the Kedgwick River. There was a tool invented in the Restigouche valley called the Bannister Brake, a mechanism that controlled a steel cable attached to the sleds and anchored to a tree so the teamsters could manage their descent down steep slopes to the river.

Today the work of three teams of men and horses can be done by three machines: the feller buncher that cuts the trees, the harvester that limbs and cuts them to length and the forwarder that picks them up, loads them on a trailer and drives them to the roadside. The spring river drives have been replaced by roads cut through the forest along which runs a steady flow of diesel engines and eighteen-wheelers, night and day, all year long.

These days the Kedgwick museum is seldom visited, the campground more often than not empty and showing its age. I was the only visitor during the hours I was there, and the monument created with such pride and attention to detail felt like an abandoned movie set. David Adams Richards wrote about the men who worked in the lumber camps in *The Friends of Meager Fortune*, which tells the story of one last great log drive and the lives of the lumbermen and teamsters who worked through a hard winter on his fictional Good Friday Mountain. He wrote of a monument to the teamsters on the mountain, visible from the truck roads that now cut through the forest. "It is such a little tribute to them, really," Richards wrote. "The woods are muted and stilled and broken and bulldozed away, by machinery none of these men could have foreseen. Nor could they have foreseen our great skyscraper mills that turn our logs into soft toilet paper for softer arses. Our companies owned by other countries.... On the roads at times, almost dark, I meet the tractor trailers bringing the logs out — those great trucks carrying twenty times the wood of those sleds.... What in the world would they think? Their sled wouldn't be as high as one of the tires of those trucks I meet along the myriad roads. Yet they had given their life for it all."

Many of the settlers in the Restigouche valley came to the river out of great hardship. They were descended from the starving Irish who came to the valley in sailing ships during the Great Potato Famine or from the Acadians who had either escaped the expulsion by hiding in the remote northern wilderness or returned home from exile in the years that followed. André Arpin's grandparents, Albert and Eliza, moved from Montreal to a farm in the community of Kedgwick River after they lost two of their children in the same week during a flu epidemic. They were seeking a new start in the remote river valley far from the misery of the big city. Albert's brother sent seeds by mail and Albert and Eliza began to grow food that they sold to families in the community, sometimes taking in children from other families who couldn't afford to feed them. André's father, Leopold, was a farmer who also worked as a river warden and handyman for the lodges on the river. In 1984, he built a stone monument on the roadside at the crest of Broderick's Hill with a small plaque that reads: "To the memory of the rugged men who before mechanization travelled this hill, ate, and rested at the Broderick Home on their way to the camps of the Kedgwick."

3 I left the forestry museum and drove down a side road on the outskirts of the village to visit Charles Thériault, a documentary filmmaker who for years has been engaged in a project he calls "an experiment in social awareness." For months I had been following his work on a web page he created with the title, "Is Our Forest Really Ours?" I found Charles in his yard working with André Arpin sawing logs with a portable mill. Charles and his wife Betty St. Pierre live in a house they built using straw bales covered in a layer of plaster for walls. They drive a sky-blue vintage Mercedes that runs on used vegetable oil. When I arrived the car was parked in front of the cottage, decorated for Charles's latest campaign, running as the candidate for the Green Party in the fall provincial election. Charles and Betty run an informal dog rescue service, and a pack of mixed breeds, including a large pregnant basset hound, was running loose in the yard. I stepped out among them and left the door open for Cody to follow but he decided that he would rather wait in the car.

I sat with Charles and André at a table in the shade of the outdoor summer kitchen while Betty bathed the dogs in a plastic pool to cool them in the heat of the afternoon. Charles was taking a break from his awareness project to prepare for the election campaign. By this time he had produced twenty-eight short documentary films in English and

French about forestry, the economics of Crown land management and the environment. Charles is a memorable frontman in the films, with a grey goatee, bright blue eyes and trademark newsboy cap. He knows that when the objective is to raise awareness about matters of complex public policy, it takes some showmanship to keep an audience engaged.

He began his advocacy in 2012 after a delegation from Kedgwick had gone to Fredericton to ask the government for an increased allocation of Crown timber. The Kedgwick mill wasn't running year-round and the people in the town thought the problem was that it needed more Crown wood. In Fredericton they were told the Kedgwick mill had already been allocated enough wood to run year-round and that prompted Charles to begin asking questions about the missing wood and then about the management of Crown forests in the province in general. Soon after that he started making films.

He began the series by interviewing the historian Bill Parenteau who explained how, in his view, the province had become a "client state" decades ago when the big paper companies began exercising greater control over the province's affairs than the elected members of the legislature. "It's a situation in which there really is a deficit in terms of democratic decision-making about our natural resources," Parenteau said.

Charles decided a social awareness campaign was the first step in reversing that deficit. People can only begin to advocate for reform when they understand the workings of the system they want to change. He argues that if Crown land is the people's land, it should be managed for the benefit of communities rather than for the profit margins of a handful of large companies. The government counters that it has been managing Crown land in such a way to ensure that that the big companies are profitable so they will keep the mills that create jobs in rural communities running. But by 2012, in the wake of the housing collapse in the United States, the industry in New Brunswick was in decline and Charles thought it was time to reconsider this approach. He wanted the public to have access to information about a forest-management system that leases all Crown forestland to just six large companies.

Since then he has interviewed foresters, academic researchers, private woodlot owners and former politicians and offered tutorials in reading satellite maps online. He interviewed a scoutmaster who showed him how the Crown land around his summer camp had been clearcut, and he travelled to Nictau to interview the canoe maker Bill Miller after his old maple syrup shack on the hill above his canoe workshop was demolished during a cut on a Crown lease. He visited Sacré Coeur, Quebec, to tell the story of a thrice-bankrupt mill reborn as a worker's co-operative.

Charles and André told me how the citizens of communities like Kedgwick have been trapped in a state of dependency that has deepened in the age of mechanization. Operators of feller bunchers, tree harvesters and forwarders act as contractors for the lumber companies, carrying loans and maintenance responsibilities for machines that almost always must be replaced with new ones about the time they make their final payments on the old ones. Mill workers' fortunes rise and fall with the inevitable boom-and-bust cycles of the industry. These same companies own some of the fishing lodges on the river. "The whole thing keeps the community far from being resilient," André said. "We have to be dependent on big industry to survive and that's wrong. Because whenever they want, they just leave us, and everything collapses. There's a corporate capture that keeps us from being self-sufficient, self-sustaining. We become either servants on the river as guides or we become workers in the woods for the big companies. They've always got you by the neck."

Both Charles and André were taken aback by the 2014 forestry deal signed with J.D. Irving Ltd. and other forestry companies that guaranteed an increase of 20 per cent in the wood supply from Crown land in exchange for commitments to further investments in their mills. When the deal was announced in the months leading up to a provincial election, the premier spoke in nostalgic language about "putting boots in the woods," arguing that the forest industry was in crisis and needed more Crown timber in order to make investments to modernize the industry for the future. Charles devoted several episodes in his awareness project to the deal that he characterized as "giving away the keys to the candy store." What was remarkable about this deal was that it locked all future governments into the agreement, subtracting the inconvenient exercise of democracy from the business equation.

In February 2014, J.D. Irving Ltd. signed a memorandum of understanding with the government that guaranteed an increase in the allowable cut on its Crown leases in exchange for investing approximately $513 million in its mills "subject to substitution at Irving's discretion with reasonable alternatives of approximately equivalent value." This was predicated on "certainty of increased wood supply, competitive wood costs and reduced costs in Irving's forestry operations in the Province." The deal was for an initial term of twenty-five years. If the agreement was breached, for example by a new government, the deal acknowledged that "the non-breaching party could suffer significant and irreparable harm," and if appropriate compensation was not offered, the dispute would be resolved out of court through a special arbitration process also outlined in the memorandum.

For years André Arpin has worried about the impact of overharvesting the forest around the streams and brooks that regulate the temperature of the river. He is also concerned about the industry's reliance on the softwood it is growing on plantations in a region where hardwoods also want to grow, pitting the industry in a perpetual war against nature. The industry is constantly striving to grow a new forest for the type of mill it wants to run, rather than building an industry that relies on the trees that grow naturally in the valley. "We sustain something that is not sustainable," André said. "What would be the most resilient against climate change? It's a mixed forest. What would be the most resilient for the community? It would be a mixed forest, and a mixed access to a mixed resource. Then we can adapt. But being caught in a system where you only have spruce, you create a monopoly over the whole resource."

In the spring of 2015, Charles along with André and his wife, Francine Lévesque, and other concerned citizens founded a coalition called EcoVie to oppose the spraying of the herbicide N-(phosphonomethyl)glycine, commonly known as glysophate. They began distributing a red stop sign reading "Non a l'arrosage N.B.," "Stop Spraying New Brunswick" that is now displayed at homes and businesses throughout the Restigouche valley. The publicly funded glysophate spray program mists clearcuts to kill the trees that regenerate naturally in order to make room for the softwood plantations. Glysophate is the active ingredient in a variety of herbicides, including Roundup, one of the signature products of the multi-billion-dollar agrochemical company Monsanto. Scientists are not certain what makes glysophate work other than that it stops plants from using a compound called shikimic acid that produces the amino acids needed to make plant proteins. Because humans don't use shikimic acid in the way that plants do, glysophate has been considered safe since it was registered in 1974, although it has since been declared a probable carcinogen by the World Health Organization.

The anti-spray coalition in New Brunswick argues that along with the health concerns for rural communities, the use of glysophate is creating a landscape where the natural diversity of plants, including hardwood trees and shrubs, has been diminished. This eliminates the habitat that supports an interrelated food web, from insects to small mammals to deer and moose populations that feed on raspberries, hardwood saplings and grasses. The coalition is also concerned about the as-yet-unknown and unintended consequences of the spray program, not without reason, for we are now just beginning to understand the extent of the legacy of other chemical applications from the past.

In 1952, the government of New Brunswick and the three big paper-makers — Bathurst, Fraser and International Paper — created Forest Protection Limited to launch a large-scale assault using the insecticide DDT on an outbreak of spruce budworm that was killing trees, particularly in the north of the province. DDT, or dichlorodiphenyltrichloroethane, is a synthetic insecticide that began to be widely used to combat mosquitos and lice during the Second World War and in the years that followed to control insects in farming and the forest industry. In 1948, the scientist who discovered the insect-killing properties of DDT was awarded the Nobel Prize in medicine.

DDT is a particularly effective insecticide because of its stability and persistence in the environment, and it was considered a miracle chemical because it appeared to cause no immediate harm to humans. When my father was a boy in Tampa during the 1950s, he and his friends rode their bikes behind the spray trucks that released clouds of DDT through his neighbourhood to eradicate mosquitos.

In the summer of 1957, CBC television reporter Kingsley Brown produced a short documentary report on "the biggest forest conservation project in history," battling the spruce budworm epidemic that threatened "the very heart of New Brunswick's economy." The government had built fourteen airstrips in the remote northern forests and assembled 220 spray planes, the largest pesticide fleet in the world, flown by retired air force and veteran American crop-duster pilots. They misted DDT from the air while on the ground research teams were "waging war at an equally relentless pace."

"Before man, the forest was harvested by the budworm, and now man and the budworm are competing for the existing crop, and the budworm must be killed," Brown said from his location at the "Budworm City" research station. The formula was 12 per cent DDT mixed with light oil and distributed through spray nozzles from the planes. More than two million hectares of forest were sprayed in New Brunswick and half a million in Quebec. "To New Brunswickers these days, one of the finest sights in the sky is the little spray plane with its deadly cargo of DDT," the reporter said in his sign off.

Rachel Carson was sick with cancer when she wrote *Silent Spring* but kept her illness secret so that it would not interfere with the message she was convinced she had a moral obligation to deliver. The zoologist was living on an island off the coast of Maine in a house she bought with the earnings from her book *The Sea Around Us*, which was first published as a magazine article in the *New Yorker* in 1951 and became an international bestseller. "Silent Spring" was first published in three parts in the *New Yorker* beginning in June 1962. "We poison the gnats in a lake and the poison travels from link to link of the food chain and soon the birds of the lake margins become its victims," she wrote. "We spray our elms and the following springs are silent of robin song, not because we sprayed the robins directly but because the poison travelled step by step, through the now familiar elm-leaf-earthworm cycle. These are matters of record, observable, part of the visible world around us. They reflect the web of life — or death — that scientists know as ecology."

Her book begins its exploration of "Rivers of Death" on the Miramichi River in New Brunswick where she tells the story of how the spraying of DDT in the 1950s to control the spruce budworm killed millions of juvenile salmon and other fish species and disrupted their reproductive cycles. Carson's story of the use of DDT spans the globe to rivers in Maine, Montana, British Columbia, California, Alabama, Louisiana, the Philippines, China, Vietnam, Thailand and Indonesia. She opens her story on a salmon river in New Brunswick not because the spray program was singular there but because the government's salmon-counting stations documented the kill with remarkable precision.

As she anticipated, the chemical industry immediately attacked her work. A spokesman for the insecticide manufacturer American Cyanamid, interviewed by CBS news wearing a white lab coat in his research laboratory, said: "Miss Carson maintains that the balance of nature is a major force in the survival of man, whereas the modern chemist, the modern biologist and scientist believes that man is steadily controlling nature." Carson, appearing on CBS television to answer the charge, replied: "Now, to those people, apparently, the balance of nature was something that was repealed as soon as man came on the scene. Well, you might just as well assume that you could repeal the law of gravity."

Rachel Carson died in the spring of 1964, the legacy of her work leading to the writing of the first Environmental Protection Act in the United States and the awakening of a conservation movement.

The New Brunswick government continued to spray DDT until 1968 and then turned to other insecticides. Five decades after the last DDT application, researchers found that high levels of DDT remained in the sediments of five remote lakes, including Upsalquitch Lake in the headwaters of the Restigouche. The fact that the insecticide persists so strongly and at such high levels in the environment surprised and alarmed scientists who participated in the study. "New Brunswick was ground zero for DDT to fight outbreaks of forest insects," lead researcher Josh Kurek of Mount Allison University told the CBC. "These are some of the highest values in Canada. It's likely there are hundreds and hundreds of lakes across our beautifully forested province that probably contain a similar story."

Carson's work prompted governments to assume the role as the regulator of the use of chemicals in the environment. I was born the same year as the publication of *Silent Spring*, so all of my experience is in the time of environmental regulation that she helped to shape. But when I returned to her writing, I began to understand how we missed her point. She was writing not only to sound the alarm about the chemical composition of pesticides and herbicides but also to argue in defence of ecologies in nature. "The history of life on earth is a history of the interaction of living things and their surroundings," she wrote. "To an overwhelming extent, the physical form and the habits of the earth's vegetation and its animal life have been molded and directed by the environment. Over the whole span of earthly time, the opposite effect, in which life modifies its surroundings, has been relatively slight. It is only within the moment of time represented by the twentieth century that one species—man—has acquired significant power to alter the nature of his world, and it is only within the past twenty-five years that this power has achieved such magnitude that it endangers the whole earth and its life." Time was the essential ingredient in the building of nature's equilibrium and balance. "Now in the modern world, there is no time. The speed with which new hazards are created reflects the impetuous and heedless pace of man, rather than the deliberate pace of nature."

The response to *Silent Spring* has been not to find ways to preserve the integrity of natural systems and ecologies, and where still possible to protect wild spaces, but to find new chemical compounds to eradicate insects and unwanted plants that interfere with industrial forestry and agriculture. So now this pesticide or that herbicide applied in these amounts is deemed safe until new science recognizes that it is not. The kind of high-risk behaviour that so concerned Rachel Carson has continued throughout my lifetime, only now it is done with the blessing of government regulators.

Rachel Carson had one more book in mind before she became too ill to write, an idea that came to her as she observed changes in the sea outside her Maine island home that she recognized were a result of anthropogenic disruptions in the climate. "We live in an age of rising seas," she wrote. We knew it was unusually hot the afternoon the Expeditionary Force took to the river, but we didn't learn until later that the summer had been one of the hottest on record in the valley and the water temperatures in the river broke records, rising at one point above 27°C, a temperature lethal for salmon. We know that the release of excessive amounts of carbon dioxide into the atmosphere has disrupted the climate and hydrological cycles of the Earth. As the Earth warms, more water evaporates and is suspended longer in the lower atmosphere by warmer air. On the river this causes more intense rainstorms and extended periods of drought, as well as changes in the cycle of snowmelt and flows.

By the summer of my season on the river the Earth's temperature had risen more than 1°C above the average temperature in the late nineteenth century. The truly dangerous consequences of climate change for natural systems and human life will begin if temperatures rise another degree above pre-industrial levels. Yet the debate in political circles is stuck at the threshold of what, if any, action should be taken. In this same year the senior energy adviser to the president of the United States told a United Nations conference that no country should have to sacrifice its economic prosperity or energy security in pursuit of environmental sustainability. When I read that statement, I thought of what the deputy said to the old Bolshevik in the novel *Darkness at Noon*: "The principle that the end justifies the means is and remains the only rule of political ethics; anything else is just vague chatter and melts away between one's fingers." The deputy was referring to the expendability of human beings

in the cause of political revolution, but when we justify upending the
life-sustaining equilibrium of the Earth in the cause of the never-ending
progression and expansion of modern economies, are we not engaging in
the same kind of calculation?

In New Brunswick there has long been a sharp division in the public
discourse about industrial use of natural resources and the imperative of
conservation; either we accept the risks or we're opposed to the creation
of jobs. When tourists and naturalists raised alarms about the landscape
of herbicide-soaked clearcuts around Mount Carleton Park, Mike Legere,
the executive director of the Forest NB industry lobby, said the viewscape
of cuts presented an opportunity for the public and tourists to see "the co-
existence of intensely and semi-intensely managed forests with the park."
The minister of natural resources said the government doesn't manage the
forest for "view ways," as if the alarms raised were about the disturbance
of a lookout rather than substantial concerns about what it means to
remove a stretch of forest from the face of the Earth, as if there is no
connection between what is beautiful and what is good in our world.

The with or against divide means there is little informed public
discussion about the protection of wild spaces or what we might consider
acceptable levels of risk. Charles Thériault is trying to change the nature
of the conversation. Strangely, the people on the conservation side of the
debate, like Charles and André Arpin, are often characterized as radicals
and the proponents of industrial development as conservatives. In fact, it's
the conservationists who are promoting a traditional conservative agenda
that suggests we should understand all the risks before we decide on a
course of action.

Later in the afternoon I left my car in Charles Thériault's yard and
André Arpin drove me into the valley, down the road toward the Larry's
Gulch Lodge. On a bluff just above the final descent to the river, he
turned his truck into a large clearcut on a block of harvested Crown
land that had not yet been sprayed or replanted. All around us stands of
poplar and birch saplings had taken root. André showed me how the cut
had come right to the edge of a wetland and seasonal creek. These water

sources feed a brook that in turn spills into the river below the Larry's Gulch Lodge. The hollow where the wetland had been was now a long band of rotting tree limbs broken by occasional puddles of stagnant water with fresh tracks of moose in the black mud beside them. Across a long section of the wetland, no buffer of trees had been left at all.

We climbed back into his truck and drove down the hill and parked near the lodge above the main river flowing through the ribbon of buffer forest that blocked the view of the big cut up on the hill. André wanted me to see the connection between what had happened up there with what was happening down here. I followed him down to the shore, scrambling over a series of small cliffs to the mouth of the brook below the lodge. Like so many feeder streams in the valley now, it is filled with gravel and has a diminished flow that spreads out over the shoreline, warming in the sun as it trickles into the main river.

We walked back upriver and stopped in to visit Jacques Heroux, the manager of Larry's Gulch, who was in his office doing paperwork. It was changeover day, so no guests were in camp and the guides and staff had the day off. Heroux is a retired senior civil servant and an author of books on salmon fishing and flies who had taken over the operation of the lodge at the beginning of the season. He took us on a tour across the porch and into the main meeting room where there is a two-sided stone fireplace and a coffee table decorated with a painting of a large salmon. On the wall are framed photographs of Princess Louise, including one of her standing on the porch of a lodge in a long skirt, scarf and short stove-pipe hat holding a fly rod beside a guide who is lifting up a large salmon. Guests at the Gulch are sometimes told that this is a photograph of the princess and Larry Vicaire, but the photograph was taken on the Grand Cascapédia River in Quebec, where she and the Marquis of Lorne built Lorne Cottage and did most of their salmon fishing in the years following their trip to the Restigouche in 1879. The man holding the salmon on the porch beside the princess is her river guide, but he isn't Larry Vicaire.

As I wandered through the lodge, Cody jumped up on the couch in front of the fireplace and lay down for a nap. He is allowed to do this at home and was unaware that it was bad manners at a fine Restigouche lodge so I sent him back out onto the lawn to wait for us there. We took a walk to the old ice house that was still filled with snow in the heat of the summer afternoon although it's been years since salmon were boxed and packed in ice there. I corralled the terrier and André drove me back to Charles's house and my car. I left them to resume their sawing project and drove back down to the Little Main.

That evening Cody and I motored upstream to the mouth of Five Finger Brook where an angler was casting from his canoe in the deep run below the outflow of the stream. He was anchored tight against the bank opposite the brook, approaching the pool from a position that we call the inside-out. I anchored below him to watch and we struck up a conversation as he took a series of short drops down through the pool. He told me that inside-out was the proper way to fish this pool so the fly would pass at the right speed and angle over the salmon that cycle up through the run. Sure enough, a few drops down, a salmon exploded from the water and took his fly.

The sun was setting so I pulled anchor and headed back downriver. Early the next morning, just after sunrise, Cody and I came back up to the pool, motored slowly past the mouth of the brook, tucked in tight along the right-hand bank where I dropped the anchor and started casting from the inside out. I hooked a salmon on the second drop, creating a moment of excitement for me but more so for the terrier, who almost went over the side of the canoe in pursuit of the fish. This is how river lessons are learned, in each day we spend on the water, one season at a time.

That afternoon I paid a visit to André Savoie, one of Marie-Christine's drivers I have come to know over the years. He lives in a two-storey house that was once a hotel opened by his grandparents in 1913 to serve the visitors brought to the town on the railway line. The old railway station still stands just down the street, several blocks back from the main highway. The railway line is now for industrial use only, operated by a subsidiary of Irving Transportation Services, which is in turn owned by J.D. Irving Ltd. When K.C. Irving bought the forestlands of the New

Brunswick Railway Company in 1943, including the lands around the upper Little Main Restigouche, the Canadian Pacific Railway continued to operate the railway assets.

In 1994 the CPR abandoned the line and since then J.D. Irving has been operating a private railway under its original name, the New Brunswick Southern Railway Company. Years ago the old hotel's third storey burned and it was redesigned at its current height with a new roof. The sign hanging over the porch now reads Hotel André Savoie. André renovated the old hotel, stripping paint, refinishing the original carved door frames and floor, and restoring the winding staircase that leads to the bedrooms that once again have numbers on the doors. André makes a living doing carpentry, shuttling canoes and telling stories to river travellers for Marie-Christine. He operates a small sawmill of his own nearby that produces cedar posts and boards.

After a look around Andre's hotel home, we took a drive to the upper end of Stillwater Brook where a beaver dam has created a small lake that André told me is filled with trout. The route followed unmarked logging roads and I wanted André to show me how to get there, thinking I might fish the brook in future seasons. When we parked beside the Stillwater lake, Cody jumped out of the car and ran face first into a skunk, ending my tour with André that afternoon. I dropped André at home and drove to Saint-Quentin with the windows open where I bought towels, a bottle of pet deodorizer and some heavily perfumed shampoo, the kind that is marketed to teenage boys. In my experience, and I have more of it than I would wish on anyone, the tomato juice solution for a skunked dog is an urban myth. After a long session with a squirming dog in the river, I had a gleaming white terrier who smelled ready to attend a junior high school dance. In the morning the flow of the Little Main had dropped too low for me to motor up over the gravel bars into the pools above and Cody was starting to smell of skunk again so I decided it was time to load the boat on the trailer and go home.

4 A week later, early on a Saturday morning, I was just about to leave for the Fredericton farmer's market with Deb when my phone rang. John Crompton was on the line and said, "Today's a good day. Can you come now?" I said that I could and told Deb that I had to drive to Moncton to meet my pilot, who was going to fly me over the Restigouche valley. John Crompton is a Moncton anesthetist and the president of the Conservation Council of New Brunswick. He also happens to be a pilot and the owner of a Cherokee Piper 6. For weeks I had been calling him, hoping he could fly me over the river so I could see the valley from the air. Now he had a free day and the skies were clear. I packed a notebook and my camera and hit the highway for the two-hour drive to Moncton.

I met him at a gas station near the Moncton airport and followed him to his hangar. We rolled the plane out of the bay doors, filled it with fuel and took off heading north toward the shore of Chaleur Bay. John's father had been a pilot of small planes, and the two of them had once crossed the Atlantic together in a four-seater. The Cherokee 6 was built in 1967 and has since had a few modern electronics installed, but it is still a plane that its pilot has to fly, both hands on the yoke. The sky was slightly hazy, the smoke from a summer of wildfires in British Columbia having pushed across the continent and into the atmosphere on the east coast. Still, it was plenty clear enough to see and I took photographs of the expansive views through the window while we spoke through our headsets.

Of all the environmental issues the council is addressing, John Crompton is most concerned about the consequences of clearcutting forests. Whenever he gets the chance, he takes politicians up in the air to show them how the centre of the province "has been completely shaved" over the past three decades. When we flew over a band of mixed forest that followed the deep cut of a river that winds north into Chaleur Bay, John told me we were passing over the Jacquet River Gorge, the largest protected natural area in the province, twenty-six thousand hectares of Crown land set aside in 2003. The boundaries of the protected area are clearly defined in the sea of cuts.

At the coast we banked west across the white sand beaches of Charlo and the port of Dalhousie and the Mi'gmaq community at the mouth of the Eel River, turning southwest toward the Restigouche estuary. We flew over the string of islands in the delta and turned upriver at the mouth of the Matapédia. What we saw on the lower end of the river was a valley largely intact, with mixed forest growing on the hills far back from the band of water. I marked the rust-coloured roof of the lodge at Brandy Brook and the line of the cold stream flowing down the hill into the pool. With expanded buffer zones, the Restigouche Wilderness Waterway park would extend this kind of forest far into the hills and through all the deep valleys of the winding tributaries.

As we flew farther upriver, clearcuts in the forest began to appear, the most recent ones gaping holes of plowed brown earth divided by dirt roads. Some of the older cuts have been left to regenerate naturally, others have been replanted with spruce in various stages of growth. We saw more cuts the farther we flew upstream. We passed over Larry's Gulch Lodge where a helicopter had landed on the back lawn and Archie Rogers's lodge on the bluff below the mouth of Kedgwick. Up the Kedgwick and Little Main, the cuts in the hills stretched as far as I could see, the narrow band of buffer forest bending along the banks of the river. Beyond the buffer zones, the cuts ranged far up the hillsides, narrower bands of trees lining the brooks that descend into the river. Almost none of this activity can be seen from the vantage point of the river.

We continued up the valley of the Little Main until John announced he had to turn back before we ran short of fuel so we banked southeast, charting a course directly across the middle of the province toward the Moncton airport. All the way back we passed over one clearcut after another, up and over the tops of the Appalachian hills, down into the valleys and around lakes, long logging roads slicing through what had once been a rich blanket of Acadian forest. Now, after decades in the industry barber's chair, the land wore a crewcut with short back and sides. The monoculture tree plantations of dark green spruce stand out because they don't look like the natural forest that is a mixed shade of greens. You might even mistake this for farmland, only there are no barns or farmhouses on this land of a thousand cuts. By the time we landed in Moncton and I was helping John push the Piper back into the hangar I admit I was a little shaken by the size of the industrial footprint. Like most of us I had imagined that the interior of the province still maintained at least some of the characteristics of the forest primeval when in fact it is no longer that at all. John Crompton had allowed me to see it with my own eyes, and I was grateful for that.

5 In late August I received a telephone call from Danny Bird at the Kedgwick Lodge telling me that he had a couple of open days. He asked if I would like to come up and fish. I drove north with an overnight bag and my fly rod and spent two nights in the old lodge, visiting with Danny and fishing in the morning and evening in the canoe guided by Herbie Martin and Rene Martin.

When I walked down to the floating dock the first evening I saw the canoe dance that plays up and down the river when it's time to go fishing. The guides were waiting, idling their canoes in the current opposite the lodge in a neat row, each one dropping down and then motoring to the side of the dock when their guests arrived fly rod in hand, so they can step into the canoe without getting their feet wet. A guest at a Restigouche lodge can fish in a pair of dress shoes. A Restigouche canoe is perfectly organized, the seat dry in any weather with blankets and tarps on hand to lay over the knees of the guest. The guide has a small collection of flies on board that have recently been attracting fish and a spool of clear leader line to replace the one you had tied to your flyline that would break if you hooked a large fish.

In the days when the anglers were harvesting fish the guides cleaned and scaled the salmon, packed them in ice in wooden boxes and marked them for shipping with stencils and black paint. The old brass stencils that once were used to mark the salmon boxes still hang on the wall of a shed at the Kedgwick Lodge. Some lodges operated smokehouses where guides developed special recipes to cure fish before they were shipped.

The water was low and the fishing was slow during my stay at the Kedgwick Lodge but I cast flies over the hundreds of salmon we could see cycling through Jimmy's Hole. From time to time a salmon would jump out of the water and crash back down into the pool sending a wake to both banks, or one would roll its back above the surface, or swirl and chase my fly. A young moose came down to the river behind us to drink. The Mi'gmaw word for salmon is *plamu*; the word for a fish disturbing the surface of the water is *gwisit*. As the sun rose higher and the light filled the pool, the fish retreated into deeper water. "We know when we're not wanted," Herbie said before asking Rene in Mi'gmaq to pull the anchor.

The Mi'gmaw word for canoe is *gwidn*, which becomes the root of the words, *gwidéman*, you are canoeing, *gwidniktuk*, you and some kind of material are aboard a canoe, and *gwidnigen*, you are a canoe maker. The example offered to illustrate the word *gwidnigen* in *Metallic's Mi'gmaq-English Reference Dictionary*, published by the linguist Emmanuel Metallic in 2005, is "Rene Martin in Listuguj, Quebec."

Rene Martin is a quiet and humble man who would not tell you unless you asked that he is a master craftsman and keeper of the tradition of building birchbark canoes. He has conducted workshops in communities throughout Mi'gmaq territory and beyond, ensuring his traditional knowledge of the craft is passed on to future generations. One of the most impressive bark canoes at the Canadian Museum of History in Gatineau, Quebec, is a long Mi'gmaw ocean canoe with its distinctive high, sloping gunwales outfitted with a mast for sailing, built by Rene Martin at Listuguj in 1991.

The temperature had dropped overnight on my last morning at the lodge and a heavy mist had formed on the river. I woke early and walked the grounds to take photographs at first light, and then came back inside to join Danny for coffee by the fire he had roaring in the fireplace. Later Herbie and Rene picked me up at the dock and we motored up to the

Junction Pool. We stopped to fish Campbell's on the way and then had to pole over the gravel bar above because the water was too low to run the motor the rest of the way to the Junction. We spent the morning engaged in casting and carrying on an extended conversation, dropping through the Junction and following a few skittish fish around the mouth of Kedgwick before motoring down to the lodge at noon. I thanked my outstanding guides and Danny, packed up and headed home.

6 Rene Martin, *gwidnigen*, respected elder at Listiguj, has another story that he doesn't volunteer unless asked, of his harrowing encounter with the Quebec Provincial Police on June 11, 1981, a day that changed the course of history in his community. At 11:20 a.m. more than three hundred Quebec Provincial Police in riot gear and ninety game wardens in motorboats and helicopters converged on the community of Listuguj to stop the Mi'gmaq from netting salmon in the river.

Rene was walking near the bridge when a policeman pointed at him. He ran, jumped down the bank into the river and started swimming. What happened next was documented in the film *Incident at Restigouche*, written and produced by Abenaki filmmaker Alanis Obomsawin. She had come to Listuguj to tell the story of what she recognized was "the biggest and most violent action against Indians in Canada for over half a century."

Alanis Obamsawin was born in New Hampshire and as a young woman moved to Montreal, where she worked as a model, singer and teacher before joining the National Film Board of Canada in 1967 as its first Indigenous filmmaker. When she heard of the raid at Listuguj on the news, she assembled a crew and came to the river to reconstruct the events through interviews with witnesses.

Among the people she interviewed when she arrived was Rene Martin. "I ran right in the water," he told her. "And I stayed in the water until one of the choppers came right towards me and I said, 'I'm going to give up right now.' And it was one of the QPP officers who grabbed me by the hair. They brought me up the hill and they threw me on the ground and stomped on me. They put the cuffs on me and then they picked me up by the hair. Once we got to the van they stopped, and the guy that was on the other side pulled my hair up again and punched my face." In her film, Obamsawin included a series of black-and-white still photographs of a soaked and distraught Rene Martin handcuffed and flanked by two officers in helmets and face shields, one with his right hand holding the thin young man by the hair. Martin was one of a dozen Mi'gmaw residents that day who were arrested and jailed in New Carlisle, Quebec.

With this raid the Mi'gmaq of Listuguj had once again been swept into political struggles with origins beyond their traditional lands. In 1972, in response to declines in salmon returns, the provincial and federal governments had imposed a five-year moratorium on commercial salmon fishing in Chaleur Bay. The moratorium was extended to 1981, at which point the government reopened a limited commercial fishery on the New Brunswick side of the Restigouche estuary. The commercial fishery on the Quebec side of the river remained closed. On the New Brunswick side the fishery was managed by the federal government, but on the other side management authority had been granted to the Quebec provincial government in 1922. Compounding this confusion, the federal government maintained that the community at Listuguj, although located in Quebec, fell under the federal jurisdiction of the Indian Act.

Listuguj was caught in the middle of this jurisdictional muddle. When the moratorium on commercial fishing was imposed in the bay, the Quebec government began charging Mi'gmaw fishermen with illegal netting, once again making their fishery a crime.

Further complicating the web of river politics, the political objective of the Quebec government under Premier René Lévesque and the Parti Québécois was to secede from Canada. One step toward a more progressive, independent Quebec was the cancellation of fishing and hunting leases on public land that had been managed for the past century like those in New Brunswick, leasing fishing rights on the Restigouche, and other rivers and lakes, to wealthy sportsmen and clubs. In 1980 the Quebec minister of recreation, fish and game, Lucien Lessard, cancelled leases on 155,000 square miles of public land and created a new system called *zones d'exploitation contrôlée*, commonly referred to as ZECs, to manage sport fishing and hunting. These locally run co-operatives were open to anyone and financed by user fees. The ZECs were designed to include all local communities in the management of their own resources. The only gap in the ZEC organizational charts, and it was a significant one, was a place for Indigenous communities such as Listuguj.

The incident at Restigouche was set in motion on June 9, 1981, when Lucien Lessard, acting on the instruction of the premier and his cabinet, sent a message to Chief Alphonse Metallic at Listuguj telling him to remove all nets from the estuary within thirty-six hours or face the consequences. Lessard's position was that the Mi'gmaw nets were blocking the migration of salmon at the mouth of the river, and he wanted them to limit their fishing to seventy-two hours during three consecutive days during the week. The Mi'gmaq were fishing for six consecutive twelve-hour nights. They refused to comply with the order and kept fishing.

On June 11 the Quebec police cut the telephone lines to the Listuguj community and sent in the troops. Police cars lined the roads in and around the community, helicopters landed on the bridge and the boats roared up the river. Lines of police marched through the town carrying long nightsticks and wearing helmets with face shields. They began making rough arrests, some of them referring to the Mi'gmaq as *sauvages*.

Obomsawin interviewed a young man named Donald Germain, whose appearance in the film has become one of the iconic images from the 1981 raid. She filmed him beside the railway tracks where he stood in front of a Canadian National boxcar, wearing a green hard hat with a red feather tucked in the side as he told of his violent encounter with police.

On the morning of the raid, Germain said he was standing near the tracks when a police officer spoke to him in French. "We didn't understand what he was saying so we stood aside," Germain said. "And he says, 'Get out of the way.' But where could you go? You couldn't jump in the river. So we stood there. They had enough room to go by. As soon as they came up to us, they started beating us up." The police handcuffed Germain and pushed and dragged him to the head of the wharf. "I was staggering," Germain said. "The guy tells me to kneel." He paused for a beat to push down a swell of emotion. "I wasn't going to kneel for anybody, so I got knocked down over there again."

In the spring of 1981 Chief Metallic was fifty-four years old and well versed in Canadian politics. He was a gregarious and gentle man who had worked in the woods in his youth, lived for a time in Montreal and studied at Laval University. He had worked for the Department of Indian Affairs, written an English–Mi'gmaq lexicon that he distributed to households in the community and had ambitious plans for Listuguj, including opening early Mi'gmaw language immersion schools. The raid outraged him, and he was prepared to stand his ground. What the people on the river needed was help, so he sent out the call.

Indigenous people from all over North America came to Listuguj, and when the police retreated, they helped to build sandbag barriers on the borders of the community. The National Indian Brotherhood relocated its chiefs' conference from Victoria, British Columbia, to Listuguj, and Mohawks blocked the Mercier Bridge in Montreal during rush hour. Federal Indian Affairs minister John Munroe came to the reserve and declared that the Quebec government's actions were outside its jurisdiction. "Mr. Monroe should have stayed home and shut up," Lévesque told reporters.

On June 20 at five a.m. there was a second raid, but this time the community was better prepared, manning the barricades at the entrance to the community. Still the wardens came back up the river in their boats and seized nets and salmon. Three days later Lessard visited the community and, after meeting with the chief, settled on an uneasy truce. Listuguj was unyielding in its position that the Quebec government had no jurisdiction to control or manage its fishing on the river.

When Obomsawin met with the National Film Board program committee to secure funding to continue the Restigouche film and conduct more interviews, a coordinator of production projects, who was also a National Film Board producer, told Obomsawin that it would be inappropriate for her to interview white people. "I could have gotten into a big fight right there, but I chose to say nothing," Obomsawin later recalled. "And, of course, I did the interviews that I wanted to do." She invited Lucien Lessard to sit for a formal interview. He accepted and flew to Montreal. She met him at the airport, took him to lunch and then set up for the interview in a sunlit room in her home, situating herself on camera across from the minister.

Obomsawin opened with some general questions. Would Lessard do it the same way if he had to do it again, and did the premier and his cabinet consult him before he made his decision to conduct the raid? Then she pushed herself forward in her chair and turned the conversation to the heart of the matter.

"When you came to Restigouche, I was outraged by what you said to the band council," she said, speaking in French. "It was dreadful. The chief said, 'You French Canadians are asking for sovereignty here in Quebec. You are saying it's your country, and you want to be independent in your country. We are surprised that you don't understand us Indian people and our sovereignty on our land.' And you answered, 'You cannot ask for sovereignty because to have sovereignty one must have one's own culture, language and land.'" She allowed her words in French to linger beyond the English translation that she provided in the film: *sa langue et sa terre.*

"How far does that sovereignty go?" Lessard replied. "It's a question of definition. Does it go as far as for example control of the whole resource? Certain native chiefs are creating illusions for the native people: 'The

Gaspé Peninsula, New Brunswick, Nova Scotia, it belongs to us.' Do you mean to tell me at this point that Montreal too belongs to you?"

"Of course, all of Canada belongs to us," Obomsawin said.

"Are you saying you are going to exclude us?" he asked.

"Did we tell you to get the hell out of here?" she replied, raising her voice pushing herself toward Lessard and touching the arm of his chair. "We never said that. We always shared. You took, took, took. Instead of being proud of us, you talked of your history, your Quebec. The history of Quebec does not begin with the French Canadians."

When Lessard began to explain how the Genesis account of Adam and Eve and the Biblical command to grow and multiply explained the present-day population of Quebec, she cut him off. "You are not going to tell me the apple story," she said. Lessard was moving toward the argument of yes, we understand that you have been wronged but we all must adjust to the new reality. Obomsawin wasn't going there.

At the end of the interview, Obomsawin asked the minister if there was anything else he would like to say. Lessard apologized for what had happened. *Je m'excuse énormément.* He said his visit to the community on June 23 and the hospitality he had been offered even under the circumstances of those weeks had touched him deeply.

In the months that followed, some of those arrested settled their cases out of court and paid a twenty-five-dollar fine. Two men, one of them Donald Germain, refused to settle and went to trial. They were found guilty of resisting arrest and received fines of $250 and a year of probation. Both convictions were reversed on appeal.

Meanwhile, Obomsawin was fighting another battle of her own within the National Film Board to complete *Incident at Restigouche*. When she returned to the program committee for funding to finish the film, the same coordinator of production projects reminded the filmmaker that she had been told not to interview white people. Obomsawin could stay silent no longer. She told the committee member she wasn't going to be instructed about who she could or could not interview. It was more than

a matter of editorial independence. She knew that the interview with
Lessard had become a critical chapter in the story she intended to tell,
and that no one could have faced the minister in the way that she did. In
the end, Obomsawin made the film she wanted to make, the film board
supported her, and *Incident at Restigouche* was finally released in 1984.
"I'm very attached to the community in Restigouche," Obomsawin said
years later. "Today, it has become a very important film for the history
of our people."

What few understood at the time was that the events of 1981 would
mark a turning point for the Mi'gmaq of Listuguj. The community had
come together and rallied in a defining act of resistance. The *Globe and
Mail* correspondent William Johnson, who had been covering the story
from the beginning, recognized that he was witnessing the beginning
of a new season on the river. "Things will never be again as they were,"
he wrote. "Neither in Restigouche, nor in reserves across Canada.
Restigouche is now a symbol, and a lesson, perhaps a turning point
for the whole Indian movement for self-assertion." The community at
Listuguj began to face the work that lay ahead with new energy and a
new generation of leaders who could take up the work of those who, in
the years before the Restigouche raids, had been preparing a foundation
for them.

Among them was a Harvard-educated lawyer from the Chickasaw
Nation and Oklahoma Cheyenne tribe named James (Sa'ke'j) Youngblood
Henderson. He had travelled to Nova Scotia in the 1970s to visit the
Potolek First Nation, the home community of his wife Marie Battiste, a
Mi'gmaw author and educator. There he met Alex Denny, the charismatic
former president of the Union of Nova Scotia Indians and *kji-keptin*
(grand captain) of the Mi'gmaq Grand Council. Denny asked the couple
to join him in his work and they moved to Nova Scotia to do so.

"The Mi'kmaq proved resilient; they survived the poverty and
suffering, and in the 1970s most had retained their knowledge system
and language," Henderson later wrote. "But any belief in their traditions
was contradicted by the world they were forced to live in, leaving them

tormented, confused and resigned." Denny recognized the significance of the treaties the Mi'gmaq had signed with the British in the 1700s and he was determined to unite his people under them, giving the documents new life and meaning by combining both written and oral records.

Denny argued that the treaties were being read the wrong way. "The Mi'kmaw treaties with the British kings did not bestow upon the Mi'kmaq any rights, he clarified; rather, the Mi'kmaq gave certain rights to the British king for the benefit of British settlers in Mi'kmaw territory," Henderson wrote of Denny's mission. "As such, the settlers had unlawfully benefited more from the treaties than had the Mi'kmaq. The Mi'kmaq then already had everything they needed to be self-sufficient. Neither the British nor the French had anything essential for the Mi'kmaq, as their ancestors had told the European missionaries and colonists."

Denny was determined to show that the treaties should be read as the reverse of subsequent Canadian law. "In the rest of Canadian law, he taught, everyone had to be granted powers and rights by the mystical Crown," Henderson wrote. "In the treaties, however, Mi'kmaq retained sovereignty, law, their knowledge system, freedom of religion and their territory for themselves; they never granted the kings any power over those ancestral rights."

Denny sent research teams to the archives and prepared to test the treaties in the courts. He asked Youngblood Henderson to prepare a brief arguing that the federal government was violating the International Covenant on Civil and Political Rights for the Human Rights Committee of the United Nations. In the fall of 1980, the year before the raids at Listuguj, Alex Denny presented the UN with a letter that reads, in part:

> The people of our tribal society are victims of violations of fundamental freedoms and human rights by the government of Canada: Canada has and continues to deny our right to self-determination; Canada has and continues to involuntarily confiscate our territory despite the terms

of our treaties; Canada has and continues to deprive our people of its own means of subsistence; and Canada has and continues to enact and enforce laws and policies destructive of our family life and inimical to the proper education of our children.

We speak plainly, so that there is no misunderstanding. For three centuries, we have honoured and lived by our Treaty of protection and free association with the British Crown. We have remained at peace with British subjects everywhere, and our young men have given their lives, as we had promised, in defense of British lives in foreign wars. As the original government of the Mi'kmaq Nationimuow from time out of mind, and as signatories and keepers of the great chain of union and association with Great Britain, we, the Mawai'omi, have guided our people in spiritual and secular affairs in freedom and dignity, in our own way, without compulsion or injustice.... They tell us we no longer are a protected State, but a minority group of "Indians," subject absolutely to their discretion and control, exercising the rights of property, self-determination, and family life only at their will. They offer our people political peonage and the destiny of dependence upon financial relief. This we cannot accept.

Two years later Queen Elizabeth II came to Canada to proclaim the new Canadian constitution on Parliament Hill. The patriation of the constitution, championed by Prime Minister Pierre Trudeau, came after years of contentious negotiations with the provinces and proceeded in the end without the approval of the separatist government in Quebec. However, the Quebec holdout didn't diminish the significance of the event for the Mi'gmaq and other Indigenous nations in Canada, for section 35 of the Constitution Act provided hard-won legal protection for all existing Indigenous treaties and land rights. For the Mi'gmaq, it confirmed Denny's argument for the significance of the Peace and Friendship treaties the Mi'gmaq had signed with the British in 1725, 1726, 1752, 1760, 1761, 1778 and 1779 that confirmed their right to continue to harvest fish and wildlife without ceding any land title or other rights.

Still, the broad principles in section 35 had to be made real in law and practice, a process that is still playing out on the rivers and in the forests and in the courts. During the 1980s and 1990s the federal government negotiated fishing agreements with Listuguj that imposed quotas on the annual catch. All the while there was constant pressure from anglers upriver to reduce these quotas. As far as the Mi'gmaq were concerned, they were being asked to leave salmon in the river so they could be hooked on flylines upriver. Between 1989 and 1992 the Quebec government again began charging Listuguj fishermen with illegal netting.

In 1990 the Supreme Court of Canada handed down its first major decision regarding the Constitution Act's protection of Indigenous rights to fish in a ruling that acquitted a driftnetter named Ronald Edward Sparrow of illegally fishing in the Fraser River in British Columbia. In the years that followed, the federal government negotiated a series of communal fishing agreements and quotas with various Indigenous communities to conform with the legal framework established in the Sparrow decision. The people of Listuguj had already been down that road and decided to take another course altogether.

On May 19, 1993, the Listuguj Mi'gmaq First Nation government assumed management of its salmon fishery in the Restigouche River by creating, passing and enforcing its own law, independent of the federal and provincial governments. The community created a force of rangers to patrol the river and began to operate a fishery not under a bylaw of the Indian Act but according to Mi'gmaw law, that states: "We the indigenous peoples of Gespe'gewa'gi are vested by Gisiteget with sacred responsibilities for stewardship of the land, waters and all living things."

In June 1993, a Royal Commission on Aboriginal Peoples, appointed by the federal government in the wake of a disastrous standoff between Mohawks, police and the army in Oka, Quebec, was holding public hearings across the country and had scheduled two days in Lisutguj. Chief Brenda Gideon Miller was the first to address the panel. She began by referring to the missionary Chrestien Le Clercq's 1691 account of a speech delivered by a Mi'gmaw leader on the subject of freedom and political sovereignty. She spoke in Mi'gmaq, translating the French missionary's recollection of the address back into its original language: "As to us, we find all our riches and conveniences among ourselves, without trouble and without exposing our lives to dangers in which you find yourselves constantly through your long voyages. And, while feeling compassion for you in the sweetness of our repose, we wonder at the anxieties and cares which you give yourselves night and day in order to load your ship with fish... Now tell me this one little thing, if you have a sense: which two is wiser and happier? He who labours without ceasing and only obtains, with great trouble, enough to live on, or he who rests in comfort and finds all that he needs in the pleasure of hunting and fishing? Learn now, my brother, once for all, that there is no Mi'gmaq who does not consider himself infinitely more happy and more powerful than the French."

The chief told the panel that her reference to the speech was to illustrate the quality of her ancestors and to dispel "any argument that my forefathers were uncivilized or incapable of organization. It is clear that the thoughts are logical, expressing rational and abstract ideas. Whether these concepts are encrypted upon parchments of hide or paper are of little consequence to the Mi'gmaq. The fact remains our forefathers understood good government. They understood basic freedoms and, most importantly, individual freedoms." A similar expression of freedom is codified in the Canadian Charter of Rights and Freedoms, she reminded the panel.

The chief spoke of the great rivers that were highways for the Mi'gmaq, a link to trade routes inland and along the coastlines, a source of food and medicines. Rivers allowed various Mi'gmaq district leaders to meet to discuss the affairs of Mi'gma'gi. When snow and ice came to the estuary families moved to the shelter of the deep forest near hunting grounds.

This seasonal migration caused the British and the French to refer to them as nomadic people when in fact they moved through their territory in concert with the seasons.

She then explained that the Listuguj Mi'gmaq First Nation government had decided to assert its jurisdiction within its traditional territory. It had a mandate from the community members to proceed in this direction and had informed Canadian governments of their intentions. "It has not been an easy one for them to swallow. We are prepared to discuss these matters with other governments, but we cannot forestall this process by seeking the permission of other governments. The Mi'gmaq community of Listuguj has reached this stage in its own evolution. We believe that we have embarked on a critical path that has the potential for benefit by government, by Nations, by our brothers and sisters. This critical path leads to what you refer to as 'self-government' in modern day contemporary terms, but one we refer to as 'the rebirth of our Nation.'"

At Listuguj, the new fishery law was the beginning of a hard-won renaissance. The community formed agreements with municipalities and governments on both sides of the river related to infrastructure, education, policing, social welfare and forestry. It opened a school that allowed children to study in Mi'gmaq from the beginning of their formal education. Challenging roads lay ahead, but the direction was clear.

In 1999 the Supreme Court of Canada handed down a decision that affirmed the right of Mi'gmaq to hunt and fish and earn a moderate livelihood throughout their traditional territory in a landmark legal test of the Peace and Friendship treaties. Six years earlier, Donald Marshall Jr. of the Membertou First Nation had been charged and convicted of illegally fishing eels in Pomquet Harbour, Nova Scotia, and selling them without a license. His lawyers argued he was allowed to catch and sell fish under the Peace and Friendship treaties. The Supreme Court overturned his conviction, affirming both the written and oral substance of the treaties of 1760 and 1761. "This appeal should be allowed because nothing less would uphold the honour and integrity of the Crown in its dealings with the Mi'kmaq people to secure their peace and friendship," the court ruled. "The trade arrangement must be interpreted in a manner which gives meaning and substance to the oral promises made by the Crown during the treaty negotiations."

While the victory was celebrated in Mi'gmaw and Wolastoqey communities, the legal language of the court still needed to be promulgated in practice on the water. In the wake of the Marshall decision, Mi'gmaq in the community of Esgenoôpetitj set lobster traps in Miramichi Bay. The non-Indigenous lobster fishermen objected to this intrusion into their valuable fishery and federal fisheries officers took to the water and confronted the Mi'gmaw boats. Some of them were swamped and rammed by armed federal fisheries officers, events that hearkened back to the raids at Listuguj eighteen years earlier. Once again, Alanis Obomsawin was on the scene with a documentary crew recording the events. The Listuguj government sent a delegation to Esgenoôpetitj to assist. The Listuguj Rangers came with a convoy of boats on trailers and launched them in Miramichi Bay to protect the Esgenoôpetitj lobster boats.

Among them was Fred Metallic, one of the new generation of leaders in the Listuguj community. Metallic grew up in the 1960s and 1970s, attending Roman Catholic school and Ste-Anne's Church, where he served as an altar boy. He had a newspaper route in the community that took him hours to complete because he often stopped for cookies and milk and occasional spiritual guidance from Listuguj elders. He recalls one elder telling him, "Don't look at what you see. Look at what you don't see."

His father, Isaac, was a river fisherman who taught his son to catch smelt, trout and salmon. And the river was where Metallic received his education in the stories of his people and their connection to the river and the valley. "On the river, with my father and my uncles, we spoke mostly in Mi'gmaw," Metallic later wrote. "I learned not only how to fish, but I learned that our family is historically connected to this territory. I learned about *ta'n tett tle'iawultieg*—how we truly belong in this territory." From his mother, Eunice, he learned that his people had always shared the fish they took from the river and, in sharing, extended their family. He came to understand that the political system in his territory was grounded in connections with one another and the natural world around them.

Fred Metallic left home as a young man to become a steelworker, building skyscrapers in New York City and Boston. When he returned home, he began seeking guidance from elders. He recalls being on the powwow grounds in Machias, Maine, when an elder led him into a nearby church. "You never know where you are going to hear the things you need to hear," the elder told him. And so he kept searching and listened to the lessons of the river.

He went on to earn a PhD in Environmental Studies from York University in Toronto, the first Indigenous student at a Canadian university to write a dissertation in his own language without translation and defend it in his home community. Metallic's doctoral thesis examined how the stories of his elders and the character of his language of action and associations offer us a way of understanding traditional Mi'gmaq laws and ways of governing. He argued that the language itself offers a guide to living with nature within a social and political order. As he wrote his dissertation, he kept returning to the question of how we come to know what we know. He faced a number of obstacles, including his insistence on writing in Mi'gmaq and his determination to hold his thesis defence in Listuguj, adding fourteen members from his community to the examining panel. He said he was now a holder of knowledge, and the community would hold him accountable just as he was responsible to his people and the river.

Leanne Betasamosake Simpson, a Michi Saagiig Nishnaabeg teacher, artist and author, was one of the members of his dissertation committee. She recalled that some of the professors at York suggested it might be difficult to hold a thesis defence in a remote community far from Toronto but Metallic stood his ground. "He insisted because his dissertation was about building a different kind of relationship between his nation and Canada, between his community and the university," she later wrote. "The defense was unlike anything I have ever witnessed within the academy."

In October 2010 three hundred people came to the bingo hall in
Listuguj to witness Metallic's thesis defence, including band councillors,
members of the Mi'gmaq Grand Council, relatives and friends. The
defence was conducted in Mi'gmaq and the questioning led by Listuguj
elders. There were songs and prayers and a feast that went on into the
night. "It was one of the most moving events I have ever witnessed, and
it changed me," Simpson said. "It challenged me to be less cynical about
academics and institutions because the strength and persistence of this
one Mi'gmaw man and the support of this community, changed things."

Metallic returned to the river and the bay and as his father had taught
him he fished salmon and trapped rock crab and lobster. He began
passing on his knowledge to his children. Metallic would become the
director of natural resources at Listuguj and a member of the Mi'gmaq
Grand Council.

"We have a right to live this way," he once said. "And we use the
language of what we call the colonizers today. We have to go to court,
and we have to talk like lawyers, and we have to defend ourselves like
lawyers and to speak that language. As soon as we change those words in
English, we change the meaning. We no longer communicate with our
ancestors. I don't want to validate or affirm who I am through the eyes
of the Canadian government. I don't want to affirm and validate myself
through Canadian society's image of who I am. I want to validate myself
as a Mi'gmaw person, but I want to do it with Mi'gmaw people, and I
want to do it in a good way, so that I can say to my children, be proud to
be Mi'gmaq. Be proud that you dream in Mi'gmaq. The fire is still lit.
We have to be sure that the fire stays lit."

Every year on June 11, about the time the salmon begin returning
to the river and the boats go back on the water, the community hangs
banners from telephone poles along the sides of the road. On some
banners is a drawing of a salmon with a braided rope extending from its
mouth, on others a photograph of Donald Germain taken from Alanis
Obamsawin's film, with the words "June 11, 1981, *Migwitetm'nej*. We

remember." The community holds a parade and the Listuguj Rangers take to the river flying flags from their boats.

The Mi'gmaq of Listuguj were shining more light on their own story in each new season. What remained was to begin the process of telling it to the other people of the river, including the owners of the old moneyed lodges of the Restigouche.

7 Since the beginning of my Restigouche journey, I had been corresponding with a retired Anglican clergyman named Stephen Booth who lives in Chester, Nova Scotia. I had been told that he was doing research among the various communities in the Restigouche valley and I wanted to find out more about his work. We arranged to meet for lunch when he was driving through New Brunswick, and we continued to correspond over the months that followed.

Stephen was born in Lancashire, in the northwest of England, in 1943. When he was seventeen his family emigrated to Lenox, Massachusetts, a community in the Berkshires, a three-hour drive from New York City, where families from the same class of Gilded Age aristocrats who had come to the Restigouche built expansive summer mansions. By the time Stephen Booth and his family arrived, economic times had changed and the grand old summer homes had for the most part been converted into public buildings, business centres or museums. Stephen left Lenox to attend Amherst College and then the Episcopal Seminary of the Southwest in Austin, Texas, where he also studied history. In 1971 he came to Canada and spent three decades as a parish priest, university tutor and chaplain in Toronto. In 2003 he and his wife returned to Lenox to care for his aging father, and he became the Rector at Trinity Episcopal Church. This stone Norman Revival church designed by Stanford White's firm was created for the summer population and paid for by the members of the congregation. President Chester Arthur laid the cornerstone for the church in the fall of 1885, the year before his death, and it was completed three years later when a Tiffany stained-glass window was installed in his memory.

Stephen Booth is a soft-spoken, thoughtful man. In our early conversations it seemed to me that he was choosing his words carefully and I didn't understand why. It took time for me to realize that in recent years he had gone through an intellectual and spiritual transformation that couldn't be explained in one meeting or in a series of telephone calls and an exchange of notes. It wasn't that he didn't want me to know what had happened in his life but rather that it was difficult to put into words.

First of all I learned that, despite the coincidence of his family moving into what had once been the summer neighbourhood of the American aristocracy, Stephen had entered the world of Restigouche salmon lodges through the back door. For three decades he had been fishing waters on the Upsalquitch River at a modest private lodge called Watiqua. The lodge was founded before the First World War by the Nova Scotian businessman William Black, who had purchased land from farmers on both sides of the Upsalquitch River that came with riparian rights to several pools, beginning just above the mouth of Bogan Brook. He built what was and remains a rustic log camp with stone fireplaces and sleeping quarters for six along a ramshackle covered porch and a kitchen and dining building behind. The old ice house is beside the road, and below that is the dock where the six fishing guests share three canoes with guides.

William Black willed a share of Watiqua to all his descendants, including Stephen Booth's wife, Gillian, who is William Black's great-granddaughter. Stephen began travelling to the Upsalquitch camp for five days each summer with a group of family members or friends, eventually settling on a regular group of six. These trips to the river were about fly fishing, relaxing in the lodge and nothing more. He knew little of the history of the river or of the people who lived in the valley and worked at Watiqua as cooks, cleaners and guides. He knew even less about the Mi'gmaq People at Listuguj and Ugpi'Ganjig.

Every summer he and his friends drove to the old camp where they settled in and fished, perhaps taking a drive to Campbellton to pick up supplies. Like most anglers, he had heard the stories of the good old days when more fish were in the river. Like most anglers, he considered himself to be a conservationist in the sense that he had joined the community that practised catch and release. That was the context of his five summer days each year for three decades, a period he later would describe as his years of "disengaged ignorance" on the river.

And there was one more thing. He had been educated in England and the United States and had lived in North America since 1960. He shared what he considered to be a commonly held view about his place in the world. He never gave much thought to the stories of Indigenous people and vaguely supported ideas about the need for their assimilation into Canadian society. "I was proud of having our feet all over the world," he said. "I don't see it that way anymore."

The seasons of change for Stephen began in the fall of 2010 when he was living in Lenox and decided to attend the annual meeting of the Restigouche River Camp Owners' Association, held at the University Club in New York City, as the representative for Watiqua. On the morning of November 11 he arrived at the University Club at Fifty-Fourth Street and Fifth Avenue, surely one of the grandest clubhouses in the world. Completed in 1899, the club was designed by Stanford White's firm in what is known as the Mediterranean Revival Italian Renaissance palazzo-style. The building is six storeys tall but appears at street level to be three. It is built of pink granite with bronze window railings and offers wood-panelled meeting rooms and a spectacular library with vaulted ceilings. It is the kind of club where you are greeted by a doorman who ensures that you are properly dressed.

For a number of years before this meeting in New York, the Restigouche Riparian Association (the precursor to the Camp Owners' Association) had been reaching out to the Listuguj community with a view to limiting the netting in the estuary. It seemed relations were improving, and the camp owners hoped they could make some kind of a deal. Among the agenda items for the New York meeting was "Economic development opportunities and the gill-net fishery." If there were more jobs on land in the community and ways the camp owners might assist in their development, they reasoned, there would be fewer nets in the river. Fewer nets in the river would mean more salmon travelling upstream to the pools near their lodges.

The camp owners had invited Listuguj Chief Allison Metallic to come to New York City to attend the meeting. Allison Metallic, the son of the chief who led the community through the crisis of the Quebec government raids in 1981, was a long-time leader in the Listuguj community and in the wider Mi'gmaq Nation, having been chair of the Grand Council and a facilitator in the confrontation between the federal government and the people of Esgenoôpetitj in the wake of the Marshall decision. "I want to make sure that my grandchildren and great-grandchildren have the opportunity to practise their language and culture," he said in an interview after being elected chief in 2008. "I want them to know that they are Mi'gmaq and be proud of that. We have a history of being the first people in the Gaspésie, and this is something that we need to be proud of. We do not doubt our history. We can also be proud of the fact that our ancestors preserved our culture and language as well as they did."

When Allison Metallic spoke at the University Club that evening, Booth recalls, the chief paid no attention to the "economic development" description on the agenda and instead began telling stories of the long history of his people and their territory. Then he asked his assistant to show the group Alanis Obomsawin's documentary, *Incident at Restigouche*. It was the first time Stephen Booth had seen the film and heard the stories of the Mi'gmaq of Listuguj.

When a Listuguj delegation returned to the University Club the following year it included Fred Metallic. Stephen Booth struck up a conversation with Metallic, and they found common ground in remembering the years they had both lived in Toronto. Over time they became friends, and Metallic became a mentor for Stephen when, after he retired from his Lennox parish in 2011, he began a research project in the Restigouche valley as part of his doctoral studies at the University of Guelph.

The subject of Booth's dissertation was the intercultural conflict over the salmon and fishing rights on the Restigouche River. As part of his research, he began conducting a series of interviews with lodge owners, non-Indigenous French and English residents in the river valley and people from the community of Listuguj. As his research progressed, Fred Metallic encouraged Stephen to ask himself, "How have I come to know what I know?" Could he be freed from the confines of his own language to begin to understand new narratives in the river valley? It's a long and difficult journey to be sure. I knew that Stephen was farther along this road than I was but when I returned to the river in September to complete my journey to the sea, I could at least say that I had become a fellow traveller.

8 On September 10, I drove back north into the valley, this time by myself with the Miller, my camera and notebooks, a load of camping gear and a cooler of food and drink. When I arrived at the top of Broderick's Hill, a brown cloud was rising below me and for a heartbeat I thought the forest was on fire, until I realized that I was watching the suspended dust rising from the road as the trucks streamed out of the valley with loads of logs. I checked into a room at Chalets Restigouche and had dinner that night with André, Rémi and Marie-Christine at her house up the hill. In a clearing behind the house Rémi had spent the day laying the foundation for a workshop he would build that fall for his Waagansis paddle-making business. The New Brunswick election was just two weeks away and André's wife, Francine Levesque, was attending meetings in her role as regional head of the Green Party's campaign.

We drank red wine before dinner and talked politics. Earlier in the day the Liberal premier had announced that if he were elected, he would create a new provincial park. Although he didn't name a location, we assumed that he was referring to the Restigouche Wilderness Waterway. This was encouraging news, but we'd all been around long enough to know a promise made in the heat of an election campaign is a long way from a done deal. Rémi barbecued pork on the deck while Marie-Christine prepared beets, green beans, zucchini and a cucumber salad, all of which she had grown in her gardens. After dinner I drove back down the hill and went over my lists and studied my maps to plan for the trip ahead.

In the morning it had started to rain. Shortly after eight a.m. I drove up Broderick's Hill and parked on the side of the road where I had cell reception so I could make a call home and send a few texts before I met Marie-Christine for the drive to Two Brooks landing. During the few minutes I was parked there, six transport trucks heading upriver to pick up loads of logs drove past me and down over the hill, one pulling a giant dump truck with tank-like treads on a trailer.

An hour later I checked out and drove across the bridge, transferred the trailer with the Miller to Marie-Christine's truck and piled my gear in the back. We drove back up Broderick's Hill, past the forestry museum and mill, up across the ridge and down the long dirt road through the ruins of the cuts toward the river. Our conversation that morning returned to the plans for the park and how it might upgrade access roads and create camping facilities that, on the stretch of river I was about to run, are few and far between. Marie-Christine said the development of the park could improve the experience of river travellers, but she doesn't want it to change the character of the valley or increase the number of canoes on the river. She said we should not lose sight of the park's primary purpose, that is to preserve the valley and the river as a wild space and to protect the ecology of the Restigouche watershed.

The warden's camp above the landing was closed for the season, the windows covered with plywood shutters. We drove at a crawl over the steep, boulder-strewn, rutted landing road to the edge of the river. We lifted the Miller off the trailer, carried it down to the river and placed it in the shallows. I piled my gear on the beach, waiting to load the canoe until after Marie-Christine drove back up the hill. I stood on the beach in the mid-morning silence, happy just to be there with the river again. The current was running flat and calm, the mists suspended in long bands along the tops of the hillsides. Just after I finished loading the canoe, two others appeared above me, each with one paddler and a load of camping gear. I waited on the shore and let them pass. When they were well ahead of me and had disappeared around the corner, I pushed off. They were the last canoes I would see on the water all the way down to the tidewater. A light rain began to fall. I laid my pole across the gunwales, pulled on my jacket and rain pants and prepared to get wet.

At the end of the long bend below Two Brooks, I floated past Red Pine Mountain Lodge on the Quebec side of the river, now closed for the season. Red Pine looks much like the Kedgwick Lodge and Camp Harmony, built of the same squared timbers with a rough, railed porch, shingled roof and stone chimneys. The front steps had been removed and the windows shuttered. Below the rugged Red Pine ledge pools I entered what for me has always been one of the most sublime stretches of water in the river system. Here the flow channels between towering cliffs, the pull of the current is strong and the deep valley echoes with the sound of water brushing the shore.

For a long time it was just me and the flow and the silent slipping of the canoe through the forest until from a distance I could see the new cabin at Cheuter's Brook with a red tin roof that Stanford White surely would have demanded be removed. The Cheuter's Brook Club is a cluster of small cabins owned by a consortium of Canadian businessmen who acquired the eight-kilometre lease of fishing rights for the upset price of $59,700 in 2013. Below Cheuter's, I approached the Chamberlain Shoals, a turbulent stretch that can be one of the more difficult rapids on the river. There's a clear passage so long as you remember to stay left. If you don't stay left, you suddenly meet a small waterfall-like drop that Deb once ran into by mistake on one of our Expeditionary Force trips. I watched her go over the top and thought she was safely through—until Cody was washed off the bow by a whitecap and she jumped overboard to retrieve him creating a few moments of drama that ended with a wet dog back riding in the canoe and his wet and shaken rescuer sitting on a rock ledge below the rapid.

I rode the band of water down the left side away from the rocks and the drop. Soon the rain started to fall harder so I decided it was time to get off the river and under shelter. Early in the afternoon when I reached the campsite at the mouth of Jardine Brook I anchored in the shallows, walked in to the shore and hung a tarp over a picnic table by tying one side to the trees high on the bank and supporting it below with two tent poles I had brought with me. I put the gas stove on the table and heated a pot of chili that I had prepared before I left and packed in the cooler. I made a cup of coffee and sat under the tarp and waited for the rain to let up and when it did I packed up and pushed back into the flow.

Later in the afternoon I worked my way through the Chain of Rocks, guiding the canoe along threads of current that swirl among a maze of giant boulders rounded and smoothed by time and the river's flow. Below the Chain of Rocks, I began the descent down a long straight run above the Brandy Brook Lodge, winding through a series of ledges and boulders. Brandy Brook is Stanford White's most memorable Restigouche creation, built along the contours of the hill with five stone chimneys above the cold brook where Larry Vicaire and Princess Louise had camped 140 years earlier.

Brandy Brook Lodge was closed but I could see a man standing on the shore downstream from the mouth of the brook casting a flyline, so I steered well out to the right beyond him and when I was far enough below turned back across the pool and anchored by the shore. I walked up the bank and asked him if he would mind if I watched him fish for a while, and he said he was happy to have the company. He was a Matapédia River guide from Campbellton who had permission to fish the pool now that the lodge was closed for the season. He had a video camera hanging around his neck and fish were coming to his fly every few casts. Like most guides on the river, his casting motion was effortless, his line extending far out into the pool and landing on the water with a whisper. He hooked and released a grilse and then another, passing the rod to me to land and release the second one while he focused on making a proper video.

I stayed on the shore waiting for him to hook another fish until I realized it was getting late. I needed to get myself downriver so that I could find the camping place I was aiming for on Mockler's Island before dark. I bailed the rainwater out of the bottom of the canoe and drifted down into the lower end of the Brandy Brook Pool. The current slackened in the deep water, and it was slower going than I expected. There is no way to rush on the river, and I was losing my light as I searched for the channel to the left that would tell me I had come to the head of Mockler's Island. Rémi had advised me to run around the island on the right side and then pole back up the inside to the camping place because the passage down the top side might be impassible in low water. But by the time I found the channel, I realized I would be poling back up in complete darkness and decided to enter from the top. I found a slim passage on the right bank and slipped through, anchoring beside the stone beach below.

When I searched for a place to set up the tent, I found that the main camping place was in a clearing in the woods in the middle of the island. Rather than set up in an area that was by then dark and dripping wet, I picked a spot on the beach, tossed aside the largest stones, unloaded and raised the tent and put my sleeping bag, mat and dry bag inside. I started a fire with dry kindling I had carried with me, warmed carrot soup on the gas stove and poured a glass of Scotch. The rain started again so I checked to make sure the canoe anchor was secure, covered the gear on the rocks with a tarp and climbed into the tent. I changed into dry clothes, read for a time by flashlight and fell asleep to the sound of rain falling on the tent. When I woke at first light, the rain had stopped. I built a fire with the last of my dry kindling and made coffee, then wandered up and down the shoreline to explore and gather driftwood.

All my life I've been comfortable spending time alone. And while I have spent many days on rivers by myself, I hadn't often done a trip of this kind on my own. That morning I was surrounded by such a heavy mist that I felt as if I were camping in the middle of a cloud. I could see the shore directly across from my campsite but I couldn't see beyond the head or the tail of the island. I returned with an armload of wood, boiled another pot of water and made more coffee. I sat on the wooden canoe chair and dried my feet by the fire. I was in no hurry to leave.

I cooked eggs over the fire and wrapped them in a flour tortilla for breakfast and spent some time drying my gear on the beach before packing. Then I lifted the canoe onto its side to drain the water, reloaded and followed the channel down to the tail of the island. I picked up a downriver breeze below Mockler's and soon the sun was cutting through the mist and the stones on the river bottom lit up before me. About a kilometre below the island I stopped on the Quebec shore to change into shorts and a T-shirt. The river slowed as I floated through a low-lying flood plain where there are summer trailers and modest cottages in an area with public access to the river. An expanse of blue sky opened above me. I passed by a series of islands until I arrived at the mouth of the Upsalquitch River, where I turned my canoe into the shore in front of Camp Harmony, which was closed for the season. It's easy to see why Dean Sage chose this place to build his Restigouche lodge on a bluff in the breeze with unimpeded views far up and down the valley. And he had the Upsalquitch at his doorstep, a river that is as fine as any in the Restigouche system, with its own lines and character and particular river customs.

Years ago my father and mother would spend a week or so every summer visiting an old cabin several kilometres upstream on the Upsalquitch. One of my mother's relatives from New England, Arthur Howe, had come to the cabin and fished these waters a couple of decades earlier when he and a group of friends had secured a river lease here. The old camp was nicknamed the Upsalquitch Parr and Beaver Club after a slow fishing trip that produced nothing more than juvenile salmon parr and beaver sightings. The old cabin and the farm behind it had been purchased by a retired policeman from Maine and his wife whom my parents had befriended. The Crown lease was no longer associated with the old cabin by the time my parents began visiting. They would arrange to stay in August when my father could receive permission from the leaseholder to fish the Home Pool in front of the camp in the mornings and evenings. In those days an eccentric bachelor named Tucker Cluett of Blue Hill, Maine, held the lease. He bought MacLennan Lodge just downriver from the old cabin in 1980 and ran it until his death in 2000.

The *New York Times* columnist Pete Bodo, who fished for many years at MacLennan Lodge, wrote of Cluett's passing and his special relationship with the people of the valley. "Tucker, who was free from pretension, threw all his energy into making the camp an enchanted place. But what really distinguished him from many other camp owners was that he wanted his staff to enjoy the same camp experience as the fanciest of his guests." In this way the lodge "became Tucker's unlikely second home, complete with a family of five": the guides, Ollie Marshall and David and Shane Mann, who are brothers; and the cooks and housekeepers, Nancy Firth and Ann Murray.

My parents were fond of Tucker as well, and my father once introduced him to me on a visit to the river. Tucker, whom I remember was a thin man with short grey hair wearing stained khaki pants and sneakers, told me that his role at MacLennan Lodge was less like a river lord and more like a "chore boy." Maybe it was because he was a Mainer, who tend to be salt-of-the-earth types, or maybe it was just because he was Tucker, but MacLennan Lodge was the kind of place where they sometimes shot fireworks through hula hoops on the Fourth of July, or where, as Bodo reported, the boss filled Ollie's shoes with rocks.

"He wasn't like our boss," David Mann told Bodo. "He was more like a brother."

"Tucker fit in better here than we ever imagined," Nancy said. "I think we brought out something in him that he could only express here."

During the years my father and mother came to the Upsalquitch, Tucker Cluett closed his lodge at the end of July, so my father and mother had the water mainly to themselves in August. One summer Deb and I visited my parents there on our way back from a trip down the Patapédia River, arriving just in time for a late lunch, extended with bottles of wine long into the afternoon in what had become only the essence of a screened porch attached to the front of the old cabin. The structure sagged with rot, and the torn screens flapped in the summer breeze.

Some years later I received a letter from Arthur Howe after he read an article I had published that made mention of the Upsalquitch. "When I begin to toss at four a.m. with disturbing thoughts about the state of the world, that's where my mind turns," Howe wrote. "I escape the restlessness of pre-dawn hours by imagining that I am getting into my waders on the porch of UPBC, walking upstream to Mann's Run and fishing down through Plum and Home Pool, moving from familiar rocks and eddy to the next, before the end of which I'm usually asleep. Or if less ambitious, I just lie on the porch in one of the ancient lounge chairs, listening to the river and watching the moving water through the diffused light between fluttering leaves. If we played some small part in leading you to the water where you drank deeply, we are the more delighted."

In the summer of 2016, Arthur Howe's youngest son, Tom, who inherited his father's love of the outdoors and is now a fishing companion and friend of mine, drove from his home in New Hampshire to the river that had captured his father's imagination and, for so many years, flowed through his dreams. He swam out in the river opposite the old camp and poured a portion of his father's ashes into water where the salmon rest along the ledges in the heart of the pool.

9 Much of the land in the Upsalquitch watershed is now part of what is known as Crown Lease 1, 421,350 hectares of industrial forestland leased to a company called AV Group that runs the mill in Atholville across the river from Listuguj. AV Group is owned by the multinational corporation Aditya Birla, based in India. It operates in twenty-five countries and is worth some $40 billion. AV Group employs about three hundred people in its Atholville mill and is considered one of the recent success stories in the boom-and-bust history of mills here, having rescued the financially troubled Fraser mill in 1998.

Aditya Birla's business is the production of viscose fibre used to make rayon thread. It markets itself as a green company that makes clothing from natural fibres grown, among other places, in the forests of New Brunswick. The process of making rayon threads from wood fibre has been known for a century as a cheaper alternative to silk and linen. Rayon is soft and highly absorbent and receives dyes well. Today rayon is used to make dresses, pants and shirts, denim, bed linens, cushions and baby wipes. Aditya Birla owns companies that make all those things. AV Group clearcuts the forests and replants with softwood trees, produces dried pulp, transports the sheets by rail and truck to the port in Halifax, Nova Scotia, and loads them onto container vessels bound for plants in India, where they are converted into rayon and consumer goods shipped back into North America's bottomless consumer market.

For a long time foresters have recognized that pulping trees for fibre is the last option for the New Brunswick Crown forests that have long been "thoroughly mined" of the best available saw logs. Viscose fibre is most commonly made out of fast-growing trees such as eucalyptus, beech or pine, or bamboo and sugar cane in warmer climates. The Restigouche valley grows trees in its short summer seasons, but slowly. It's a precarious business to bank on a crop that takes six decades to mature before harvest. And there is the added uncertainty that the climate in which the seedlings are planted now will not be the climate in which they are harvested.

The process to produce rayon from the trees harvested here requires the use of a toxic chemical called carbon disulfide that the factories emit into the air and water. Rayon production further pollutes the already contaminated rivers of India, and rayon products eventually join the mountains of throwaway clothes and fabric in landfills. The chemical processes used to produce them stops the fibres from breaking down for generations. Researchers are finding rayon fibres in the ocean, washed into the sea from wastewater outflows. I had beached my canoe late that September morning at the mouth of a fragile Restigouche tributary that flows through the forests that allow us all to be consumers of rayon clothing, bedsheets and moistened wipes. The water flowing past me and merging with the big river is now part of this global supply chain that has become invisible in the modern consumer world.

10 In the spring of 1902, Dean Sage, then sixty-one, travelled from New York to Camp Harmony for his usual season of fishing. He fished the morning of June 23 and died during his afternoon nap at the lodge. The guides at Camp Harmony poled a casket up from Matapédia that evening. Sage's friend and fishing companion Joseph Twitchell described the scene he witnessed in the *Hartford Courant*: "Mr. Sage's body laid upon two canoes fastened together, was borne down the stream over the flowing waters between the leafy banks so familiar to him and celebrated by his pen, on its way home. An impressive scene to contemplate is that of the first stage of the sad journey, and not without beauty." The *New York Times* made note of Sage's famous Restigouche book in his obituary: "Its author's death (from apoplexy) occurred at the headquarters of the Camp Harmony Angling Club on the banks of the river whose piscatorial attractions it so delightfully describes."

Apparently Dean Sage wasn't altogether pleased with Stanford White's Camp Harmony design, complaining to a friend that he found it to be "a little squatty." Nonetheless, White, with his long moustache and red hair, continued to be a celebrity on the river, travelling through the valley he had graced with his architectural gifts and joining the Restigouche Salmon Club as a full member in 1887. On June 25, 1906, White's dark secrets caught up with him when he was murdered at his table in the garden theatre on the Madison Square Garden rooftop, which he had designed. He was shot point-blank by Henry Kendall Thaw, the volatile millionaire husband of Evelyn Nesbit, a young New York model and actress who testified at her husband's trial that White had raped her when she was sixteen and he was forty-seven. According to newspaper reports on the "Trial of the Century" in New York, Thaw surrendered to police after telling the dead architect, "You ruined my wife."

In articles written about the river, the encounter between White and Nesbit has been described as a seduction, perhaps because it follows more easily the comfortable narrative of noble salmon anglers on the Restigouche and their rustic lodges designed by the most famous New York City architect of his day. According to Nesbit's testimony, she was drugged and unconscious before she woke up naked next to White with blood on the sheets. In 2019 the *Atlantic Salmon Journal* published a feature on White and the famous Night Hawk salmon fly he had designed. "White attracted and was attracted to women," the author wrote. "One of those ladies was Evelyn Nesbit." The article suggests White had an affair with Nesbit when she was married to Thaw, who was "a milquetoast sort of man, but he provided the financial security Nesbit and her mother craved."

Thaw was a lot of things, but milquetoast was not one of them. He was tried twice for murder. The first trial ended in a hung jury, the second found him not guilty for reasons of insanity. He later escaped from the mental institution where he was being held and made a run for the Canadian border, stopping in Lenox, Massachusetts, for lunch on the way, before being caught and returned to custody. Two decades after the murder, Thaw said, "Under the same circumstances, I'd kill him tomorrow."

I stopped at the Rafting Grounds landing below Camp Harmony for lunch. Dozens of Canada geese were resting on the far shore before their migration south for the winter. A birdwatcher was sitting in a lawn chair on the bank with her scope on a tripod. I made a sandwich, opened a beer, sat with my feet in the water and had a rest. Just below the Rafting Grounds landing is Runnymede Lodge, purchased by the tobacco merchant brothers Joseph and Edgar Cullman in 1953. The Cullman family now leases a kilometre of Crown water just above the

Rafting Grounds that it won at auction in 2013 for $12,000. For years, the Cullman brothers were central figures in the management of the Restigouche River, Edgar serving as the chair of the Restigouche Riparian Association for more than twenty-five years. More recently, Edgar Cullman Jr. has served as the chair of the Camp Owners Association.

More than two decades ago I dropped by Runnymede unannounced and found Joseph Cullman at home on his screened porch with Nelson Bryant, the outdoor editor of the *New York Times*, and Joan Wulff, a soft-spoken celebrity angler, the widow of a famous sport-fishing writer and documentary producer named Lee Wulff. It was cocktail hour before the evening fishing. The grey-bearded Bryant was smoking a pipe. I was a newspaper reporter on assignment and Cullman, then eighty-three years old, welcomed me in and allowed me to turn on a tape recorder and ask about his views on salmon conservation and the river. Cullman was small in stature but clearly not one to be trifled with. He had been the hard-driving chief executive officer of Philip Morris Inc. for twenty-one years and had greatly increased the value of the tobacco company during his tenure. That afternoon Cullman spoke of the imperative of conservation and his financial support for the work of the Atlantic Salmon Federation. In his view, the decline in the salmon runs was caused by changing conditions for salmon at sea, pollution in rivers and oceans, and Mi'gmaw nets. "The Indians stand out as the only people who are flagrantly ignoring the principles of conservation," he said.

"The larger philosophical question interests me," Bryant interjected. "There's no question that the Indians in this country and the United States got screwed. But we've reached the stage where the important thing is the conservation of the resource. If you conduct yourself in such a fashion as to damage or destroy the conservation efforts, then in the end you have nothing, and the Indian has always been cited as a working conservationist. You know, they didn't clean everything out. They moved around. But it seems to me a point comes when the resource is threatened, when you've got to join hands, or you have nothing. And I think that's where we are now."

It was a familiar narrative that persists today, resting on the tenuous premise that angling is and has always been an act of conservation. In fact, the Mi'gmaw practice of spearing salmon was a form of selective harvest they were forced to give up at a time when anglers with fly rods indiscriminately hooked salmon and then speared them with a gaff on the beaches beside their pools. The practice of catch and release is a recent development, introduced as a conservation measure of last resort. What is most difficult for the salmon conservation movement to face now is that after decades of organizing a well-financed and politically connected campaign, the population decline has continued. As someone who once advocated for this movement, I understand that it's hard to accept that while we were busy saving the salmon, we lost the thread of the long story of the river itself.

Just downriver from Runnymede I floated over a stretch of water known as Grog Brook where for years the newspaper magnate Joseph Pulitzer kept a lodge, and more than a century ago Charles Akroyd chased down a netsman's canoe. The wind shifted and I fought a gentle headwind through most of the afternoon. As I approached the mouth of the Matapédia, I stayed close to the Quebec shoreline then turned up a side channel on the left side of an island and poled the canoe upstream and under the bridge that crosses the river in the middle of the town. Several motor canoes were anchored beside a small dock. I left the Miller there and walked up to a campground run by the outfitter Nature Adventure that rents canoes and runs guided trips throughout this end of the river system. I paid for two nights at a campsite and a couple bundles of firewood. I heard the train whistle as it passed the station behind the Restigouche Salmon Club on the other side of the river as I carried my gear up a short path and set up the tent in the field alongside some shade trees.

11 Weeks ago, when I had mapped this final stage of the trip, I had planned to canoe up the Matapédia but now I saw that the dry summer had made an upstream passage impossible. Even the rain of the day before had raised water levels only a fraction of an inch. I thought I was stuck until early in the evening when, during a walk across the bridge and through the town, I saw a sign on a car in the parking lot beside a gas station that said "Rent Me" in French. The next morning, I walked across the bridge and rented the car, drove down to the campsite, loaded my fly rod, waders and cooler in the back and then crossed back over the river to the office of the Corporation de Gestion des Rivières Matapédia et Patapédia. The corporation was formed in 1989 as one of the *zones d'exploitation contrôlée* that René Lévesque's government had formed after it cancelled sporting leases on rivers and lakes in Quebec. This ZEC is a non-profit, community-based manager of three Restigouche tributaries: the Patapédia, the Matapédia and its tributary, the Causapscal. The corporation also manages *la réserve faunique Dunière* in the valley for hunters.

The corporation sells a variety of fishing, hunting and tourism experiences. Some of the fishing is sold by lottery and requires a guiding service, but large stretches of the river are open to the public with a day licence. In the small office beside the highway, I bought a non-resident Quebec fishing licence for forty dollars and a day ticket to fish the pools upriver for sixty dollars. This included a map that listed more than a hundred named and numbered pools where I could fish. I drove upriver, my map and licences on the seat beside me, through small towns periodically connected by old red covered bridges to their neighbours on the other shore. The change in the river culture on the Quebec shore was striking. Every pool was clearly marked with parking spaces for anglers, some with picnic tables and rod racks. Small roadside shops on the way upriver sold angling supplies and hand-tied fishing flies. The corporation keeps an up-to-date website with weather information, water levels and fishing statistics and has developed ethics guidelines for sharing the pools.

The system is designed to bring people to the river, not keep them away. About a thousand visitors a year access fishing through the corporation that employs about a hundred people.

In the town of Causapscal is a salmon museum called Matamajaw, created from the remains of an old lodge built by George Stephen, the Montreal banker and president of the Canadian Pacific Railway who later became Baron Mount Stephen, the first Canadian to receive a British peerage. Across the street from the museum is a stone statue of two salmon, one leaping in the air, the other wrapped about its tail. The inscription reads *Le Roi de nos rivières*, the king of our rivers. Just below the museum is the pool called *Les Fourches*, where the Causapscal River rushes into the Matapédia. There is a picnic area on one side of the river and a playground on the other. It's all public space and I could have fished the pool with my day ticket if I had wanted. Instead, I took a walk across the bridge with my camera and watched an angler who was swinging a fly just below the outflow of the Causapscal hook a large salmon that he released back into the river.

I followed the directions on the map to a pool downriver called Matalik, where I knew there were salmon holding in the deep water. I had no great expectation that I would hook one on a hot September day in low water, but I figured it would be a spectacle and I might meet river travellers along the way. I parked on the shoulder of the road above the pool, pulled on my waders, strung up my fly rod and followed the path down beneath a small bridge that crossed a stream that for the first time in anyone's memory was dry.

Matalik Pool is down below the brook where the flow runs through a rapid then drops into a deep hole and through a series of ledges and boulders at the tail. The road runs close to the bank and the shoreline has been artificially reinforced with large quarried rocks. There was a flat-bottomed boat anchored on the road side of the pool for anglers to use in higher water. I waded across the shallows at the head of the pool just as an angler was releasing a salmon below me. His group left as soon as the fish swam away, and for a time, I had the pool to myself. I waded down along the shore, casting out into the deep water where I hooked a large trout that I released, and then spent some time casting to salmon I could see lying among the boulders in the tail. They thrashed about and boiled on the surface, and sometimes chased but never took my fly.

As the sun rose higher and the fish moved out of the tail into deeper water, I waded back across the river and walked up the hill to the car, where I took a sandwich from the cooler and carried it up to a clearing high above the pool. I sat on the guardrail beside the road and looked down on hundreds of salmon resting in a mass in the centre. I spent the better part of the afternoon back down by the river, talking with a couple of young river guides from the Gaspé Peninsula who were here fishing on their day off (guides tend to do that) and later with Peter Firth, a veteran guide from Matapédia who had arrived with two clients from New England. Peter began guiding when he was eighteen years old, starting his career at the Tobique Salmon Club that had relocated to the Matapédia after the construction of the Saint John River dams. That afternoon Peter was wearing a ball cap given to him by a Mi'gmaw friend, that read Native Pride under the picture of an eagle's head. He had rolled his chest waders down to his waist in the heat of the afternoon, and we sat in the shade on the shore and talked while he watched his clients cast through the pool. I discovered that Peter is a friend of David LeBlanc and helps with the Restigouche River Watershed Management Council's salmon counts in the fall. Over the years he has worked both as an employee of the camps and as a freelance guide.

He said the Watershed Management Council and the ZEC have helped to create a sense of community stewardship of the river. Peter's brother Richard was one of the founders of the ZEC and was its manager for decades. "It allowed local people to decide where the money was reinvested," Peter said. Still, he expressed concerns about the future of the river. He worries about logging and land use in the watershed and the drying of the brook above the pool, although he speculated that some cold water might still be seeping into the river below the surface. He worries about changing weather patterns that have disrupted fish habitat and spawning cycles. When someone on the shore suggested that Mi'gmaw nets were contributing to the salmon decline, Firth answered with a gentle but firm intervention: "The problem is not the Indians; the problem is mankind. We are the ones who emptied the oceans. It's not the Indians with their nets."

I stayed on the shore talking with Peter Firth until the early evening when we saw the flashes of tiny herring, locally known as gaspereau, skittering across the surface of the water, hatched from tiny eggs deposited in the spring. After a summer of feeding in fresh water, they were beginning their migration downriver to the sea. These flashes in the last sunlight of the day were a reminder that the cycles of life were still turning despite the drought and all of our worries about the changing order of the natural world. On the river, the beautiful is always close at hand. I left Peter Firth there with his clients and drove back downriver to my campsite, arriving just after dark.

12 Months later I thought of my trip up the Matapédia River when Alanis Obomsawin, now eighty-seven years old and with more than fifty films in her catalogue, came to Fredericton to receive an honorary degree from my university. At a dinner the night before convocation, she spoke of the changes she has witnessed in Canadian society.

"Many people fought their whole lives against the discrimination of the Indian Act and its discrimination against our people," she said. "When the sacred smoke of the sweet grass rises over me, in kindness I see the other face of truth. There is love, there is peace in my heart. A gentle day is here.

"Hey, hey, my mother the Earth. Hey, hey, my father the sky. No, our people don't have to die. Someday they will find their place on Earth again. Our young are now strong, and many begin to understand the real healing will come from within and through our ancestors. Going back to some of our ways, ceremonies, spiritual expression, we are going somewhere where we have never been. We have doctors, lawyers, judges, teachers, many of our young people are well educated. Changes are here. This is a time when Canadians are healing. There is a feeling that they want to see justice done to our people."

In his dissertation, Stephen Booth concluded that while he found promising new conversations in the valley among the various cultural groups along the river, he feared the expanse that lay between the Mi'gmaq and Western views of our relationship to the salmon and the created world in general would be difficult to cross. In particular, he noted, the "quasi-evangelical" mission of the government and conservation groups to "save the salmon" remains a concept that Indigenous people consider to be "logical nonsense and moral anathema."

Early in my Restigouche journey I met a scientist named Carole-Anne Gillis over an early morning coffee in Campbellton. She is the research director at the Gespe'gewaq Mi'gmaq Resource Council, a non-profit organization created by the Mi'gmaq communities in the Restigouche estuary to integrate traditional knowledge and modern science that will help guide public policy. Carole-Anne grew up in Matapédia in a river family that settled here after a forest fire swept through the Miramichi region in 1828. Four generations of guides, including her father, have worked on the river. One of her uncles was manager of Camp Harmony for decades, and her cousins and uncles have been or now are managers, wardens and guides at camps up and down the river. Her father was guiding at the Restigouche Salmon Club the summer morning in 1983 when the old clubhouse burned. He and other guides broke through a door with a fire axe and ran into the building to save luggage and passports, antiques, rods and reels, and anything else they could carry until they were driven away by the flames.

Carole-Anne took her first steps as a toddler in Richard Firth's home, and Peter Firth's son Michael, who is also a river guide, taught her how to skate. "We are all so intertwined in Matapédia," she says. She speaks English and French, has a doctorate from the Institut National de la Recherche Scientifique and now manages various research projects on the river and in the bay. She was on her way the morning we met to participate in a shoreline cleanup at Eel River Bar.

"When I went to school there was just one way of describing things," she says. "Since then I have come to realize that there are other ways of knowing." Her awakening began when she was conducting research for the council, taking tissue samples from eels to map food webs in the river. By analyzing the chemical composition of the tissue samples, in particular concentrations of nitrogen and carbon, she situated the eels in the food chain. When all the samples were analyzed, she had a problem: four sets of outlier data placed the eels higher in the food web than the salmon. From the point of view of modern science, the data made no sense because the eels are scavengers and are not feeding on salmon. The outlier tissue samples remained a mystery until one day when she was working in Listuguj at a boat landing near the powwow grounds and she watched a group of Mi'gmaw salmon fishers cleaning their catch and feeding the eels in the river. They were returning the gills and guts they did not need back into the river ecosystem as they had done for generations. This explained the outlier tissue samples, an understanding she could not have reached in her laboratory.

What she saw at the landing in Listuguj allowed Gillis to complete her food web. But more than that it opened her eyes to how humans interact with natural systems. We generally think of human interaction with the environment on a global scale, through carbon emissions or pollution from large industry, when in fact each of us is intimately connected to the ecologies that surround us in the countless small movements of our lives.

Among her many projects, Carole-Anne Gillis is now part of a team studying cold-water refuges on the river. Since 2011, the council has identified more than 1,800 refuges throughout the Restigouche watershed by flying over the rivers by helicopter, capturing images using high resolution and thermal cameras. These images allowed the team to measure and map surface water temperature. The larger the thermal refuges, the more important they are for fish populations that need cold water to survive in the heat of the summer.

Using this data, they have mapped the drainage areas of thermal refuges and developed plans to correct land-use practices that diminish sources of cold water. The council's goal is to increase the resilience of the river system as the climate warms. The council has now identified ten critical cold-water refuges on the Matapédia, including Matalik Pool where the stream ran dry in the summer of 2018, and has been meeting with landowners to discuss ways to protect the sources of cold water to make sure they are persistent over time.

"The salmon is the one that brings us all together," Carole-Anne Gillis says. "We all care for it. It is what binds us even though there have been conflicts. No matter the differences in ways of knowing, we create a respectful space to learn from one another."

The council's executive director, John Vicaire, notes how much traditional knowledge can be found in the Mi'gmaw language itself. For example, the Mi'gmaw word for the month of November is related to the word *gep't'g*, to freeze over. This is the time of year when the river has frozen in the past. Now in a changing climate the variations in the cycle of freezing and thawing, and the timing of the ice run in the spring and the composition of river ice, is transforming the river in ways we are only beginning to understand. Traditional knowledge can help situate the long life of the river in the context of what is happening now. John Vicaire is also an accomplished photographer, and the council is using aerial images captured by a drone to collect baseline information that will allow researchers to track how the landscapes in the watershed are changing in each new season.

The council promotes stewardship and builds relationships among various communities in the valley. The council assists with the Harmony Project launched in 2001 as a way to bring together young people in the neighbouring communities of Listuguj and Pointe-à-la-Croix on the Quebec side of the river to address generations of misunderstanding, discrimination and violence. The Harmony Project organizes students from kindergarten to sixth grade to participate in picnics, skating, bowling, hockey games and visits to farms, libraries and museums. They also plant trees together alongside the Restigouche River and join in an annual ceremonial signing of a Harmony Treaty. The program has expanded to include more neighbouring communities in the river valley, changing attitudes one generation at a time, trusting that children are surely the most powerful source of reconciliation.

Since 2014 the council has assisted Listuguj Fisheries in the organization of annual salmon summits. A recent summit at Listuguj included representatives from Mi'gmaq communities, conservation groups, the ZEC in Matapédia, the camp owners and provincial and federal governments. Stephen Booth gave the keynote address. On the first day there was a presentation on the Harmony Project and a panel discussion about the salmon and the river that included Fred Metallic, Listuguj researcher Pamela Isaac, David LeBlanc and Danny Bird. On the second day David LeBlanc presented a report on the Restigouche salmon returns. The summit ended with a smudging ceremony and a talking circle.

Meanwhile, members of the camp owners' association continue to meet with Mi'gmaq communities. In 2017 they gathered at Ugpi'Ganjig, the first time that they had come together in a Mi'gmaq community. They met again the following summer at a new tourism destination on the New Brunswick shore, the Restigouche Experience Centre built by the city of Campbellton. The main item on the agenda that year was the story of the river told at the centre. The tourism information centre that includes a museum and restaurant is situated directly across the river from Listuguj and is designed along the lines of one of the old Stanford White fishing lodges. The displays are primarily about the history of salmon angling. There's a collection of antique fly-fishing rods and one old Mi'gmaw fishing spear. There is a handful of historical photographs of Mi'gmaw and Wolastoqey guides on the river.

Under the title "The Mi'gmaq and the Salmon," the narrative in one of the panels reads as follows: "The season when salmon swam upriver was manna from heaven for the Mi'gmaq. This fish held an important place in their diet, their culture, and their economy. It obviously provided families with a food source and was even used as a substitute food item whenever hunters were out of luck during the fall. From the 17th to the 19th centuries, salmon were also a commodity to be traded with the Europeans.... Water held an important place in the Mi'gmaq tradition. A nomadic people who lived from hunting and fishing, the Mi'gmaq were excellent navigators and used watercourses to canoe across the territory. They pitched camp at the mouth of a river, where they would find fish in abundance. Villages thus came into being along the Restigouche River."

In this account, the verbs in the past tense effortlessly dismiss the existence and relevance of the Mi'gmaq in the present tense. A visitor might be left with the impression that the Mi'gmaq People no longer inhabit the river valley, despite the fact that their fishing boats and the Listuguj Rangers can be seen from the windows of the experience centre. The sport-fishing story dominates the museum. There's a wall display of various flies, photographs of harvesting river ice for the camps and an early Johnson outboard motor from 1927. A large angling canoe hangs from the rafters above a stone fireplace. Along the hallway is a mural map of all the fishing camps on the river, starting with Boston Brook on the Little Main, marking each lodge all the way down to Tide Head and Atholville. The community of Listuguj was not on the map.

After the meeting in the summer of 2018, the Listuguj government released a statement that said: "It was agreed upon to evaluate and review the current history that is being displayed at the Centre to include both the history of multiple generations of guides and anglers along with the history of the Mi'gmaq and Gespe'gewa'gi. Acknowledging the darkness in our collective history is the first step to reconciliation and to ensure that history does not repeat itself."

There have been some steps taken to acknowledge the long story of Gespe'gewa'gi in the city of Campbellton. In the fall of 2019, a memorial map was erected on the waterfront with an inscription in Mi'gmaq that translates as follows: "You are currently located on the unceded traditional territory of the Mi'gmaq of Gespe'gewa'gi, which is the seventh district of

Mi'gma'gi. The Mi'gmaq have been here since time immemorial and have been stewards of the land for generations. Over the course of time the Mi'gmaq have endured and remained strong and resilient in the face of adversity. As long as the rivers flow and the animals roam and grandfather sun is there, we shall always overcome to protect who we are." In the same season, the Mi'gmaq flag was raised over Campbellton city hall. Stephen Booth continues to travel to the river valley to try to facilitate plans to rewrite the narrative at the Restigouche Experience Centre.

Fred Metallic is looking to the future, forging a connection to the stories and teachings of his elders without leaving his people in the past. He often thinks about what kind of ancestor he will be. In a conversation in his office at Listuguj, he told me how Mi'gmaw creation myths describe the birth of the atmosphere and how language is drawn from the energy that moves over the water and through the natural world.

In the spring, when the *plamu* return to the river a great assembly forms in the valley. The old salmon lead the younger ones back to the waters where their lives began. "Every year when the salmon come back, all of that comes back again, the energy comes back, the ecology forms," Fred Metallic says. "We were born into a family. We haven't learned what that means. Our teachers come back every spring."

That day he spoke of how eagles have returned to the river. He said a biologist would say the eagles have returned because they have found new sources of food. A Listuguj elder told him the eagles have come back to acknowledge the strength and resilience of the Mi'gmaq communities in the valley. "It is because we are picking up our bundles," he said.

13 On the morning of the last day of my season on the river, I had arranged to meet Alan Madden, the former Restigouche biologist who, early in the spring, had directed me to Waagansis Brook. Weeks ago, I had called and asked him to reserve a day so we could run the lower section of the river together to the head of tide. He said he would wait for me at the mouth of the Matapédia on the beach down the hill from the Restigouche Salmon Club headquarters. That morning I set my alarm to wake before dawn, drove the rental car across the river, parked it by the gas station and dropped the key in the after-hours box. I walked back across the bridge and down into the campsite, made coffee and broke down the camp, carried the gear to the river and loaded the canoe. I pulled anchor and poled down the side channel to the main river, across the tail of the island and the outflow of the Matapédia to the beach where Alan was waiting with a small cooler that served as both lunch pail and gear box. He had with him his fishing rod and a wooden paddle. He was wearing faded jeans and a dark purple long-sleeved shirt, rubber boots and a floppy green hat. He stepped into the front of the canoe and we pushed off into the current. He stood in the front leaning on his paddle watching for rocks, from time to time turning all the way around so we could have a proper conversation. I stood in the back with the pole, keeping the nose of the canoe pointed downstream.

There was still heavy mist down in the valley as we floated through the big pool below the mouth of the river, passing the giant bridge piers that Sandford Fleming had designed for the Intercolonial Railway almost a century and a half ago. We were twenty-five kilometres west of Chaleur Bay where the river splinters into a maze of cross and side channels that flow around more than two dozen uninhabited islands, creating wild spaces for nesting ducks and bald eagles; a myriad of fish species; beavers, mink and otters; marsh grasses and fiddlehead ferns; tangles of wild grape and alders; and stands of towering maples, poplars and spruce. All this rich landscape stretched out before us, and Alan had many things to show me.

As the heat of the sun burned away the mists, Alan began a lecture in river history and science that continued throughout our September morning canoe run. A train rumbled past us along the Quebec shore as we followed the channel down past the highest island in the archipelago, called Bell's. It is long and substantial with a stand of mature hardwoods and spruce in the centre. "That island has wild grape on it, just like the islands on the Saint John River down below Fredericton," Alan said.

When the current pulled us closer to the Quebec shoreline, Alan pointed and said, "There's milkweed right there," and asked me to land the canoe so we could have a closer look. Above the stand of milkweed, a cluster of staghorn sumac trees was growing, their leaves just beginning to turn, always among the first to mark the changing season. Milkweed is the tall broad-leafed perennial flowering plant that is an essential link for the monarch butterflies that migrate between the shores of this northern river and the Sierra Madre Mountains of Mexico. Alan stepped out onto the shore and walked up to the milkweed stand, whose flowers had already bloomed and released their silky seeds into the wind. He broke one of the stems to show me the milky latex inside and explained how the life cycle of monarch butterflies runs through four generations in a single season. No one knows how these butterflies, hatched in the valley of the Restigouche River, find their way to Mexico and back again, any more than we understand how the salmon find their way to Greenland and back to these waters through vast oceans. All we know for sure is that they come to this shoreline because they are meant to do so.

We eased the canoe back into the flow along the north side of Long Island where we floated across a stretch of shallow water and steady current above a wide expanse of fine gravel. This bed of gravel is the most important spawning area in the lower river because here the water flows at the precise speed that allows female salmon to dig their nests and deposit their eggs among the tiny stones. When we floated across a scattering of larger stones farther downriver, Alan noted that this bottom known as rubble wasn't suitable for spawning. "Real big gravel we call rubble," he said.

We floated past a grassy island and he showed me where a colony of bank swallows, a species of tiny birds with brown heads and white chests that live in holes they dig deep into the soft shoreline, nests on the muddy bank of the meander. The population of bank swallows in North America has declined by as much as 40 per cent in recent decades. "That colony has been here since I've been here," Alan said.

Some things haven't changed in his lifetime on the river, but others have. He spoke that afternoon about the annual reports of Max Mowat, who was the head warden of the Restigouche Riparian Association from 1895 to 1945. Alan has read most of these reports. On one day in October in the early 1940s, Mowat counted four thousand spawning salmon in just the first four miles of the Main Restigouche from the mouth of the Kedgwick River down to Cheyne. During the past forty years, government counts found no more than two thousand salmon in the entire length of the river. "It's all relative really," Alan said. "We can't even comprehend how many fish there were in the nineteen-thirties, and people in the nineteen-thirties couldn't even comprehend how many fish there were in the seventeen-thirties."

Bank beavers are thriving in the lower river, the signs of their digging and cutting and mud-and-stick lodges, both in use and abandoned, littered every channel through the islands. In a pool beside a gravel island we saw a small school of silver striped bass swim past, a native population of fish that has experienced a remarkable resurgence all along this coastline in a time when the salmon populations have declined. I turned the canoe back upstream and we both took a few casts in their direction, but we weren't fishing in any serious way.

At midday we stopped for lunch on a narrow sandspit on the tail of an island above Morrisey Rock, a high cliff through which the Intercolonial Railway engineers had cut a tunnel in the 1870s. I anchored the canoe off the point, and we set up chairs and watched the currents swirl where the two channels met below us to form one.

Early in the afternoon, as we approached the Tide Head beach, we saw remnants of the log drives, old hand-sawn timbers half buried in the river bottom and the remains of the square-box boom structures, worn and battered but still holding in the current. In the decades since the log drives stopped scouring the river bottom and the Restigouche works to heal itself from the wounds of the logging industry's first incursions into the valley, Alan Madden has watched the river marshes gradually reform.

There is more healing to be done here and all along the shore of Chaleur Bay, where bones of the industrial dream in these ancient Appalachian hills are now scattered far and wide. Some we can see, but most are hidden and unaccounted for beneath the breakers along the coastline, in the soil, in the sediments of lakes and streams and in the atmosphere far above us, the legacy of a time when we imagined ourselves to be the measure of all things. So much has come and gone in this measure that is but a heartbeat in the life of the wild river.

I poled the canoe into the shallows near the public docks down below the Tide Head beach where Alan had parked his car. As he was wading into the beach, he turned back to tell me that for many years he has kept a record of the people he fishes with. Because we had both taken a few casts, he said he would put my name in his book when he returned home. And he told me he doesn't list just anyone in the book, only those he considers to be friends. I told him it was an honour to be included.

In the months that followed that day on the river, I have reflected on the many things I learned from this generous man, the most important being how to keep my eyes fixed upon the miracles of creation. A day on the river with Alan Madden is a reminder that every form of life in every realm of nature reveals something beautiful and marvellous in each moment of its passing.

I poled back upstream to the Tide Head landing where I anchored the canoe and unloaded my gear on the beach. Marie-Christine arrived with my car and trailer about a half an hour later. On the drive home I began the long process of unravelling all I had seen and all I had learned.

The one thing I knew for certain then was that I had spent a season following the flow of a great river and I would try to find the right words to say what that means.

14 In the spring of 2019 both my city and the Restigouche valley were flooded again by the spring freshet. The floods in and around Fredericton reached levels about the same or higher than the previous year, my neighbours and I once again sandbagging our homes and pumping water from our basements, once again facing the uneasy realization that the river may really have irrevocably changed. In the Restigouche valley, after a long winter of heavy snowfalls, the ice run came hard and fast. CN Railway moved loaded cars onto the old Intercolonial Bridge to anchor the tracks. The river breached its banks and poured into the streets of Matapédia, flooding homes and businesses and pushing piles of ice onto roadways that had to be cleared with bulldozers and loaders when the water receded. It was another season of dire warnings from climate scientists and politicians debating the urgent need for bold action, or at the very least, flood mitigation.

In mid-June I took a few days off from writing and headed back north to the river valley with the core members of the Restigouche Expeditionary Force. Lucy and Ruth had requested a river trip at the end of their school year. We knew these requests from teenagers will become increasingly rare, so Deb and I packed the canoes and assembled the gear, and we headed for the river late in the afternoon after their last exam. This time we left Cody at home in the care of a friend. We have realized that while he loves canoeing, he dislikes camping; for now, he's a day tripper.

We spent the night in a cabin by the Little Main and arrived at Arpin headquarters in a light rain on the morning of June 14. When we pulled into the driveway, I could see that André Arpin had had a busy winter and spring after his work on the election campaign ended. In the September election, his friend Charles Thériault finished second in his riding to the Liberal candidate, a much stronger showing than the last time around but still a long way from winning the seat.

André's response was to turn his attention back to the world of the river, where he can make change with his own hands. He installed a sheet of solar panels on the roof of an old school bus that had been retired after years of transporting paddlers through the valley. To house the storage batteries, he built an insulated room inside the bus with a window that a thermostat-controlled arm opens and closes automatically to regulate the temperature. The solar panels supply all the power to his home, and he is planning to refine and modify the system to supply the business as well. Marie-Christine asked him to paint the yellow bus green so it would blend into the yard, which he did, and then he hung a large sign over the back window that reads "Protegéon la diversité de nos Forests," protect the diversity of our forests.

André also modified the greenhouse built onto the side of his wood-working shop, and after a tour of the solar bus, he showed me his tomato plants in bloom and cucumbers that were ready for harvest. The green-house grows food, and the sun heats the shop in winter. He turns on the heat by opening the connecting door and windows.

While I was talking with André and touring his latest projects, Deb, Lucy and Ruth were in the office in discussions with Louise to change our travel plans. Another group of paddlers was preparing to leave about the time we arrived, and they were heading for the same camping spot we had planned on using that evening. When I joined them, I was told the Expeditionary Force preferred to have its own space on this river trip. Louise suggested we return to the Kedgwick Forks, where we had taken our first trip together five years earlier.

We loaded our gear into one of the company trucks, attached the canoe trailer and Samy, a young member of the Arpin team from Saint-Quentin, drove us an hour and a half north, across muddy logging roads to the Forks. We unloaded in the clearing beside the pool, washed the mud off the canoes, assembled a quick lunch and then launched in the upper Kedgwick, the teenagers paddling Deb's canoe and the two of us following in the Miller. Late in the afternoon we stopped on an island just below Rapids Depot to set up camp. A canoe with a guide and angler from the Kedgwick Salmon Club motored up and anchored at the tail of the island to fish the run alongside our campsite. The guide warned us that thunderheads were moving downriver, so Deb and I turned over the Prospecteur on the beach, stashed as much gear as we could underneath and set up the tent. Just as we were starting to make dinner, the storm arrived, flashing and booming and dropping rain in sheets on the island. The guide and angler retreated to the lodge below, and we all took shelter in the tent. The storm crashed and flashed over the island for the next hour. When the thunder and lightning moved on downriver and we had only to face a hard rain, Deb and I stepped out of the tent. I held an umbrella over the stove while she prepared an emergency Kedgwick storm dinner of sausage risotto that I passed to the grateful teenagers, still sheltering in the tent.

In the morning the sun returned, and we spent a long day wrapped in river time that included an expansive lunch break on a beach downstream. Lawn chairs and gin and tonics were on the menu. We spent the next night at Falls Brook on a high bank between the roaring falls and the confluence of the brook and the river. It rained again in the evening. We had the tent and a tarp strung in the trees and it didn't seem to matter. Deb cooked a lasagna in the Dutch oven by the fire, and for dessert Lucy and Ruth continued their tradition of outdoor baking, creating a fine lemon blueberry cake using the same campfire oven method. In the morning we floated to the mouth of the river, the teenagers once again in their own canoe, Deb and I following and admiring them as they slipped downstream, framed in spring greens and blue sky.

A couple of days later I headed north again with my friend Butch Dalton to fish Red Bank, the Crown Reserve stretch that we had booked through the winter lottery. It was just the two of us on this trip, travelling in Butch's Sharpe canoe from Downs Gulch landing and riding a nice flow of water for two hours downriver to the cabin. When we had everything stowed inside, we went fishing, motoring all the way down to the lower boundary of the stretch at White Brook Island and slowly fishing drops on our way back upstream.

Our friend Marty Stewart wasn't with us in person on this trip but whenever we are on the river, he is there with us in spirit. Above the pool called Wishart's, there's a trench in the river we call Marty's Pothole. It's the kind of place that will never be on any river map, belonging only to those who have the eyes and experience to see it. Over the years Marty has often dropped anchor and found fish there. That afternoon we anchored alongside the upper end of Marty's Pothole and after a couple of drops I hooked a large salmon, bright and silver and strong that must have weighed at least twenty pounds. The salmon stripped a hundred metres of line off my reel as Butch brought the canoe to shore. I stepped out of the canoe and saw the salmon jumping near the shore on the other side of the river where the current was strong. I turned the salmon as quickly as I could, reeling it back into the shallows where Butch released it back into the river.

During the rest of the trip we had several salmon following or splashing at our flies but no hookups. It didn't matter. As we always do, Butch and I had long conversations in the canoe and took afternoon naps. We watched an eagle riding the updrafts along the shoreline in front of the cabin. The trees on the hillsides cast long shadows over the water, and we refilled ourselves with the river's grace. David Adams Richards once wrote about the "spiritual readjustment" we draw from time spent at these kinds of river camps. "For here is another life, not only the life of the fly and the rod, but a life that says that so much of our concerns—which we put so much stock in and trouble ourselves so much about—does not matter in the least. We have too much, we fret too much, we hoard away too much for ourselves. These camps can and always do tell us this if we listen to them and the water running below them. That human kindness matters, and companionship, and our love and protection for those who are far away from us at that moment, but not much else."

The second evening when Butch and I had motored back down to fish the pool at White Brook Island, we watched a pair of Canada geese standing at attention as six newly hatched grey goslings appeared on the shore for what may have been their first encounter with the river. The goslings waddled upstream along the shore of the island bobbing their heads into the puddles of water between the stones, the parents following behind, their eyes never leaving their new brood. They couldn't have chosen a more suitable place to nest and bring new life into the world.

The next morning we found salmon leaping and splashing at the Shingle, a deep hole close to the bank on the long run below Red Bank where for as long as we have been coming here the fish have been stopping and resting on their way upriver. Early in the afternoon we cleaned the cabin, packed the Sharpe and motored up to Downs Gulch landing where we loaded the canoe on the trailer and drove down into Kedgwick River. Butch left me there and I caught a ride with Marie-Christine and Rémi to Campbellton where I checked into a motel.

The following morning I met Stephen Booth in the lobby of the motel before sunrise and we drove across the bridge into Listuguj and parked by the shore. It was June 21, the summer solstice, the longest day of the year that reminds us how the light from the sky and the movements of the sun and the Earth still shape our lives. We who live in northern countries always feel the primeval pull of these extended hours of light.

The acknowledgement and celebration of solstice is still marked around the world across all languages and cultures, and that morning the Gespe'gewaq Mi'gmaq Resource Council had planned a solstice ceremony on the beach beside the river. John Vicaire brought firewood in the back of his truck to light the fire on the beach. Glenda Wysote-LaBillois, an elder from Listuguj who operates the Sacred Fire Healing Lodge in Ugpi'Ganjig, performed the solstice ceremony that on this day was both ritual and a lesson for the visitors to her community. David LeBlanc and Carole-Anne Gillis were there, along with Jesse Allain and Alex Giroux of Nature Adventure in Matapédia and Nathan Wilbur of the Atlantic Salmon Federation.

Glenda began by singing the Mi'gmaq honour song, an anthem of resurgence and resistance, a call for her people to be proud of who they are and have been and an invocation to live with honour and respect for the world as the creator intended. We took pinches of tobacco and scattered them over the fire as she said prayers in a sequence to the four corners of the Earth: to the south for the women, to the west for the men, to the north for the elders who walk in our shadows and to the east for the children who are the gifts of creation.

Shortly after six a.m. the small boats of Listuguj appeared on the river, slipping through the mist toward their nets across the flat calm of the estuary. Glenda passed an eagle feather around the fire, inviting each of us to hold it and say a few words about the season that had passed and the new season ahead. The longest day of the year, she said, is the day that connects us in time present to time past and time future. As we spoke and passed the feather, the Restigouche stretched out before us, silent and powerful, an ancient river shining in the first light of a new day.

Just after sunrise, Glenda closed the solstice ceremony with a story that had been passed on to her from her elders, about a man who danced beside a tree for ninety days. He danced until he and the tree became one.

We left the beach together and gathered for breakfast at Restaurant Chez Claudine in Pointe-a-la-Croix, Quebec, on the outskirts of Listuguj. We sat around a long table and talked about the new season on the river, the developing plans for the Restigouche Wilderness Waterway, the work of the council, John's passion for photography and Glenda's worries about how young people will stay connected to their language and the flow of the river in an age when the mediated world that appears on their screens consumes so much of their attention. The words spoken over breakfast were in Mi'gmaq, French and English, all bound together by the stories and lives of the people of the valley and the river.

Since the beginning of my journey I had been following the lines of this river on maps, and there I could see how its shapes resemble trees, the main stem linked to tributary branches that reach up into headwater hills, the braids of its delta extending like roots into the sea. We find these branching patterns all around us in the natural world: in the primary and lateral roots of plants, in the veins of leaves, in the antlers of deer, in the shape of the currents of the Gulf Stream, in arteries and capillaries, in the bronchi and bronchioles of our lungs. Life emerges in branching patterns, the new taking shape from what came before. When Charles Darwin first began to refine his thinking about the flow of evolutionary life, he sketched the branches of trees in his notebooks.

Rivers participate in nature's branching patterns, but their motion is of a different kind. The water that flows through the branching patterns of rivers moves in the opposite direction of the growth of trees, each river branch contributing to the creation of the larger stream of water below. The wild river's origins are not in its main stem but in countless branches that flow into ever larger streams that eventually merge into one.

Late that morning, we drove back up through the valley, tracing the lines where the light shimmers down into the deep cut and the wild river bends through its branches, swaying like trees on the hillsides dance in the winds.

Acknowledgements

The research for this book was supported by a creation grant from the New Brunswick Arts Board.

I want to thank the team at Goose Lane Editions for their support, hard work and dedication to this project: publisher Susanne Alexander, editor Susan Renouf, art director Julie Scriver, and manager of many moving parts Alan Sheppard.

I want to thank my colleagues at St. Thomas University who listened to me talk about the book and pointed me in directions I needed to go, in particular Jane Jenkins, Patrick Malcolmson, Tom Bateman, Michael Camp, Jamie Gillies, Angela Wisniewski and Matt Dinan. Tony Tremblay encouraged me in the early days and later read several passages and offered essential criticism. Alan Hall, my friend and sometimes teaching partner, read a draft manuscript, offered valuable suggestions and gave me the courage to go on. Michael Pallotto provided invaluable research, thoughtful criticism and guidance. I also want to thank Jeffrey Carleton for his friendship and support.

John Leroux located the drawings and paintings of Maria and Edmund Head at the Beaverbrook Art Gallery. Katy Haralampides taught me everything I know about the science of rivers. Gordon Yamazaki offered scientific advice and river companionship and kept me out of the weeds. Bill Taylor allowed me to raid his library. The author Jim Marriner generously shared his research and deep knowledge of New Brunswick history. Roy MacGregor long ago encouraged me to write about this river and later wrote a forward to the book.

I am grateful for Stephen Booth, who shared his time and research, opened doors and drove me home and helped me work through difficult issues with grace and humility. I am also grateful for the time spent and knowledge of the river offered by David LeBlanc, Fred Metallic, Carole-Anne Gillis, Peter Firth and Charles Thériault.

Cecelia Brooks, David Adams Richards and Freeman Patterson graciously read the manuscript, while Alanis Obomsawin and James (Sa'ke'j) Youngblood Henderson read sections. My friend and fishing companion Tom Howe helped me define the issues of the book.

To my friend Danny Bird, I give full credit for the idea of a Restigouche book in the first place (yes, I remember) and for putting up with endless queries and supporting me and the project in more ways than I can count.

I thank the gifted artist and scientist Lena Beckley for creating the book's beautiful maps.

I received more than support from my network in Kedgwick River: André Arpin, Francine Lévesque, Rémi Bergeron, Louise Poirier, Dominic Leblanc, André Savoie and Samy Querry. Manon and Pascal Arpin provided me a home away from home.

Marie-Christine Arpin has been with me on and off the water since I set out to write about her river, offering logistical support, encouragement and friendship.

I am grateful for all my fellow river travellers: Michelle Pinfold, Will Taylor and Charlotte Taylor, Alan Madden and the indomitable Tommy Colwell. My daughters, my son, my mother and father, my sisters and brother, Tim and Carolyn Nobes, have been with me on all the journeys that matter most.

My long-time Restigouche companions and steadfast friends Butch Dalton and Marty Stewart have guided me through a lot more than fishing trips and always remind me what being on the river is really about.

Finally, to the members of the Restigouche Expeditionary Force: my beautiful daughter Lucy Nobes Lee, Ruth Christie, and Deb Nobes, team leader and my partner on the great adventure, whose sensible judgment and loving eyes are on every page—there are new seasons ahead of us.

Notes

Time

1

The American journalist is Charles Hallock, who wrote under the name Penman. The article "The Restigouche" was published in *Harper's New Monthly* in 1868.

3

The newspaper editor referred to here is Neil Reynolds, who outlined his views on the moral purpose of journalism in the introduction to my book *Home Pool: The Fight to Save the Atlantic Salmon* (Fredericton: Goose Lane Editions, 1996).

The reference is to T.S. Eliot's poem "Four Quartets." I adopt the words from the poem "unweave" and "unwind" at the end of the chapter.

4

Moses Perley wrote many reports on his field inquiries for the colonial government, including *Report on the Fisheries of the Gulf of St. Lawrence* (Fredericton: Queen's Printer, 1849) and *Report on the Sea and River Fisheries of New Brunswick, within the Gulf of St. Lawrence and Bay of Chaleur* (Fredericton: Queen's Printer, 1850).

6

The portage routes are described by historian Peter Thomas in his book *Lost Land of Moses: The Age of Discovery on New Brunswick's Salmon Rivers* (Fredericton: Goose Lane Editions, 2001). Peter Thomas's fascinating book has been an invaluable resource throughout my research.

The story of the mapping of the Canadian and United States border is told by New Brunswick author and journalist Jacques Poitras in his book

Imaginary Line: Life on an Unfinished Border (Fredericton: Goose Lane Editions, 2011).

Abraham Gesner produced several reports for the colonial government including *First Report on the Geological Survey of the Province of New Brunswick* (1839), *Report on the Geological Survey of the Province of New Brunswick: with a Topographical Account of the Public Lands and the Districts Explored* (1842), and *New Brunswick with Notes for Emigrants* (1847).

Allison Mitcham's *Prophet of the Wilderness: A Biography of Abraham Gesner* (Hantsport, NS: Lancelot Press, 1995) offers an account of Gesner's life.

Miguasha National Park, now a UNESCO World Heritage site, provides a wealth of information on its history and value as research area.

Charles Lyell's *Principles of Geology* was published in three volumes between 1830 and 1833.

An account of Abraham Gesner and Charles Lyell's travels together in Canada is found in Howard J. Falcon-Lang, "A History of Research at the Joggins Fossil Cliffs of Nova Scotia, Canada, the World's Finest Pennsylvanian Section," *Proceedings of the Geologists' Association* 117, no. 4 (2006).

Charles Lyell's travels in New Brunswick in 1852 have been documented by Randall F. Miller of the New Brunswick Museum. Arthur Hamilton Gordon's "Wilderness Journeys in New Brunswick" was published in the collection *Vacation Tourists and Notes of Travel, 1862-3*, ed. F. Galton (London: Macmillan, 1864).

The story of Gabriel Acquin is told by Karen Perley in "Gabe," *New Brunswick Manuscripts in Archaeology* 41 (2005).

The photographs and the story of the photographer is found in Ronald Rees and Joshua Green, *Slow Seconds: The Photography of George Thomas Taylor* (Fredericton: Goose Lane Editions, 2019).

7

I was guided here by *The Last Billion Years: A Geological History of the Maritime Provinces of Canada* by the Atlantic Geoscience Society (Halifax: Nimbus, 2001) and *Underground New Brunswick: Stories of Archaeology*, eds. Paul Erickson and Jonathan Fowler (Halifax: Nimbus, 2013).

The groundbreaking book *Nta'ugwaqanminen Our Story: Evolution of the Gespe'gewa'gi Mi'gmaq* by Gespe'gewa'gi Mi'gmawei Mawiomi (Black Point, NS: Fernwood, 2016) has been a valuable resource throughout.

8

A brief history of the Ste-Anne's church is found in Vetta LaPointe Faulds's *The Way it was Along My Bay Volume 5: Campbellton and the River Communities of Atholville, Tide Head, Flatlands and Ristigouche* (Island View, NB: Rhyme for Reason, 2010).

9

The Aristotle references relate mainly to his *Parts of Animals* and *Metaphysics*. In understanding the science of Aristotle, I was assisted by Armand Marie Leroi's fascinating book *The Lagoon: How Aristotle Invented Science* (New York: Penguin, 2015).

The Thomas Aquinas reference is from the *Summa Theologica* 1.47.1.

I refer here to Pope Francis's *Laudato Si'. Encyclical Letter on Care for Our Common Home*, May 24, 2015.

Among the various accounts of Mi'gmaw creation, Stephen Augustine's is found in *Visioning a Mi'kmaw Humanities: Indigenizing the Academy*, ed. Marie Battiste (Sydney, NS: Cape Breton University Press, 2016). James (Sa'ke'j) Youngblood Henderson's commentary on the creation account in the same volume is also invaluable. Marie Battiste's creation account is found in *The Mi'kmaw Concordat* by James (Sa'ke'j) Youngblood Henderson (Black Point, NS: Fernwood, 1997).

Fred Metallic's essay "Strengthening our relations in Gespe'gewa'gi, the Seventh District of Mi'gma'gi" is found in Leanne Simpson's excellent edited collection, *Lighting the Eighth Fire: The Liberation, Resurgence and Protection of Indigenous Nations* (Winnipeg: Arbiter Ring Publishing, 2008). I was also assisted by Fred Metallic's fine essay "Treaty and Mi'gmewey," which is found in the collection *Living Treaties: Narrating Mi'kmaw Treaty Relations*, ed. Marie Battiste (Sydney, NS: Cape Breton University Press, 2016).

I have also been assisted in my research by the dissertation "Uncommon Waters: Intercultural Conflict over the Atlantic Salmon of the Restigouche Watershed" by Stephen P. Booth (University of Guelph: February, 2019).

The reference is to Descartes, *Discourse on Method*.

On human affairs in the eighteenth century, I was assisted by my father's guide in these matters, Karl Barth's *Protestant Thought: From Rousseau to Ritschl* (New York: Harper, 1959).

Sandford Fleming's memoir *Terrestrial Time* was published in London. Fleming's *The Intercolonial: A Historical Sketch of the Inception, Location,*

Construction and Completion of the Line of Railway Uniting the Inland and Atlantic Provinces of the Dominion was published in Montreal and London in 1876.

I reference T.S. Eliot's "Four Quartets": After the kingfisher's wing / Has answered light to light, and is silent, the light is still / At the still point of the turning world.

10

John Rowan's *The Emigrant and Sportsman in Canada: Some Experiences of an Old Country Settler with Sketches of Canadian Life, Sporting Adventures, with Observations on the Forests and Fauna* was published in London in 1876.

The essential work of historian Bill Parenteau has been invaluable throughout, including, "'Care, Control and Supervision': Native People in the Canadian Atlantic Salmon Fishery, 1867-1900," *Canadian Historical Review* 79, no. 1 (March 1998); "A 'Very Determined Opposition to the Law': Conservation, Angling Leases, and Social Conflict in the Canadian Atlantic Salmon Fishery, 1867-1914," *Environmental History* 9, no. 3 (July 2004); "Looking Backward, Looking Ahead: History and Future of the New Brunswick Forest Industries," *Acadiensis* 42, no. 2 (2013); "The Woods Transformed: The Emergence of the Pulp and Paper Industry in New Brunswick, 1918-1931," *Acadiensis* 22, no. 1 (1992).

I refer here to the testimony reported in "Eel River Bar First Nation Inquiry, Eel River Dam Claim" by Indian Claims Commission, Government of Canada, December 1997.

For mercury pollution in Chaleur Bay, see Christine Garron et al., "Mercury Contamination of Marine Sediments and Blue Mussels (*Mytilus edulis*) in the Vicinity of a Mercury Cell Chlor-Alkali Plant in Dalhousie, New Brunswick, Canada," *Water Quality Research Journal* 40, no. 1 (February 2005).

The quotation from David Adams Richards is from his essay "We Told Them They Were Building a Dream" from in his collection *Murder and Other Essays* (Toronto: Penguin Random House, 2019).

12

On Stanford White's architecture I was assisted by Gary Hughes's invaluable study "Beaux-Arts in the Forest? Stanford White's Fishing Lodges in New Brunswick," *Journal of the Society for the Study of Architecture* 26, nos. 1-2 (2001).

The story of the Broderick family is told in Father B.M. Broderick's indispensible book, *Memories of the Kedgwick River*, self-published in 1994.

13

The Voyages of Jacques Cartier with an introduction by Ramsay Cook was published by University of Toronto Press in 1993.

Chrestien Le Clercq's *New Relation of Gaspesia (Nouvelle Relation de la Gaspésie)*, translated with an introduction by William F. Ganong, was published in Toronto by the Champlain Society in 1910.

I refer here to Thomas King's *The Inconvenient Indian: A Curious Account of Native People in North America* (Toronto: Random House, 2012).

I was assisted here by the book *The Battle of the Restigouche* by Judith Beattie and Bernard Pothier, published by Parks Canada in 1978, and by the wealth of information on display at the National Historic Site.

L.S.F. Upton's *Micmac and Colonists* was published by the University of British Columbia Press in 1979.

15

K.C. Irving's official biography by Douglas How and Ralph Costello is *K.C.: The Biography of K.C. Irving* (Toronto: Key Porter, 1993).

The story of the New Brunswick and Canada Railway Company and Wolastoqey territory is outlined by Andrea Bear Nicholas in her forward to *The Travel Journals of Tappan Adney, Vol. 2, 1891-1896*, ed. C. Ted Behne (Fredericton: Goose Lane Editions, 2014).

Water

1

I was assisted here and throughout by Marq DeVilliers's book *Water* (Toronto: Stoddart, 1999).

The story of the work of astrochemist Ewine van Dishoeck appears in the November 1, 2018, edition of *Quanta Magazine*: "All the water that we see here on Earth, all the molecules that we have in our bodies were already formed on the surfaces of the grains in the cloud out of which our solar system collapsed."

3

For more on the long history of farming on the Wolastoq, see Jason Hall, "Maliseet Cultivation and Climatic Resilience on the Wəlastəkw/ St. John River During the Little Ice Age," *Acadiensis* XLIV, no. 2 (Summer/ Autumn 2015).

I refer here to the report "Recovery Potential Assessment for Outer Bay of Fundy Atlantic Salmon," Department of Fisheries and Oceans Canada, 2014.

4

My edition of Aldo Leopold's classic *Sand Country Almanac* was published by Oxford University Press in 1968.

6

The quotation here is from *The Mi'kmaw Concordat* by James (Sa'ke'j) Youngblood Henderson (Black Point, NS: Fernwood, 1997).

D. James M. Marriner's excellent and carefully researched book has been more than helpful throughout: *Tight Lines Mean Bright Fish: The Larry's Gulch Story* (Mader's Cove, NS: Gale's End Press, 2013).

Charles Hallock's account of Princess Louise is found in *The Salmon Fisher*, published in 1890 by Harris Publishing.

7

I have been assisted by Al Carter's book *The Next Best Thing to Heaven: The Ristigouche Salmon Club 1880-1998*, privately published. Note that the club officially uses the variation Ristigouche. I have referred to the Restigouche Salmon Club throughout to avoid confusion. "A Letter From Stanford White to Robert Goelet, August 19, 1897," was privately printed by Charles B. Wood II as a keepsake for an evening at the Anglers' Club of New York.

8

Campbell Hardy's *Sporting Adventures in the New World; or Days and Nights of Moose-Hunting in the Pine Forests of Acadia* was published in London in 1855. His *Forest Life in Acadia* was published in London in 1869.

9

I was assisted in this chapter by Charles Hallock's 1868 article "The Restigouche" (published under the pseudonym Penman) in *Harper's New*

Monthly and by Peter Thomas's fine research about the contentious and mysterious "Penman."

10

For the story of Princess Louise, Larry Vicaire and the Restigouche, I was assisted by the work of Peter Thomas and Jim Marriner, the *Globe and Mail* archives and Abraham Lansing, *Recollections*, ed. C.E. Fitch (New York: De Vinne, 1909).

11

My edition of Alexis De Toqueville's *Democracy in America* was translated by Harvey C. Mansfield and Delba Winthrop (Chicago: University of Chicago Press, 2000).

Thomas Nelson Page, *Marse Chan: A Tale of Old Virginia* was published in New York in 1884.

Charles Akroyd's *Diary of a Veteran Sportsman* was published by Robert Carruthers & Sons in 1926. Alan Madden alerted me to the value of this volume.

12

I am grateful for the assistance of Jim Marriner here, both in his published work and in various memos and documents in his collection that he generously provided.

The history of the Restigouche River Riparian Association is told by Allan and Sterling McNeish in their book *Voices From Out of the River*, privately published in 2005.

13

Jack Russell's account of his Restigouche adventure is found in his book, *Jill and I and the Salmon* (Boston: Little Brown, 1950). My copy came from the collection of author Peter D. Clark, who sold it to me one Saturday morning at the Fredericton Farmer's Market.

14

Philip K. Bock's *The Micmac Indians of Restigouche: History and Contemporary Description* was published by the National Museum of Canada in 1966.

17

The story of Hubbard Brook and an overview of the research there is found in Richard T. Holmes and Gene E. Likens, *Hubbard Brook, the Story of a Forest Ecosystem* (New Haven, CT and London: Yale University Press, 2016).

Flow

1

I was assisted in my understanding of rivers by my patient and steadfast friend Katy Haralampides, professor of civil engineering at the University of New Brunswick. She directed me toward the work of Robert Newbury. The quotation here is from Newbury's "Rivers and the Art of Stream Restoration," *Natural and Anthropogenic Influences in Fluvial Geomorphology*, Geophysical Monographs Series 89, ed. John E. Costa et al. (Washington: American Geophysical Union, 1995).

2

David Adams Richards's novel *Friends of Meager Fortune* was published by Random House in 2006.

3

I was assisted here by the *New Yorker*'s archives and its article "The Right Way to Remember Rachel Carson" by Jill Lepore, March 26, 2018.

5

The life of Alanis Obomsawin is told in Randolph Lewis, *Alanis Obomsawin: The Vision of a Native Filmmaker* (Lincoln: University of Nebraska Press, 2006).

"The Long Walk of Alanis Obomsawin," published by *Cinema Canada* in June 1987, describes her interaction with the NFB funding committee.

Alanis Obomsawin's complete film library is available on the National Film Board website.

James (Sa'ke'j) Youngblood Henderson's fine essay on the work and legacy of Alex Denny is found in the collection *Living Treaties: Narrating Mi'kmaw Treaty Relations*, ed. Marie Battiste (Sydney, NS: Cape Breton University Press, 2016).

"Making First Nations Law: The Listuguj Mi'gmaq Fishery" was published by the National Centre for First Nations Governance Native Nations Institute for Leadership, Management, and Policy in 2010.

I refer here to the published transcript of the presentation by Brenda Gideon Miller, Listuguj Mi'gmaq First Nation Government, at the Royal Commission on Aboriginal Peoples, Restigouche, Quebec, June 17, 1993.

Leanne Betasamosake Simpson wrote about Fred Metallic's thesis defense on her blog *Elsipogtog Everywhere* and a shortened audio version aired on CBC New Brunswick's radio program *Shift* on October 21, 2013.

9

The reference to the forests being "thoroughly mined" is found in Nancy Holloway, Glen A. Jordan and Burtt M. Smith, "Management of New Brunswick's Crown forest during the twentieth century," *Forestry Chronicle* 84, no. 4 (July/August, 2008).

10

The Story of Runnymede Lodge by Wilfred M. Carter was privately published in 2001.

14

The quote is from David Adams Richards's *Lines on the Water: A Fisherman's Life on the Miramichi*, published by Doubleday in 1998.

Oliver Sacks writes of Charles Darwin sketching trees in his notebook in his essay "Darwin and the Meaning of Flowers," part of the collection *The River of Consciousness* (New York: Vintage Books, 2017).

A journalist, lecturer, and bestselling writer, Philip Lee began his career as an investigative reporter on Canada's east coast. *Restigouche* emerged from his long-standing interest in rivers and the people who love them. His first book, *Home Pool: The Fight to Save the Atlantic Salmon*, grew out of his award-winning reporting on the decline of the Atlantic salmon. Lee is also the author of *Frank: The Life and Politics of Frank McKenna*, a national bestseller, and *Bittersweet: Confessions of a Twice-Married Man*, which was long-listed for the BC National Award for Canadian Non-Fiction.

A professor at St. Thomas University in Fredericton, Lee developed the Dalton Camp lecture series, broadcast annually by CBC Radio's *Ideas* and edited *The Next Big Thing* (a published collection from the lectures). When he is not writing and teaching, Lee spends as much time as he can following the currents of rivers.

Photo: Deb Nobes